Poor Parents

Poor Parents

SOCIAL POLICY AND THE 'CYCLE OF DEPRIVATION'

Bill Jordan

Department of Sociology
University of Exeter

ROUTLEDGE & KEGAN PAUL
London and Boston

First published in 1974
by Routledge & Kegan Paul Ltd
Broadway House, 68-74 Carter Lane,
London EC4V 5EL and
9 Park Street,
Boston, Mass. 02108, USA

Set in ten point Pilgrim on eleven point body
and printed in Great Britain by
Northumberland Press Limited
Gateshead

ISBN 0 7100 7852 8 (c)
      0 7100 7853 6 (p)

Library of Congress Catalog Card No. 74-77195

Contents

Preface

This book started from a profound sense of discomfort that I have been feeling for several years about developments in the social services. I have seen these developments from the position of a social worker in one of the statutory services; from the position of a university lecturer teaching people in a professional social work course; and most recently (and most vividly) from my involvement as an associate member of a Claimants' Union. In each of these roles I have felt that the direction of change has been towards the increased isolation, separation, stigmatisation and the reinforcement of a sense of rejection by larger society of a group of people who are the consumers of the Welfare State's provisions.

These changes have come about with the connivance of a number of different interests, whose usually well-intentioned 'remedies' for the plight of the worst-off have failed to take account of the feelings and aspirations of the people they claim to serve. There are the politicians, anxious to score paper victories over statisticians' problems; the administrators, carving out their empires; the 'poverty lobby' with its narrow definitions of human misery; and the social workers, trying to appease their 'radical' consciences. The failures of the massive upheavals in the social services in the last four years to produce a more just and a more humane society are reflected not so much in technicalities like 'low take-up rates' as in the faces of the slum-dwellers, the slogans on the walls of the waiting rooms and the sight of police being called to break up disturbances in social security offices.

My concern in this book was to try to find a method of analysing our framework of provisions for social needs which does justice to the flavour and the texture of life among those who make use of these provisions. In the main, the method I have chosen is historical. It seems to me that this approach allows us to discern certain basic principles which have been applied through the ages both to poverty relief, and to services intended to meet other forms of need; and the consequences of the application of these principles on the lives of the recipients of these services. Such an analysis shows a remarkable persistence of the very oldest principles derived from the first Poor Law, and a tendency for the newer, more shallow-rooted products of democratic compromise (like the insurance principle) to be assimilated into the old system and ultimately relegated to a subsidiary role, at least in relation to the group which has traditionally received most attention from the social services. Above all, there is a strong tendency for these old principles to reappear in new guises as successive governments employ the social services as means to accomplish their traditional tasks of reinforcing the work ethic, maintaining the sense of family responsibility, and keeping law and order.

Although my original discomfort stemmed mainly from the social policies of the Conservative Government, these policies were nearly all evident as trends in the period of the previous administration. Political opposition to Conservative policies has tended to be pragmatic and the Labour Party in opposition has not apparently evolved new principles. For instance, Mr Roy Jenkins's latest publication, *What Matters Now*, gives an analysis of poverty which is fundamentally similar to Sir Keith Joseph's in that it focuses on the inadequacies of poor families, and takes an optimistic view of the development of the social services along recent lines as the means of effective intervention in these families' lives. Furthermore the Labour Party's recent election campaign has not provided evidence of any new thinking about the social services. However, in an atmosphere of economic crisis it is more urgent than ever to consider where our social policies are leading us. The alternative to such a fundamental reassessment of our priorities is, I have suggested towards the end of this book, an increase in civil disorder and violence.

In writing this book I have received a great deal of assistance from two of my colleagues at Exeter University, Jean Packman and Una Cormack. I have also drawn a lot on things that I have learnt from members of the Newton Abbot Claimants' Union; from my clients; and from students I have taught—in particular Jim Wilson, from whose dissertation on Guaranteed Income I have borrowed shamelessly.

1
The cycle of official deprivation

In a speech to the Pre-School Playgroups Association in June 1972, Sir Keith Joseph, Secretary of State for Health and Social Security, asked, 'Why is it that, in spite of long periods of full employment and relative prosperity and the improvement in community services since the Second World War, deprivation and problems of maladjustment so conspicuously persist?' He summarised his own answer to the question as follows: 'It seems perhaps that much deprivation and maladjustment persists from generation to generation through what I have called a "cycle of deprivation". Parents who were themselves deprived in one or more ways in childhood, become in turn the parents of another generation of deprived children.'[1]

The notion of a 'cycle of deprivation' focuses attention on a cluster of social problems which appear to be closely related. The recent Secretary of State has put forward a theory which gives expression to the tendency of social policies to converge, and to concentrate on a group of people who seem to suffer disproportionately from almost every kind of disadvantage. This group's plight quite obviously requires some form of remedy; but the problem of devising social services which will meet its needs raises almost every key dilemma in the history of social policy. Sir Keith Joseph has been embroiled in the reorganisation of the social services for the past three years, and thus his theory of the 'cycle of deprivation' has considerable significance as an indication of the direction of future government interventions.

In many ways, Sir Keith Joseph's theory is characteristic of a tradition of official thinking about poverty at times when the 'paradox' of conspicuous poverty side by side with affluence is 'baffling' the authorities. This is shown, amongst other things, in the link he makes between poverty and maladjustment. He connects these two factors through the concept of 'deprivation'.[2]

> Deprivation is, I know, an imprecise term. What I am talking about are those circumstances which prevent people developing nearer their potential—physically, emotionally and intellec-

I

tually—than many do now. Deprivation takes many forms, and they interact. It shows itself for example in poverty, in emotional impoverishment, in personality disorder, in poor educational attainment, in depression and despair. It can be found at all levels of society—not only among the poor—but the most vulnerable are those already at the bottom of the economic and social ladder.

What Sir Keith Joseph is saying here could be seen as simply expressing in a different form the message repeatedly given to him and his predecessors by official reports and by academics in the field of social policy and administration. Since about 1965, governments have been continuously pressed to give special priority to certain communities and special groups within society whose needs are greater than any others'. In housing, the Milner Holland Report; in education, the Plowden Report; and in the personal social services, the Seebohm Report, all recommended a massive transfer of resources to special priority areas of maximum need. The implication of all these in combination would appear to be that a concerted policy of concentration on the needs of the most deprived communities and their inhabitants is required if the interaction of these several bad factors is not to produce a new generation of social problems. As minister in charge of both the income maintenance services and the personal social services, as well as the health service, Sir Keith Joseph was in a position to organise this redirection of resources towards those in greatest need.

However, such a reorganisation of the social services raises important questions about the ways in which they can best be provided for those who need them. In the development of the 'Welfare State' after the Second World War, the personal social services evolved quite separately from those for income maintenance. The Children's and Welfare Departments and the Mental Health Service were based on the local authorities, and developed their own ethos through the emergence of a professional identity among the social workers who staffed them. The income maintenance services were central government departments, hierarchically ordered and staffed by civil servants. However, these sharp distinctions of structure, function and staff roles have been blurred over the years by a number of changes, not least of which has been the fact that social workers, who previously dispensed little other than compassion in their relationships with their clients, have become increasingly involved in the mechanics of distributing welfare benefits in cash and kind. Ever since the Children and Young Persons Act of 1963 acknowledged the possibility of a co-existence of financial difficulties and family problems, the door has been opened to a transfer of obligations for dispensing benefits from social security to the personal social services. The creation of a unified Department of Health and Social Security has produced closer administrative links at many levels between the two kinds of services to reinforce the effects of this overlap of functions. Thus Sir Keith Joseph's theory of the 'cycle of deprivation' could be seen as confirming an established trend towards concentrating the personal social services, as well as those traditionally associated with income maintenance, on the problems of the poorest sector. This book is about the implications for the social services of this trend and the other innovations in social policy which have aimed at selecting poor families as a target group for special attention.

The justification for these policies is the notion that the poor are the group most in need of both financial benefits *and* social work support, and that in many instances these kinds of help are best given in conjunction with each other. The same theme occurs in Sir Keith Joseph's speech, in the passages which suggest that poverty and maladjustment are interconnected. He makes no direct attempt to show a causal link between them, but quotes several reputable studies which relate *emotional* deprivation to delinquency and other forms of maladjusted behaviour 'at all levels of society'. He stresses that he does not wish to imply that poverty is the only factor in 'deprivation', but 'there can be no doubt that low income plays a large part, and efforts to combat poverty must continue'.[3] In part, this seems to be a justification for the selective policies of the government in the field of income maintenance.[4]

> The Government are using all available means to [combat poverty]—by regularly increasing benefits, by introducing new ones, and by making unprecedented efforts to ensure that everyone knows of benefits they are entitled to, and can claim them with a minimum of difficulty and fuss. With the Family Income Supplement scheme, we are making a frontal attack on family poverty, and the national rent rebate scheme will complement it.

However, there is also the suggestion that the family patterns of the poor cause certain forms of deprivation which are particular to this income group, and which thus demand other forms of intervention. For instance, he mentions research which indicates that 'problem families' (distinguishable by their dependence on the welfare services), give rise to children who form a new generation of 'problem families'. He also draws attention to the 'ways and extent to which children in working-class families, particularly those with semi-skilled or unskilled fathers, are disadvantaged from birth'.[5] Hence there would seem to be justification for concentrating services on those communities and groups which contained large proportions of poor parents as a way of preventing the miseries of 'the most difficult casualties of society, the problem families, the vagrants, the alcoholics, the drug addicts, the disturbed, the delinquent and the criminal'.[6]

However, before this trend in social policy is endorsed, or Sir Keith Joseph's theory accepted, we ought to consider the evidence that exists, both about the connection between poverty and social deviance of the kind he mentions, and about the kind of social services which result from selecting the poor as a target group for special provisions. Sir Keith Joseph's theory is claimed to be derived from research findings, and may well become an important instrument of government policy. It is therefore a matter of some urgency to evaluate the theory as a potential basis for the reorganisation of the social services, much of which is already well under way.

What sociological evidence is there on the relationship between poverty and maladjustment? In the 1920s, American sociologists of the Chicago School investigated slum areas of American cities, and found that they had the highest rate of almost every kind of social deviance.[7] This gave rise to the theory that the 'social disorganisation' of such areas resulted from a breakdown of the formal institutions (such as the police, schools and the family) by which society's controls on behaviour are normally maintained. However, when this theory was tested in England, it was not verified. In 1935, Sainsbury found that suicide rates, for instance, were highest in those London boroughs which had low rates of poverty and unemployment.[8] His researches suggested that two quite different 'problem areas' of British cities could be distinguished; the first having high rates of poverty, unemployment, overcrowding, crime and psychotic mental illness, and the second having high rates of immigration, mobility, social isolation, suicide, divorce, illegitimacy and alcoholism. The former areas tended to be relatively stable working-class zones, while the latter were characterised by a shifting middle-class population, with large proportions of people living in lodgings or hotels, or in one room alone. Thus instead of a concentration of *all* social problems (including poverty and deviance) in slum zones, different forms of deviance were associated with different social characteristics, and neither problem area exactly matched the description of 'social disorganisation'. In 1957, Morris found similarly in Croydon that it was difficult to define zones of the city to which even variations in crime and delinquency could be meaningfully related.[9]

Another American sociological school has linked social deviance with low-status occupations. For instance, Merton suggested that all forms of deviant behaviour result from inequalities in access to the success goals of a society. Modern societies emphasise certain goals such as material wealth, but provide limited legitimate means for achieving them.[10]

4

It is only when a system of cultural values extols above all else certain common success goals for the population at large, while the social structure rigorously restricts or completely closes access to approved modes of reaching these goals for a considerable part of the same population, that deviant behaviour ensues on a large scale.

The greatest pressure towards deviance therefore is on the lowest-status occupational groups. American studies showed that people in the lowest socio-economic class had the highest rates not only of crime but also of psychotic mental illness.[11] However, even in the USA, the same was not true of neurosis[12] or of chronic alcoholism.[13] In this country, the highest rates for alcoholism and, until recently, drug addiction[14] were in the higher-status occupational groups. Even in the field of juvenile delinquency, a study of male probationers aged seventeen to twenty-one concluded,

> while the impoverished minority cannot be ignored, there was nevertheless every indication that the probationers and their families were for the most part well in the mainstream of Britain's affluence in the sixties. 38% were completely free from material stress.[15]

> 69·3% of those with a home had material stress scores of 0, 1 or 2. These form the largest group and are the one which, superficially at least, appear to have few problems in its material environment.[16]

These statistics suggest that there is no straightforward correlation between all forms of deviance and the lowest socio-economic class. To the contrary, a comparison I myself made between the number of people sent to prison in one year and those admitted to a mental hospital from the same area during a similar period, led to a very different conclusion. The latter outnumbered the former by more than five to one, and because of the high rates of admission for mental illness of women from higher-status occupational groups, it was possible to suggest (if deviance is measured in terms of need for institutional treatment) that the 'typical deviant' in an English Cathedral city was a middle-aged, middle-class woman.[17]

Comparisons between different societies' rates of social deviance do not support links between poverty and the forms of maladjustment mentioned by Sir Keith Joseph either. Clinard reported that the highest rates for chronic alcoholism were found in the USA, France, Sweden, Switzerland, Denmark and Australia.[18] More damagingly for Sir Keith Joseph's theory, the same six rich countries were found by Goode to have the highest rates of divorce.[19] Gibbs found that Durkheim's conclusion that most urbanised industrialised societies had higher rates of suicide than backward and poor ones was still true, though the Anglo-Saxon countries have lower rates than European countries and Japan.[20] What emerges from all these statistics is that it is only in the USA that one could speak of a consistent correlation between poverty and social deviance, and even there the pattern is not completely consistent. Throughout the rest of the world, forms of deviance other than crime are likely to be concentrated most in the richer nations, and within these nations among the higher-status social groups. In the USA, the richest nation and the most deviant, they are nearly all most prevalent among the poorest sector (i.e. by and large the urban black and immigrant groups). One is led to conclude that this says more about the particular nature of American society than it says about a connection between poverty and maladjustment, and if Sir Keith Joseph is suggesting that something similar is coming to be true in this country, presumably it implies that we are coming more closely to resemble the USA than our European neighbours.

In spite of the lack of evidence linking poverty with maladjustment in Britain, the official stereotype of the bad parent is still the poor parent. It is of a mother whose children are dirty, badly clothed and badly fed, who play in the street, truant from school, steal and do damage. Sir Keith Joseph quotes Dr Urie Bronfenbrenner's view that this country is 'the only one which exceeds the United States in willingness of children to engage in anti-social behaviour' and links this with his conclusion that 'England is the only country in our sample which shows a level of parental involvement lower than our own, with both parents, especially fathers, showing less affection, offering less companionship and intervening less frequently in the lives of their children.'[21] It appears that Sir Keith Joseph thinks these criticisms apply particularly to poor parents.

> It is where there is a combination of bad factors—problems associated with poverty, poor housing and large family size, for example—that children are most at risk.[22]

> The most vulnerable—those at the bottom of the economic and social scales—are those most likely to be affected.[23]

Here again, one looks in vain for evidence to support Sir Keith Joseph's conclusions. The obvious way of measuring the total amount of parental inadequacy and neglect in the country would be to study the numbers of children deprived of normal family life. Since these are the children whose parents have been unable or unwilling to provide for them, one would expect, if Sir Keith Joseph's theory holds water, that the rates of such children would be highest in areas where poverty was most concentrated. In fact,

Jean Packman's study found that rates of deprived children (consisting of those in the care of local authorities and voluntary organisations, in approved schools, remand homes and maladjusted schools, privately fostered and awaiting adoption) followed no such pattern.[24] Instead 'deprived children occur with more frequency where the general standards of living are high and less frequently where they are low'.[25] Total numbers of deprived children in local authority areas correlated negatively with the proportion of the population in social classes IV and V and with the proportion in mining, agriculture and manufacture. 'In addition there were two high positive correlations with indices reflecting wealth and good social conditions (+0·51 with the expectation of life at year 1; and +0·53 with the net product of the penny rate per 1,000 population).'[26]

This led her to ask 'Why should "wealthy areas" be more frequently associated with deprivation than "poor areas", and why should the south and south-east of England produce more deprived children than the north and north-west?'[27] One possible reason she suggests is 'that static and declining working-class areas retain and foster a greater degree of family solidarity and self-help than areas in which geographical and social mobility are a by-product of affluence'.[28] Another is[29]

> that child neglect, juvenile delinquency and poor standards of child care stand out (like the proverbial sore thumb) in authorities where the general standard of living is high, and by doing so may provoke a drastic reaction on the part of the statutory and voluntary services for children, so that a higher proportion of children are removed from home. The approved school figures certainly suggest that this may be so, for some of the very highest rates are to be found, not only in the industrial areas of the Midlands and the North, where delinquency rates are high, but also in the wealthy resorts and coastal towns of the South like Hastings and Brighton, Bournemouth and Bath. Juvenile mobility and seasonal invasions of trouble-‍‍ers may account, in part, for the high rates in some of these   wns, but the incongruity of the young offender in areas of relative wealth and 'middle-class respectability' is probably also an explanation.

One final study which is relevant is Janet Mattinson's *Marriage and Mental Handicap*, which was a follow-up of eighty ex-patients of a subnormality hospital who were known to have married each other. The average IQ of the sample was 61, and their average length of stay in hospital for thirteen-and-a-half years; thus they had institutionalisation as a disadvantage as well as subnormality. As far as income was concerned, nine families were living on benefits, averaging £10-£11 per week, and the rest were living on earnings, averaging £12.9s.0d per week. The largest income in any household (where both husband and wife were earning) was £19 per week (this was in 1965-8). Thus the families were poor. They had a total of forty children between them, of whom six were in care of local authorities, belonging to three families. The families' school age children were assessed by their teachers as to normality and abnormality in attitudes and behaviour; about half were placed in either category. Janet Mattinson's assessment of the pre-school children was that 'none of these twenty-three children (of thirteen families) appeared mal-nourished, consistently ill or unfairly treated, cold or unhealthily dirty'.[30] It would seem, therefore, that despite the massive disadvantages of these parents, they succeeded in producing quite a high ratio of children assessed as 'normal', and in caring for them in an acceptable manner. It may well be relevant that most of these surprisingly 'successful' families were living in a low-income area of the country, where they were possibly not the 'sore thumbs' they might have been in more affluent surroundings.

These findings may help us to re-examine Sir Keith Joseph's original question. Since we know that deprivation and maladjustment occur at all levels in society, what we might wish to discover is which particular social conditions give rise to very high rates of these undesirable factors. But we should certainly not assume that there is any direct connection between poverty on the one hand and emotional deprivation and maladjustment on the other. On the contrary, all the sociological evidence leads us to expect that the richer the society, the higher the rates of maladjustment; and within a relatively wealthy society like our own, the wealthier the community, the higher the rates of deprivation. Therefore the question we should ask is: by what processes do affluent societies give rise to high rates of deprivation and maladjustment? It is not a question of how these factors *persist*, as Sir Keith Joseph suggests, but of how they are *reinforced* by conditions of prosperity.

This question is therefore quite separate from the one about the persistence of poverty in the midst of plenty. It is perfectly proper for Sir Keith Joseph to ask why in an era of increased prosperity and improved community services some people are still *poor*. But this question has nothing to do with maladjustment. It is only confusing the issue to set up research into poverty *and* maladjustment among the poorest sector, when only the former is a distinguishing characteristic of this group.

However, this kind of confusion in official circles about such questions is not unique to this country. The distinguished administrator and academic Daniel P. Moynihan put forward in 1965 a very similar 'cycle of deprivation' theory to explain the vast

8

increase in public assistance payments throughout the USA at that time. In a report called *The Negro Family*, he explained the fact that a disproportionate share of this increase in poor relief had gone to black people in terms of the deterioration of their family patterns. 'The steady expansions ... of ... public assistance programs in general can be taken as a measure of the steady disintegration of the Negro family structure over the past genera- tion in the United States.'[31] Moynihan tried to account for the increase in poverty (as measured by relief rolls) in terms of the increase in female-headed black families, arising out of the break- down of conjugal relationships among rural immigrants who found themselves unsupported by kinship networks in a stressful and unfamiliar urban environment. However, Lurie's research revealed that the increase of female-headed families during the period in question could only possibly account for ten per cent of the welfare explosion, and concluded, 'it is clear then that the rise in the numbers of families receiving AFDC cannot be explained by the rise in the number of poor families headed by females'.[32] This discovery did not prevent Moynihan and other Federal officials continuing to treat black poverty as if it was a problem of family structure, to be tackled by a combination of relief and social work intervention.

The same sort of notion underlies Sir Keith Joseph's diagnosis of our own social services. He has suggested, in effect, that we concentrate our services' attention on the child rearing patterns of the poorest sector of our population, and that we combine a service for income support for this group with a service to help provide them with the emotional resources to give their children 'a consistent combination of love, firmness, guidance and stimu- lus'.[33] He does not imply that the same agency should fulfil both these functions. However, there is already a strong tendency to- wards local authority social service departments becoming involved in the mechanics of supplying means-tested benefits for the poorest group, and responsibilities for various discretionary payments are regularly being transferred from social security departments to local authority social services. Sir Keith Joseph's theory therefore has important implications for the future of local authority social services departments.

Hitherto social workers who staff these departments have been trained to see the problems of maladjustment and deprivation re- ferred to them under the statutes governing their functions in terms of theories of personal, family or community pathology. The role of social workers has been to intervene at any of these levels and to seek to influence situations, to re-establish the deviant member within his family and neighbourhood, by means of his relationship with his client and those in the community. But the theories which have underlain such interventions have not, for the most part, understood those forms of social pathology as connected specifically with *poverty*. Certainly theories of emotional interaction, and especially of family dynamics, have been derived from evidence from all levels of society, and especially from certain centres of research (such as the Tavistock Clinic) which specialise in working with middle-class clients. It was not therefore part of the original tradition of local authority social work to think of maladjustment as causally connected with poverty, even though social workers have increasingly, since the unification of local authority services, been involved in the business of providing poor relief.

There are therefore several important questions to consider about the application of Sir Keith Joseph's theory within these departments. First, there is simply the question of whether Sir Keith Joseph is right to suppose that maladjustment can verifiably be identified as something which is linked with poverty. But an equally important question is whether, even if maladjustment frequently is associated with poverty, the *best* services can be provided for the maladjusted on the basis that they are poor. Here again, American experience is extremely relevant. Traditionally, in the USA, public welfare agencies have been primarily poor relief authorities, and secondarily agencies concerned with child care, old people's welfare, etc. However, separate from and parallel with the casework services of the public welfare departments have been developed a whole battery of private organisations, privately financed, to which their clients pay fees, which provide casework and psychiatric counselling services for people with emotional and family problems. It is generally recognised that in terms of training of staff and the service offered to clients, these private agencies are enormously superior in quality to public welfare agencies. The public welfare agencies disburse large sums of money to generally hostile clients; the private agencies receive money in fees from clients who are generally grateful and appreciative.

The American experience of combining functions of poor relief with casework services would therefore suggest a number of conclusions. First, it would suggest that where the two are combined, the clients' attitudes towards the poor relief functions (which are often hostile, resentful and dependent) may well be carried over into casework relationships, which may be unhelpful in the resolution of emotional problems. Second, the structure of the public welfare agency may well be more geared to the poor relief functions than to casework, thus causing difficulties in the practice of those skills associated with helping people with emotional problems, and possibly deterring the more skilled and highly trained staff from taking positions in the public services. Third, it suggests that there is a demand for counselling services for family and emotional problems in the better-off sectors of society, and that such people are willing to make sacrifices to get the benefit of the best possible help with problems of this nature. It is clear that better-off people in the USA do not think that public welfare agencies provide the best service.

It is perhaps not, after all, so surprising to find that in the USA the *best* social services should not be those specifically provided for the destitute. American society has traditionally, like Britain, associated destitution with fecklessness and moral inferiority. Indeed, it has never been part of the American philosophy of social services that *public* services should exist to deal with social problems, except those problems associated with destitution, and they should be dealt with in a way that reminds the destitute person of his responsibility to work and maintain his family. The same philosophy pervaded our own social institutions until the last war and was expressed in the administration of the Poor Law. Other services were seen as appropriately provided by voluntary endeavour from the private subscriptions of prudent and thrifty members of society. This philosophy is not entirely different in kind from the one propounded by the recent Conservative Government.

It is thus not altogether unexpected that we should find in Sir Keith Joseph's theory of the 'cycle of deprivation' a basis for the counterpart in the personal social services to the principle of selectivity in the income maintenance services. This principle is a fundamental distinguishing feature of the recent Government's policies in reorganising the social security system, and the application of a 'cycle of deprivation' might possibly have equally far-reaching consequences for the personal social services. The transformation of local authority departments from casework agencies into public welfare relief authorities is already well under way, and has already transformed the functions of the local authority social worker. 'His historical ancestor is not the psychiatric social worker who returned to England from the States in 1930 after training, but the old relieving officer.'[34] One might add that his new American tutor is not Florence Hollis or Virginia Satir but Daniel P. Moynihan.

A recent study, *Social Theory and Social Policy*, has minimised the practical consequences of a commitment to selectivity. Pinker suggests that 'the academic debate (between universalism and selectivism) is more imbued with ideological imperatives than its parliamentary counterpart'. In spite of a value commitment to universalism, 'institutional model' services tend to require supplementation by selectivist services. 'Allocation takes the form of positive discrimination programmes rather than means tests.' Those who favour a 'residual model' of social services (like the recent Government) find in practical terms, some minimum framework of universalist services tends to emerge and become institutionalised, generally for reasons of administrative convenience. The overall effect on the recipient is a more uniform one than ideologists of either left or right will care to admit.[35]

In the context of democratic politics, the related concepts of relativism and proportionate justice act as a kind of catalyst, inexorably transforming universalists into reluctant selectivists and selectivists into reluctant universalists.[36]

The conflict that breaks out from time to time is largely a battle between ideological ghosts, but the echoes of their gunfire serve as necessary reminders to policy-makers that issues of principle are involved.[37]

Pinker's book is about the relation of theory to administration, and therefore inevitably somewhat remote from the everyday reality of consumers' experiences of the social services. What he says may well be true of academic and parliamentary debates, but it is certainly not true of what happens in social security offices and social services waiting rooms. The conflicts which give rise to the formation of Claimants' Unions, to occupations of offices, to violence and arrests, have all been real enough. The take-up rates for new selective benefits, the increases in social security investigators, the ever growing list of controls on abuse, of new disqualifications and penalisations of claimants, all these are not matters of academic dispute, but part of the day-to-day lives of thousands of people all over the country. These events provide as important evidence on the results of a social theory like selectivism, as do a comparison between one of Sir Keith Joseph's speeches and a new Act of Parliament. In the same way, the effects on clients of local authority social services departments of a 'cycle of deprivation' commitment to the functions of public welfare poor relief agency will be found in clients' words and actions, and not in those of politicians or academics.

In the meanwhile, however, even though the poor and the maladjusted may not form coterminous groups, official policy is likely to give them more and more in common. They already share one common problem which is part of their existence in an affluent society. They are very conspicuous. Jean Packman's simile of the 'sore thumb' applies to both, and both may well, as she suggests, increasingly provoke more drastic reactions by the authorities than they would in less prosperous conditions. This book will be concerned with the principles by which an affluent society deals with its poor and maladjusted members. I shall look at the evolution of services for both income maintenance and personal counselling, and consider the relationship that has developed between these and other social services as prosperity has increased. In this way, I hope to shed some light on the processes by which wealthier societies tend to produce higher rates of deprivation. It may also be possible to understand how these higher rates are, to some extent at least, a *product* of the social theories and social policies of more prosperous societies. We can also see how the economic policies which set out to maximise the growth in a society's prosperity require social policies which have this effect. Although 'cycle of deprivation' theories do not explain poverty or maladjustment they do have some validity. Obviously the changes which accompany economic growth are usually more adversely felt by the poor, and very often this directly affects the quality of their family life. The results of these changes can be most grimly recognised in those areas of large cities which have 'a rapid inflow of population from both outside and inside the country; heavy pressure on housing; a high illegitimacy rate; many inhabitants without the support of relatives living nearby, and a large amount of mental illness and marital breakdown'.[38] However, all this hardship and misery requires the mediation of official social agencies before it can be translated into high rates of deprivation or maladjustment. Thus in the case of child care, Jean Packman concluded that:[39]

> the children's departments themselves, their policies and practices, also bear some responsibility for the lack of uniformity of numbers in care.... Some authorities reject many more applications for care than they accept (a refusal rate of 70% in some cases, for example). In other areas the reverse is true (only 19 per cent of applications are refused in another authority).

It is therefore to the policies and practices of the official social agencies that we must look for at least part of the explanation of the greater amount of deprivation among the poor in more affluent conditions.

Linked with Sir Keith Joseph's theory of the 'cycle of deprivation' is his claim that community services have improved since the Second World War. He makes it clear that while his theory of deprivation is cyclical, his theory of social policy is of a straight line progress. The direction of this progress is claimed as being towards more generous support and assistance for the poor. But here again, if this is supposed to mean that the relative position of the poor in our society is improving, it is extremely hard to substantiate. The researches of Townsend and many others in the 1960s showed that the economic situation of the worst-off sector was worsening, and there has been little other than government rhetoric to suggest there has been an alteration in this trend.

Indeed, the deteriorating situation of the lowest income group and its need for massive subsidisation is tacitly acknowledged when Sir Keith Joseph says 'With the Family Income Supplement scheme we are making a frontal attack on poverty, and the national rent rebate scheme will complement it.'[40] I shall suggest that these selective benefits have contributed to the worsening situation of the poor by creating an enormous class of people whose circumstances have, by stigma and rationing, to be made less eligible than those of another group who do not qualify for allowances. These subsidies have added to the deprivations which result directly from economic changes a further turn of the screw in the form of deprivation by the authorities appointed to deal with poverty. It is this that I shall call 'official deprivation'.

It might be thought that in a rapidly changing and disruptive economic situation, any theory which linked poverty with maladjustment should work to the advantage of the poor, ensuring that they were given more financial support on the pretext of their disorganised behaviour. In fact, this has never been the case, because such theories have always subjugated the notion of financial *support* to the function of *regulating* the poor by means of the principles under which poor relief has been provided. It has always been a characteristic of such theories that the very processes by which financial support is *rationed* are themselves the greatest kind of moralising influence on the poor, as this very rationing is done according to principles which are themselves both edifying and instructive for poor families. The result has been that according to such theories it has been seen not only as right to deal with the poor as a separate group, apart from society and morally inferior, but also as greatly to their moral benefit to keep them short of money. Since their problem is self-control, they can learn from the control that is influenced on them. Since they do not know how to ration themselves, they can only learn by being rationed by the authorities. The converse of this is that during brief periods when the poor have not been seen as a separate inferior group, they have fared better not only from a financial point of view, through benefiting from income maintenance provisions available to the rest of society, but also they have enjoyed better social services, through participating in those available to the rest.

Thus the policies of the recent Government, so far from being 'unprecedented' as Sir Keith Joseph claims, were based on principles which are familiar both from other countries' experiences and from our own. They are based on the notion that an extension of the social services to cater for a larger sector of the population by means of welfare benefits and other interventions can always be seen as advantageous for the poor and an effective form of remedy for poverty. This kind of approach is shared by the recent Conservative Government and the leading spokesman on social policy in the Labour Party. For instance Mr Roy Jenkins in his latest publication, *What Matters Now*, proposes an expansion of the personal social services as well as higher social security benefits and new taxation provisions. The Labour Party seems more concerned to increase the provisions of social services than to challenge the principles established by the Conservative Government. However, as I hope to show later in the book, it is of the greatest importance to consider *how* social services are provided as well as in what quantity and it is possible to recognise the direction of the trends in the social services which have been predominant under both Conservative and Labour Governments since 1965 by referring to our own past history. Indeed, in a great number of respects they represent a return in principle and in detail to the old Poor Law. In later chapters I shall trace the re-emergence of these Poor Law features of our system of relief. Throughout the rest of this book, I shall suggest that the changes in the social services which have taken place since the setting up of the Welfare State have tended to be in the direction of eroding the principles embodied in the Beveridge Report, and re-establishing those of the old Poor Law system. It is this full turn in the cycle of government policy towards the poor since the Second World War that leads me to the notion of a *cycle* of official deprivation of the poor. In the next chapter I shall suggest that official thinking about deprivation and maladjustment has followed this kind of cyclical pattern for the past two hundred years.

2
Official theories of deprivation

Sir Keith Joseph's theory of the 'cycle of deprivation' and the policies of the recent Government illustrate certain themes in official thinking which have a very long history. In particular, they recall a very old dilemma about poverty and family responsibility which has faced governments since the break-up of the feudal system. Poverty and social disruption appear to threaten the family as an institution. The families of the poor seem disorganised and destructive. Social policy has to be aimed at supporting the family and encouraging members to take responsibility for each other. But equally it has to intervene in the lives of the poor to correct tendencies in their family patterns which it sees as potentially damaging.

It is important to recognise that historically poor relief and intervention in family life were not separate entities in social policy, but different aspects of the same policy commitment. Poor relief has been seen as *the* way in which the State could intervene in and regulate the family life of the poor. Indeed, destitution alone was recognised as giving the state a right to intervention and a responsibility to intervene. It was as important to this tradition of social policy to limit the powers of the State for the sake of protecting the liberty of the majority of citizens to choose their own style of family life, as it was to control the poor. Spencer, for instance, was reflecting the dominant mode of nineteenth-century social theory in his belief both that the State should 'use social services, or rather the denial of social services, as a disciplinary agent'[1] and that the extension of these services beyond the residual provisions of the Poor Law would create 'despotism of a gradual and centralized officialism, holding in its hands the resources of the community, and having behind it whatever amount of force it finds requisite to carry out its decrees and maintain what it calls order'.[2]

It is thus to the history of the Poor Law that we must turn to examine how official thinking about the relationship of poverty to family life and maladjustment has been translated into the practices of social administration. We shall see that changes in the Poor

Law over the past centuries have been seen as methods of accomplishing changes in the moral situations of the poor and their children as much as in their economic and physical well-being. The notion of separate services for families and children at all levels of society, to deal with the consequences of bereavement, separation, neglect or conflict, dates from the break-up of the Poor Law after the Second World War. Sir Keith Joseph's strategy of simultaneous intervention with financial relief and official guidance for the poor thus represents a return to an old administrative model, and there are, as we shall see, important philosophical links with the past in his theories.

The first characteristic principle of official social policy has been that financial support for the poor should be made conditional upon the willingness of the family to take responsibility for its members. Forms of separate provision for work or institutional care have traditionally been used as the means of dealing with individuals who cannot be supported within the family. The general implication of this policy is that families can, and should, with limited financial help, deal with all but the most difficult social problems that arise, but that certain very problematical situations necessitate treating individual members or the whole family within an institutional framework controlled by the state.

The first example of this principle was the Elizabethan Poor Law, which has had such a dominant influence on our social policies ever since the sixteenth century. The Poor Law Act of 1598 stipulated that 'the parents or children of every poor and impotent person, being of sufficient ability, shall at their own charges relieve and maintain every such poor person'.[3] This was the first example of the 'means test' which was extended in the 1930 Poor Law Act which stated, 'it shall be the duty of the father, grandfather, mother, grandmother, husband or child of a poor, old, blind, lame or impotent person ... if possessed of sufficient means, to relieve and maintain that person'.[4] The other side of the 1598 Poor Law consisted in the aim of 'setting to work of the children of all such whose parents shall not be thought able to keep and maintain their children', and 'the putting out of children to be apprentices'.[5]

However, clearly such a resolution cannot be followed without reference to a number of other important considerations. One of these is the sheer possibility of families maintaining their members from their joint incomes. This, in turn, demands a delicate balancing of the levels of poor relief and wages, especially at the lower end of the wage scale. It is an equally old principle of poor relief that it shall only be given to those who are unable to obtain work. The 1598 Act provided only for 'the necessary relief of the lame, impotent, old, blind and such other being poor and not able to work'.[6] The corollary of this is that those who are able to work must be willing to do so on any terms. In order to make sure that this is achieved, official policies have, by some means, to maintain a relationship between low wages and benefits which results in people preferring the former however unpleasant the work involved. It is not enough for families to take responsibility for sheltering each other; financial responsibility must be maintained through income from work whenever this is possible.

Finally, and equally important, social policy has to deal with the poverty of the poor in a way which takes account of their potential threat to law and order or, worse still, to the very established fabric of society. Here again, the official resolution of the two problems of poverty and family responsibility and of work and benefits may not necessarily be easily reconciled with the official policy over public disorder. Once again, it was the Poor Law Act of 1598 which set the tone for subsequent policies. It was passed in an atmosphere of fear surrounding the Food Riots of 1596 involving the dispossessed labourers who had lost their feudal rights to land and were wandering the country in search of a livelihood. The preamble to the Act stated:[7]

> whereas a good part of the strength of this realm consisteth in the number of good and able subjects ... and of late years more than in time past, there have been sundry towns, parishes and houses of husbandry destroyed and become desolate, whereof a great number of poor people are become wanderers, idle and loose, which is a source of infinite inconvenience.

The Act gave powers for rogues and vagabonds to be punished or put to work, and thus set a precedent for the many subsequent measures to deal punitively with the 'small minority' of applicants for poor relief who are seen as trouble-makers or abusers of the system. But even if poor relief is seen as provided only for the deserving, and as ensuring that the undeserving are penalised or excluded, there remains a problem about the total sum to be devoted to relief. Piven and Cloward have suggested that there is a direct relationship between the amount of national income spent on poor relief and a cyclical process of unemployment and public disorder followed by restoration of order and work enforcement.[8]

> Relief arrangements are ancillary to economic arrangements. Their chief function is to regulate labor, and they do that in two general ways. First, when mass unemployment leads to outbreaks of turmoil, relief programmes are ordinarily initiated or expanded to absorb and control enough of the unemployed to restore order; then, as turbulence subsides, the relief system contracts, expelling those who are needed to populate the labor market.

However, I would wish to modify this thesis slightly by reference to some subtler political factors. It seems to me that, in general terms, there may be some situations of expansion and growing prosperity which, because of a political commitment to a 'One Nation' social policy (often as a result of war) may not lead to a contracting of poor relief. Equally, there may be situations of depression or economic stagnation where poor relief is not immediately made more generously available because of a political commitment to keeping the poor in their place.

However, it is generally true to say that a situation in which conspicuous poverty and social disruption are evident, while the standards of living of better-off members of society are rising, has led to officially sponsored theories which suggest that the poor are in some way responsible for their poverty, and are poor because of some factor other than their shortage of money. These same theories tend to see the families of the poor as a breeding ground for every sort of social evil, and condemn poor parents for their neglectfulness and for causing the plight of their children. They see bad character and moral turpitude as being a major cause of deprivation and they look to correction of abuses of the system of poor relief as a way of strengthening moral fibre and the improving influences of family life.

We can see an example of a whole cycle of official policy involving all of the three important principles in the changes in the system of poor relief between 1790 and 1834. In the years following the declaration of war with France, there was a rapid increase in agricultural production accompanied by an even more rapid inflation in the price of food. Industrial production was also expanding, but hanging over this increased prosperity was the threat of revolution, represented by events in France itself. It was probably this last factor more than any other that contributed to the adoption of a policy of supplementing the low wages of agricultural workers out of the poor rates on a scale which was related to the size of families and the price of bread. This apparently generous measure of poor relief (providing benefits for those in employment for the first time in the history of the Poor Law) was justified by the Prime Minister, Pitt, because[9]

> this will make a large family a blessing, not a curse, and thus will draw a proper line of distinction between those who are able to provide for themselves by their labour, and those who, having enriched their country with a number of children, have a claim upon its assistance for support.

Piven and Cloward point out that this policy was, in part at least, connected with the fact that 'the burgeoning English textile industry solved its labour problems during the latter part of the eighteenth century by using parish children, some only four or five years old, as factory operatives'. Not only could children be an economic asset in the new industrial expansion; even where their families could not afford to feed them they formed a potential source of 'profit making poor relief' to overseers while 'manufacturers negotiated regular bargains with parish authorities, ordering lots of fifty or more children from the poorhouses'.[10] Thus the combination of political and economic expediency gave rise to a policy which encouraged the lowest-wage earners to have large families as a way of qualifying for poor relief.

This policy was by 1834 being condemned as having been responsible for the 'demoralisation' of the poor, and the creation of an 'army of paupers'. By offending the principle of family responsibility, it affected the quality of family life in a way that was decried almost equally by Chadwick and by Cobbett. In disturbing the balance between wages and benefits, it had casualised rural employment. The principle of work on any terms as a condition for benefit could only be maintained by forcing the enormous numbers of redundant country labourers to undertake tasks normally performed by animals. Between seasonal activities they were kept 'like potatoes in a pit', ready to be taken out for use when the farmers could not manage without them. Finally, it failed even to satisfy the principle of maintaining law and order. In 1830, the Labourers' Revolt, an outbreak of rioting, burning and machine smashing which took place in precisely the areas where the system of wage supplementation were most widely operated, showed that an annual expenditure of over seven million pounds on poor relief was not producing the effect that was intended. Far from being submissive in their dependence, rural paupers were dangerously volatile and potentially revolutionary.

The Poor Law Amendment Act of 1834 therefore reasserted the principles which had been abandoned since 1795. In removing the subsidies on low wages, it also took away the allowances which encouraged large families among the poor. Instead the entire responsibility for maintaining their children returned to the poor parents. It was to be no part of the Poor Law authorities' duty to provide 'that the children shall not suffer for the misconduct of their parents—the wife for that of the husband, or the husband for that of the wife'.[11] Failure to provide was to be punished, not rewarded. In future, the test of need was to take the form of the offer of admission to the workhouse, where conditions were intentionally made harsh enough to deter all but the most desperately needy. The balance between wages and poor relief was restored by the principle of 'less eligibility' intended by means of the workhouse test to ensure that the lot of those receiving relief 'shall not be made really or apparently so eligible as the situation of the independent labourer of the lowest class'.[12] In part this principle was upheld by the ways in which families were treated within the workhouse. Husbands and wives were separated from each other and from their children. Thus the bond that existed between family members was used as a means of enforcing the principle of independence and maintenance from work and wages. The alternative of the workhouse imposed not only labour at humiliating tasks, but also strict discipline and a prison-like uniformity.

Considering that Sir Keith Joseph has, in effect, reintroduced (in the Family Income Supplement) the system of allowances that Chadwick (as author of the Poor Law Report) was seeking to abolish, it is surprising to find that their theories of deprivation have some important points in common. Chadwick believed 'that the proposed change would tend powerfully to promote providence and forethought, not only in the daily concerns of life, but in the most important of all points—marriage'.[13] He had gathered evidence from those parishes where the allowance system had been discontinued, and reported that in one 'for the eight years subsequent there was, as compared with eight years preceding, a positive diminution (in population). Improvident marriages are less frequent.'[14] Sir Keith Joseph is similarly concerned to prevent large families and irresponsible parenthood.[15]

> Where parents with large families are immature and in danger themselves of marital breakdown, the more so when they are also poor and badly housed, the children are virtually sure to be deprived. Clearly, then, an understanding use of family planning could reduce the numbers afflicted by deprivation.

The explanation of this similarity may well lie in the fact that Sir Keith Joseph was already becoming alarmed at the implications of his own allowance system within three years of its first introduction.

The other common feature in their theories is the firm conviction that the great bulk of social evils ('demoralisation' in Chadwick, 'maladjustment' in Sir Keith Joseph) is to be found among the poor, and that therefore in dealing properly with the poor as a class of people in need, the authorities will simultaneously be taking the necessary steps to deal with these other social evils. For both men, any good system of poor relief is also a system for remedying a whole set of other problems. Chadwick claimed that, where the able-bodied had been[16]

> rendered independent of partial relief, 1. Their industry has been restored and improved. 2. Frugal habits have been created or strengthened. 3. The permanent demand for their labour has increased. 4. And the increase has been such, that their

wages, far from being depressed by the increased amount of labour in the market, have in general advanced. 5. The number of improvident and wretched marriages has diminished. 6. The discontent has been abated, and their moral and social condition in every way improved.

He also claimed elsewhere that the crime rate had fallen.[17] The vast difference between the two theories, of course, lies in the chosen method of poor relief. Chadwick hoped by his abolition of allowances to restore a dependent pauper class to a higher moral plane through the dignity of an independence gained by income from work. Sir Keith Joseph hopes by creating more selective benefits to increase the income of the poorest families, and appears to see their dependence on these benefits as a way of introducing more control, supervision and guidance over their performance as parents.

Chadwick's 'wages fund' theory, which led him to believe that wages would rise following the abolition of Poor Law subsidisation, did not really justify itself for another twenty years after 1834. As he to some extent recognised, the Corn Laws, which artificially inflated the price of food and encouraged rural underemployment, made at least as substantial a contribution to deprivation and misery as the Speenhamland System. In the cities, slum housing and bad sanitation (which he himself tackled with vigour), added to the sufferings of families whose wages could scarcely feed them and whose employment was uncertain. Chadwick's own short-term solution was widely adopted. 'In all extensive civilised communities ... the occurrence of extreme necessity is prevented by alms-giving.'[18] It was to charities that the poor were forced to turn as the only alternative to the workhouse test, and even in the more prosperous 1850s and 60s, there was still a large sector of the population which desperately needed this form of outdoor relief.

In spite of the difficulties of applying his administrative remedies in practice (he was bitterly disappointed by the laxity of many districts which continued to practice old abuses), Chadwick's theories were extremely influential. Until well into the twentieth century the 'principles of 1834' were quoted with reverence by the highest Poor Law authorities. The continued and increasingly conspicuous existence of poverty and degradation during the increase of prosperity did not shake his or the official faith in his original diagnosis of the problem. The real enemy was still seen as the *moral* depravity of the poorest class, and the real solution as a system of relief which dealt with this depravity and confined it as narrowly as possible to this near-incorrigible group, thus saving the much larger poor but industrious class from contamination. But the sheer size of the problem and the numbers who still sought relief required some explanation. Chadwick himself in the 1830s undertook research which revealed that over half of all claims from widows and orphans were caused by deaths of heads of families from fevers and epidemic illnesses.[19] He used these and other startling figures to argue the case for an active programme of urban sanitary reform. In the absence of adequate preventive measures, sickness and other unpredictable disasters could be recognised as giving rise to a different kind of need from that caused by 'demoralisation'. It was one of the great strengths of Chadwick's theory that it allowed the distinction to be made, which has survived to this day, between the 'deserving' and the 'undeserving' poor.

This distinction in official thinking is nowhere more vividly illustrated than in the Report of a Select Committee on the Administration of Relief of the Poor in 1864.[20] The Committee investigated the allegation that the Poor Law had 'broken down' during a very severe frost which lasted for five weeks in the winter of 1860-1, and which threw a great number of dock and other workers out of employment for this period. A large sum of voluntarily contributed money was dispensed by magistrates and clergymen quite separately from the Poor Law authorities, and 'it appeared to have been generally assumed that the machinery of the Poor Law was inadequate to meet the prevailing distress'. The Committee discovered that the weekly average number of paupers in the metropolis had risen during the five weeks from 96,752 to 135,389, but had no record of the number given voluntary relief. It then quoted the assessments of the situation given to it by the Poor Law authorities and the voluntary dispensers. 'Mr. Farnall, the Poor Law Inspector of the Metropolitan district, was of the opinion that the distress scarcely ought to bear the name of a crisis.' He added that of 15,463 men who applied for relief, only 5,233 were willing to take the workhouse or labour tests, and 'the rest were never heard of again'. On the other hand, magistrates and clergymen described the 'extreme distress' and 'awful misery' they encountered when walking round their districts, and put forward the opinion that 'but for charitable subscriptions, "there would have been a fearful loss of life from starvation"'.

This apparent contradiction in perceptions of the situation could be reconciled within the framework of official thinking. The Committee concluded 'there can be no doubt that the machinery of Poor Law administration was adequate to the occasion, and that the guardians possessed the requisite powers for raising the funds necessary for the relief of the distress'. They report a great deal of evidence from experienced Poor Law officers that they 'had not the least difficulty in relieving the applications that were made to them; their machinery was complete'. They said that they 'could have relieved in a humane and adequate manner the whole number applying', and that they 'did not require the assistance of the voluntary subscriptions of benevolent people'. In spite of this, throughout the frost,

> the guardians felt that as a protection against imposture, it was necessary, in the case of able-bodied men, to enforce the test of the workhouse.

> It appeared, however, that a very small proportion of applicants to whom relief under this test was offered, accepted it.

> Although some witnesses expressed an opinion that this reluctance to accept relief upon such conditions showed that the test was applied with harshness, yet a very considerable amount of evidence went to prove that it arose from the great facility with which the relief voluntarily contributed could be obtained.

Mr Henry S. Selfe, Magistrate of the Thames Police Court, 'considered it necessary as a condition for relief that a test of work or strict inquiry should be applied. If there were no discrimination as to relief, and undeserving persons were relieved, it doubtless tended to demoralise those who were struggling to be independent.' Although he had not dealt directly with the guardians

> he believed them to be humane, and to have a desire to perform their duty ... there was hardly a complaint against a parochial authority which was not found to be groundless.

> At the same time, there were a number of cases which the Poor Law never could touch: and he did not conceive it possible that a thoroughly official system, paid for by compulsory contributions, could be without some kind of hardship to the poor. The workhouse test, or the labour test, which no doubt was properly applied in the case of the sturdy vagrant or the idle, was wholly unfit, in his judgement, to be applied to the vast number of those who were destitute. In the eastern district of the Metropolis there were numbers of the most deserving poor who would never go near the poorhouse; they would sooner die.... No system of Poor Law relief, if devised by angels, inasmuch as it would have to be administered by men, could ever prevent the necessity for voluntary exertion, and the more of the latter the better, provided it was conducted wisely.

These words have a decidedly contemporary flavour. The problem of how to ration benefits without deterring the deserving; of how to prevent contamination of the industrious by the idle; of how simultaneously to reward thrift and punish fecklessness; all these are present-day dilemmas for the poor relief authorities. If we substitute the unemployment crisis of 1971-2 for that severe frost, we can recognise in this report many features of recent Supplementary Benefits Administration Papers, of ministerial statements and of the Fisher Report. Indeed, so succinctly does he express the current double-standard of public opinion, it is hard to believe that Mr Henry S. Selfe is not alive and well, and writing regularly to the *Daily Express*.

The notion that there existed a whole category of 'undeserving poor' whose family life-style and child-rearing practices distinguished them from the rest allowed a 'cycle of deprivation' type of theory to develop during the mid-Victorian era as an explanation of conspicuous and disruptive poverty. This kind of theory gained ground in the prosperous 1860s and '70s when, as Beatrice Webb recorded, the ruling class required an explanation of the fact that 'in the slums of the great cities, stagnant pools of deteriorated men and women, incapable of steady work, demoralising their children and all new-comers, and perpetually dragging down each other into even lower depths of mendicancy, sickness and vice'[21] were evident in spite of the growing affluence of the industrious and thrifty classes. At this time, it came to be 'the common opinion of such enlightened members of the governing class as were interested in the problem of poverty' that these conditions were caused 'by spasmodic, indiscriminate and unconditional doles'.[22] Even more alarmingly, Spencer argued that 'maudlin philanthropy' fostered social inadequates and bred 'an increasing population of imbeciles, idlers and criminals'.[23] Accordingly, the reorganisation along principles which accorded with the theory, of the thousands of charities which had grown up to relieve distress, became a high priority. It was with this aim in mind that the Charity Organisation Society, a voluntary body whose influence on official thinking for the next fifty years was very considerable, was established.

The Charity Organisation Society's (COS) consciousness of the dangers of demoralisation through alms-giving was indicated in its Second Annual Report. 'To give material relief, food or money, to everyone who asked for it on the sole conditions of their being what is commonly called deserving and in want, even after the most careful verification of these conditions, would inevitably do more harm than good.'[24] While its functions included 'the promotion of habits of providence and self-reliance, and of those social and sanitary principles, the observance of which is essential to the well-being of the poor and of the community at large', they also numbered 'the repression of mendicity and imposture, and the correction of the maladministration of charity'.[25] Their stance on family responsibility was clear. They endeavoured to help the distressed person in such a way as 'to call out for his aid the sympathy and assistance of his family and those upon whom he is in any way dependent'.[26] They saw as a necessary condition for the encouragement of these virtues that the official system of poor relief should be made 'as distasteful as possible to the applicants'.[27] However, charity existed to help those who were 'reduced to distress without fault or improvidence of their own, even persons who had not made the best use of their opportunities, but whose previous position and temperament would make the workhouse almost intolerable'.[28]

By implication, of course, this made the workhouse an appropriate way of dealing with the undeserving. Some examples of undeserving cases (at a time when the COS gave assistance to only about one-third of all applicants[29]) were contained in a report of 1873.[30]

A widow had broken her collar-bone in an accident and her son, aged 10, was in danger of losing his situation for want of boots: 'on inquiry it was found that she resorted to a public-house every evening, and broke her collar-bone while under the influence of drink'. In another case, a woman with four children applied for help, her husband having been out of work for two weeks and the family in great distress; inquiry showed that the husband was very lazy and he and his wife confirmed drunkards. A widow's plea for help was dismissed on the ground that she was of bad character, and much given to drink.

These examples show clearly how commitment to strict principles of poor relief determined the COS's policies of intervention in family life. It was these same principles that guided their dealings with the deserving cases to whom they granted assistance. In the case of another widow with three children,[31]

her character was excellent; the only difficulty was how to enable her to earn sufficient to support herself and her children independently. One of the ladies of the committee visited her and thought her so well calculated for a nurse, that training for this was suggested to her; she expressed her readiness to follow this advice if her children could be placed comfortably in schools or in a family.

In thus arranging to disperse a family in order to allow the mother to work to provide for her children's subsistence, the COS revealed its priorities in questions about family life. Even if the parental influence was a good one, it was quite acceptable to require the separation of children from their mother as a condition of providing charitable assistance; where parents were given to drink or laziness, the separation of the workhouse was necessary for the children's protection from demoralisation. While prosperous Victorians defended their rights as parents, and ruled their children with firm paternal authority, the ideology which underlay social work with the families of the poor was one of 'rescuing' children from the influence of dissolute and feckless parents. Thus Dr Barnardo fought a long battle in the courts for the right not only to care for the children of the poor, but also to arrange for their emigration to the overseas Dominions, even against the wishes of their parents.[32] The 'cycle of deprivation' theory of the first social workers did not lead them in the direction of respect for the parental rights of the poor.

It was not until the turn of the century that the social philosophy which subjugated family life to the 'principles of 1834' was effectively challenged. Beatrice Webb, who had assisted in Booth's researches into poverty in London, and had also made a study of working-class mutual aid societies, was appointed to the Royal Commission on the Poor Laws in 1905. The Commission was, in her opinion, based on 'an uneasy feeling that there had been, during the last two decades, an unwilling drift away from the principles of 1834, and one which sooner or later had to be stopped'.[33] However, fairly quickly she was able to steer it[34]

away from being an inquiry into the disease of pauperism into an investigation of the disease of destitution. For, while it was clear that the only direct way of restricting relief out of the rates to the destitute, and thus diminishing pauperism, was by making their condition less eligible than that of the lowest-paid labourer, this policy not only left undiminished the mass destitution outside the Poor Law, but also, in the case of the infant, the child, the child-bearing mother, the sick and the mentally defective, actually increased it.

She thus recognised, and tried to force her colleagues to accept, that by making services to unfortunate families and individuals and those in special kinds of situations subservient to principles of poor relief, the authorities were reinforcing the effects of these contingencies and misfortunes by making paupers out of those who suffered them.

Beatrice Webb's answer was to take[35]

all the non-able bodied (the infants and the children, the sick and the mentally defective) out of the poor law with its framework of repression, in order to transfer their treatment to the already existing framework of prevention, imperfectly embodied in the public health and education acts, administered by the County or County Borough councils. To this it was proposed to add a national scheme for old-age pensions, paid for and carried out, free from any stigma of pauperism, by a department of the central government.

Her scheme, embodied in the Minority Report of 1909, was eventually implemented in large measure, first by the transfer of many of the Poor Law authorities' powers to the local authorities in 1929 and, more important, in the setting up of the Children's Welfare and Mental Health services of the local authorities in 1948. Her recognition that such services could never be properly established under 'the framework of repression' and 'the stigma of pauperism' has not, however, been transmitted to the present generation. The very organisations which owe their existence to her imaginative perception of another kind of service for those in distress, not given solely on grounds of destitution, are rapidly taking on the features of the Poor Law authorities she sought to undermine. Sir Keith Joseph's theory of the 'cycle of deprivation' reinstates the notion that those who are deprived can best be dealt with by official agencies whose prime function is the dispensing of means-tested benefits according to Poor Law principles. It was precisely this kind of theory that Beatrice Webb was trying to discredit.

At the same time, there was another direction in which the principles of 1834 were being undermined. Although Beatrice Webb's recommendations did not win the support of Parliament, they probably influenced the passing of what was seen as in some ways an alternative to them—Lloyd George's scheme for sickness benefit based on the insurance principle, a principle which was extended to cover a limited range of unemployment under the same government. It was to a considerable extent the necessity of pleasing the new Labour Party representatives as well as the Conservative House of Lords that caused Lloyd George to adopt—on the model of Germany and New Zealand—a principle that was totally unprecedented in official policy in this country, and thus manage 'to spike the Socialist guns with essentially Conservative social measures derived from the Liberal arsenal'.[36] Political expediency in the delicate balance of power which existed in the far from stable situation immediately before the First World War accomplished the adoption of a scheme which foreshadowed the 'One Nation' concept of the Welfare State.

Although Lloyd George saw his scheme as only a beginning, and envisaged many of the developments of thirty years later, he also recognised that the insurance principle was of necessity an interim measure. He wrote to his private secretary,[37]

Insurance necessarily temporary expedient. At no distant date hope State will acknowledge full responsibility in the matter of making provision for sickness, breakdown and unemployment.

It really does so now, through Poor Law, but conditions under which this system had hitherto worked have been so harsh and humiliating that working-class pride revolts against accepting so degrading and doubtful a boon.

The insurance principle's only roots in the British tradition of social administration were found in working-class self-help organisations like the Friendly Societies, through which his scheme was organised; and it was to this stratum of respectable, provident, thrifty and deserving workers that it most appealed and applied. While the State had taken responsibility for the first time through a centrally administered fund for the misfortunes of the deserving poor, the distinctive, repressive and far more deeply-rooted traditions for dealing with the undeserving remained virtually intact.

During the 1920s and '30s the two approaches to deprivation represented by Lloyd George's institutions and those of the Poor Law co-existed and disputed the right to official endorsement, while predominantly Conservative governments faced with the chaos of mass unemployment, moved tentatively towards a more liberal interpretation of the assistance which should be given to the poor under both sets of principles. Beatrice Webb had recognised that it was unemployment that represented the greatest threat to the institutions of 1834.[38]

> So far as the able-bodied worker was concerned, all that the deterrent policy did was to induce him to accept any job which afforded more freedom and comfort than the able-bodied 'test' workhouse, which was, in fact, a penal establishment of a peculiarly repulsive character. But what if there were no jobs offering for hundreds of thousands of workers, men and women, young and old? If so, the abolition of relief, except under penal conditions, not only increased mass destitution, with its inevitable mendicancy and vagrancy, but as many witnesses asserted, actually multiplied the number of criminals; the energetic and self-willed man preferring a life of theft and fraud, with its off-chance of prison, to the certainty of daily existence in one of the able-bodied 'test' workhouses established by some boards of guardians with the approval of the Local Government Board.

Once the number of unemployed rose to millions, the validity of this argument was more readily accepted in official circles. Even so, there were times when as a matter of policy the old Poor Law principles were reasserted. In 1926, after the defeat of the General Strike,[39]

> guardians were encouraged, if necessary warned, to examine claims more closely, to refuse help to single men, to continue

relief to families only if the husband and father would enter the institution. This last device, though not commonly resorted to, meant in effect the break-up of the family.

These and other restrictions, however, did no more than reduce the number on poor relief from nearly a million and a half in 1927 to a million and a quarter in 1928. Tacit recognition was given to the failure of these repressive policies both in the gradual extension of the insurance principle during the inter-war years, and in the creation of the Unemployment Assistance Board in 1934, providing means-tested outdoor relief, without the workhouse test. For the first time in a hundred years, those who were not covered by unemployment insurance (or the somewhat arbitrary system of 'extended benefits') could apply for poor relief without the fear of institutionalisation for themselves and their families.

It could well be argued that the eventual triumph of the universalist principles in which the Welfare State was established owed more to the Second World War than to any other factor. The Government White Paper of 1944 stated that the proposed social insurance scheme was intended to be the expression of 'the solidarity and unity of the nation, which in war have been its bulwark against aggression'[40] and that, on this basis, 'in a matter so fundamental it is right for all citizens to stand together, without exclusions based on difference of status, function or wealth'.[41] Here indeed was a very different approach to problems which had hitherto been seen in terms of a ruling class dealing with the moral inferiority of its lowest stratum of subjects. However, Beveridge himself as author of the scheme, had a very limited view of the nature of the 'British revolution' he was introducing. He saw it simply as a scheme to provide for the *interruption of earnings* 'by unemployment, sickness or accident ... retirement through age ... (or) loss of support by the death of another person'.[42] Inevitably, this left a number of categories of people who required financial support from the State outside the National Insurance scheme. Thus, even though Beveridge hoped that the National Assistance Board would be a residual service, dealing only with a very small number of claimants who were not covered by the insurance principle, he left the door open for the continued existence of an institution which embodied the old principles of poor relief. Although he hoped that the benefits available to insured persons without a test of means would establish a 'national minimum' and would be a floor above which they could rise rather than (as with the Poor Law), a ceiling below which they were kept, this aim was not accomplished. In the long run, for reasons which we shall examine in the next chapter, it was the older principles which triumphed over the new. As Lloyd George had foreseen, the insurance principle was no more than a temporary expedient, and could not form the basis of a thoroughgoing assumption of responsibility by the State for all forms of income maintenance. As Lloyd George had also recognised, the theoretical framework which underlay the Poor Law *was* just such a basis, and in the absence of some new and much more comprehensive concept than the insurance principle, the old rules for the game of regulating the poor and the deprived were bound to re-emerge to assert their stranglehold on British social policy.

In the meanwhile, it is important to recognise that during the brief generation in which Beveridge's universalist principles held sway, there were established a whole set of services for those deprived of a normal, decent family life by a variety of contingencies, and that these services were to a considerable extent set free from the yoke of 1834. The distinguishing characteristic of this generation of local authority provisions was that they were, for the most part, seen as dealing primarily with deprivation and maladjustment as emotional hazards in the processes of personal development and the evolution of family life rather than as consequences of poverty. Indeed, the concept of poverty virtually disappeared, along with that of pauperism, from the literature of social policy, while there was a burgeoning interest in a multiplicity of newly-recognised forms of maladjustment and emotional deprivation. It was not that poverty itself disappeared, as has since been shown, but rather that these other problems were recognised as existing in all strata of society, and not just among an undeserving sector at the bottom; and furthermore that services for these kinds of deprivation were seen as best established, in the interests of all who suffered them, on a universalist basis, catering equally for rich and poor according to compassion for their inner sufferings more than the necessity of relieving their outer circumstances. Thus the 'rediscovery of poverty' in the latter half of the 1960s, while no doubt objectively justified, was not necessarily a step in the direction of improving services for the poor, for it has served as a ready excuse for concentrating all our social resources on the unfortunate sector for whom the old principles of poor relief are characteristically employed. It is sad, too, that a new generation of 'radical' social workers should have so singularly failed to recognise the virtues of these services in which, while more respect was paid to Freudian theories than those of Marx, the administration was at least organised along lines which gave relatively little deference to the principles of Chadwick. Sir Keith Joseph, as we shall see, has ensured that Chadwick shall make Freud and Marx equally irrelevant for those social workers in their daily round of administering means-tested benefits.

A history of the local authority Children's Departments from their creation in 1948 to their absorption by social services departments following the Seebohm Report would be a valuable case-study of one such service designed to meet the special needs of a deprived group.[43] Originally intended simply to provide the best possible substitute care for those children whose parents were unable for a number of possible reasons to provide for them, it developed into a much wider service for the prevention of deprivation and delinquency and the promotion of good child care in the home. The work of the Children's Departments thus became focused on preservation and strengthening of the family unit, helping families to resist pressures to break-up, and keeping children wherever possible with their parents. When children did have to be received into care, the emphasis was on giving them as near as possible a normal upbringing. Whereas the 1930 Poor Law stated that Public Assistance Committees should 'set to work or put out as apprentices all children whose parents are not, in the opinion of the council, able to keep them'[44] (a restatement of the Elizabethan Poor Law principle), the 1948 Children Act required 'where a child is in the care of the Local Authority, it shall be the duty of that authority to exercise their powers with respect to him so as to further his best interests, and to afford him opportunities for the proper development of his character and abilities'.[45] The 'One Nation' spirit of the original Welfare State was thus extended, by the child care service, to those who had been the most unfortunate sufferers under the 'less eligibility' principle.

This spirit did not long outlive the wartime experiences on which it was based. Within ten years of the creation of the system based on the social insurance scheme, the first breaches were being planned in the principles that Beveridge had established. The very first principle to be discarded was that of universality. In another twelve years, a government had been elected whose major social policy commitment was the substitution of selectivity for universality as the rationale for dealing with the re-emergence of conspicuous poverty in an affluent society. This will be the subject of the next chapter.

3
The triumph of the Poor Law

In order to understand how the services for children and families discussed at the end of the last chapter are again becoming subjugated to principles of poor relief, it is necessary to look in some detail at the decline of the system of social insurance which was established after the Second World War. The re-emergence of Poor Law principles as the dominant values in social policy is due in the main to the failure of the insurance principle to provide an adequate system of income maintenance. It was this failure, heralded in the 'rediscovery of poverty', assisted by changes in the structure of the local authority services themselves, that allowed the old principles signified in Sir Keith Joseph's theory of the 'cycle of deprivation' to take root once more in our social services.

Beveridge's notion of a comprehensive, universal scheme of national insurance was totally accepted in the debate of the National Insurance Bill in 1946. 'There will be no adjustment in our Bill. It is one Bill for everybody in the country' stated the Minister of National Insurance.[1] However, by 1959 an exception had already been made in allowing 'contracting-out' of the scheme for wage-related retirement pensions, by allowing employers to contract their employees out of the scheme under certain conditions. By the end of 1966 4¾ million had been contracted out, mostly men in public employment.[2] The Labour opposition at the time did not oppose contracting-out in principle, but only the method (by the employer's decision) adopted by the Conservatives. But the notion of wage-related benefits introduced in the National Insurance Act of 1959 challenged Beveridge's other principles in an even more fundamental way, and set a trend that has since (unlike the notion of contracting-out) been accelerated. It was fundamental to the concept of social insurance, according to the Beveridge Report, that benefits should be provided which were adequate *for subsistence* and at the same rate 'irrespective of the amount of the earnings which have been interrupted'.[3] He felt that this was the 'central idea' of his scheme that distinguished it from its predecessors.[4] Both in the Report and the debates which followed it, a serious attempt was made to settle flat-rate benefits at a level that would provide subsistence for the average wage earner. It was generally agreed that no provision could be made for benefits above subsistence level, and that 'some kind of supplementation from national assistance would be necessary in exceptional cases'.[5]

From the start, benefits were fixed at a very low level, based on Beveridge's own rather parsimonious calculations of the cost of necessities for subsistence in 1938. However, the pressure from the Labour Party was never in the direction of raising the real level of flat-rate benefits (e.g. to keep pace with rising *wages*), but only to review them in the light of increases in *prices*. However, in 1957 there was a significant shift in the party towards the notion of wage-related benefits on the model of the many occupational schemes that had been developed since the war. Flat-rate benefits began to be discredited;

> what we had hoped would become a milestone in our history has become a millstone round the necks of many old people.[6]

> The demand for equal benefits for all may have suited the war period when the nation was under the same physical dangers to life and property, and the immediate post-war conditions of rationing and austerity, but it soon wore thin in the more affluent fifties and sixties. With the rise and diversification of wages, the steady demand for labour that gave hope to the working man for a continuing rise in his standard of living, there came a diversification in the way people spent their earnings. This was eventually followed by a demand for diversified social insurance benefits. If men were unequal during most of their life, there was no good reason why they should be forced into a deceiving state of equality at times when their earnings ceased or were interrupted.[7]

Accordingly, the Conservative Government passed the Act providing earnings-related pensions 'prompted mainly ... by the activity of the Labour Party in opposition'.[8] By the National Insurance Act of 1966, the Labour Government extended the principle of earnings-related benefits to sickness, unemployment, industrial injuries and widows' allowances, in a measure that aroused no political controversy. 'Thus the Beveridge revolution spent itself with the rise in national prosperity.'[9]

The adoption of earnings-related benefits is an example of the way in which affluent conditions give rise to official policies which reinforce the disadvantages of the poor. The other side of this policy is that low-wage earners (who are likely to be most vulnerable to unemployment) get lower benefits when they are out of work or sick than their better-off counterparts. The motive behind the change was that 'the National Insurance Fund was for the first time £14m in the red in 1958'[10] and that forecasts had been made that 'within the next decade this deficiency will reach £260 millions a year, and in about 20 years time will exceed £400 millions a year'.[11] If flat-rate benefits were to be maintained in principle, then they could only be financed by flat-rate contributions if the latter were increased to a level that was considered politically unacceptable, and would have imposed hardship on some lower-paid workers. The necessity of increasing contributions was therefore disguised by introducing earnings-related pensions which in no way compensated for the increase in earnings-related contributions. What the 1959 Act really introduced was 'graduated additional contributions—not benefits—so as to cut down the mounting charge on the Exchequer which the National Insurance Scheme was piling up'.[12] But the real need for this change rested on the myth inherent in the insurance principle. This, the weakest basis of Beveridge's scheme, is the one of his principles which has survived. His notion was that 'the insured persons themselves can pay and like to pay' and that 'it is desirable to keep the Social Insurance Fund self-contained with defined responsibilities and defined sources of income'.[13] However, because of the employers' and the State's contributions, the insurance notion is essentially fictitious, and the scheme is certainly not comparable with private insurance. In spite of this, the suggestion made to the Labour Party in 1956 that the National Insurance Scheme should be 'removed from its present actuarial basis and should be financed wholly through the Exchequer'[14] was rejected because it was felt that the resultant increase in income tax would be less politically acceptable than the earnings-related increase in the insurance stamp. 'Psychologically and socially', argued *The Times* in support of Mr Crossman, 'the stamp ... is accepted as different in kind from taxation.'[15]

The reason for this psychological fixation is not hard to find. Historically, the only precedents for non-means tested benefits were those introduced under the insurance principle since 1911. Since the financing of social security from general taxation could not be seen as related to any insurance principle, paying benefits *as of right*, the only alternative way of paying benefits seemed to be after a means test. In the absence of some new principle for the payment of benefits (and Bevan had no such suggestion to make) the choice appeared to be between an extension of the insurance principle through earnings-related benefits and contributions, at the expense of the flat rate principle, or a return to the Poor Law. What ensued was, in fact, a mixture of the two.

The 'diversification of earnings' already referred to had not dealt kindly with some sectors of the population. Some people's wages had risen more quickly than the cost of living, but others had failed to keep up with it. Townsend and Abel-Smith's revelation in 1965 that of the 18 per cent of households in the country which were living below the National Assistance level, two-fifths were in households primarily dependent on earnings, came as a shock to many, but was a natural outcome of inflation and the unequal bargaining positions of different groups of workers. It was equally natural that these revelations should be hailed as a 'rediscovery of poverty' and should lead Townsend and others to setting up the Child Poverty Action Group. The new school of thought concentrated on drawing attention to the consequences of *low earnings* on the one hand, and *low take-up rate* of means-tested benefits on the other hand. Inevitably, therefore, the debate about poverty came to be focused on the questions of income maintenance for those in work, and on poor relief outside the insurance scheme. Indeed, there could be no other focus for it, because in the absence of some completely new principle of income maintenance for productive and non-productive members of society (and the Child Poverty Action Group initially took no such stance), the only inference could be that what was required was some improvement in the existing system of poor relief.

That system had been established under the National Assistance Act of 1948. Although the Act began with the statement 'the existing poor law shall cease to have effect', its principles were essentially the same. It was the duty of the Board to 'assist persons in Great Britain who are without resources to meet their requirements, or whose resources ... must be supplemented to meet their requirements'. In disregarding more resources than had been the practice under the Poor Law, the Board merely carried forward a trend which had developed since 1930; and in determining requirements, it merely standardised the practices of local authorities and provided new scales for the blind and the tuberculous. The point of the Beveridge scheme was not to remodel assistance on new principles, but to relegate it to a residual role, to be used only in exceptional circumstances. Instead, it came to occupy an increasingly important role as time went by. Although the annual rate of new applications for assistance hardly increased from 1949 to 1965, the total number of people receiving weekly allowances in this period increased from 1,157 thousand to 1,997 thousand during this time.[16]

Although the Ministry of Social Security Act of 1966 made no changes in these basic principles of national assistance, the Labour Government made great play of having established a *right* to supplementary benefits. In fact, this 'right' consisted in no more than a few changes in the rules governing disregarded income, a wider publicity of the existence of supplementary benefits, and an administrative system under which supplementary and contribu-

tory benefits were paid together both to pensioners and the unemployed (though they still had to be *claimed* separately). There
was a large increase in new claims for supplementary benefits in
the year of the new Act, but Atkinson has shown that this can be
explained by the increase in the level of requirements rather than
a higher rate of applications among those eligible.[17]

The failure of the measures taken by the Labour Government to
come to grips with the problems of income maintenance is vividly
illustrated in the mutual recriminations of the Government and the
Child Poverty Action Group, published by the latter in their
pamphlet *Poverty and the Labour Government*.[18] The reply by the
Minister of State at the Department of Health and Social Security
to the Group's policy statement shows the extent to which it was
possible to misunderstand the Group's confused and confusing
approach to the problem it had uncovered during this period.
In its statement, the Group was anxious to deal with the suggestion
that its activities (which included encouraging individuals to be
more aware of their 'rights' to means-tested benefits) were 'appearing to maintain the existing system by seeking to improve its
efficiency. In fact the Group has been embarrassing the system
by showing the inadequacy of its procedures.' This claim was somewhat contradicted by the one on the back of the pamphlet that
'some major successes' included 'better publicity for rate rebates
and free school meals'. The Government had clearly interpreted the
Group's approach as being calculated to increase take-up; hence
Mr Ennals's frustrated incomprehension. 'There are now some
600,000 more people (old people, widows, the sick, unemployed,
deserted wives, etc.) drawing supplementary benefits than received
national assistance—yet Child Poverty Action Group condemn us
for this achievement. You just can't win.'

In fact, it had taken not only the Government but also the Group
until 1970 to realise that something much more fundamental than
increases in family allowances and better publicity for means-tested
benefits was required. The Group had done the poor no service
in defining the problem simply in terms of poverty. For, as Chadwick had pointed out in 1834, 'it has never been deemed expedient
that ... provision should extend to the relief of poverty; that is the
state of one, who, in order to obtain a mere subsistence, is forced
to have recourse to labour'.[19] If the Group had had any regard for
the historical basis of intervention in the field of poor relief, it
would have recognised that to draw attention to a sector of the
population suffering *poverty* was to invite upon that unfortunate
segment of the community the treatment which was by tradition
reserved for *paupers*. Since there was no accepted principle in the
tradition of our social services for maintaining the income of those
who were poor, it was necessary, before anything could be done to

relieve the needs of any persons alleged to be in that state, to ensure that they were destitute. Once the charge of poverty had been made, this was fairly swiftly accomplished.

As the Child Poverty Action Group belatedly recognised in 1970, this process was already well under way during the life of the Labour Government. What the introduction of supplementary benefits and the rate rebate scheme had achieved was that[20]

> contrary to Labour Party objectives the number of persons in the population who are dependent in whole or part upon the means-tested benefits of the Supplementary Benefits Commission had increased rather than decreased to 4·0 millions by the end of 1968 compared with 2·8 millions in 1965.

What Mr Ennals had expected would gladden the Group's heart was instead recognised as a cause for concern. Furthermore, the Group acknowledged a 'basic conflict' about means-tested benefits.[21]

> Not only do these schemes exist to confer benefits according to means, but they embody social discouragement of those who are alleged to be work-shy, spend-thrift or scrounging. In some respects they have to repel, and in others to attract, custom, and it is obviously difficult for the schemes to operate without repelling at least some people who need help.

In its own clumsy and slightly repellent way, the Group was recognising that its attempt to establish 'rights' to means-tested benefits (outlined the previous year in a pamphlet called *A policy to establish the legal rights of low income families*) was doomed to failure.

In fact, it can well be argued that the notion of a 'right' to supplementary benefit resulted in a decrease in the real rights of the poorest section of claimants. This was because of a misunderstanding of the relationship between *need* on the one hand and *relief* on the other. What the Child Poverty Action Group and the Government's own researches had proved in the mid 1960s was that need existed in the form of people who were living below the level of supplementary benefit entitlement. It seemed to follow that such needs could somehow be met in supplementary benefits. But poor relief has never operated solely in terms of meeting needs. There had always been some mechanism for separating destitution resulting from misfortune from exactly the same state of neediness resulting from what was regarded as wilful or negligent behaviour. In the absence of a proper *right* to benefits—such as existed by virtue of contributions under the insurance principle—the best title to means-tested allowances is the claimant's *deservingness* (i.e. that he is forced to claim relief but through no fault of his own). Clearly the most deserving (that is the most thrifty, industrious and prudent) are not usually the most needy and vice versa, so the two criteria of need and deservingness have been in conflict in our traditional system of poor relief.

This conflict is clearly evident in the Ministry of Social Security Act of 1966. Section 13 of the Act says that 'Nothing ... shall prevent the payment of benefit in an urgent case.', an apparently overriding emphasis on need as the criterion for relief. But Section 4 (i) (b) of the second schedule of the Act says 'where there are exceptional circumstances a supplementary allowance may be reduced below the amount so calculated or may be *withheld* as may be appropriate to take account of those circumstances'. What the poster campaigns and the rest of the publicity about supplementary benefits as a 'right' tried to do was to encourage the deserving (especially the elderly) to claim by attempting to reduce the stigma attached to an agency which relieved need. But this in turn had two effects on the most needy. On the one hand, the increase in volume of supplementary benefits work meant that their needs were given lower priority, as compared with the much larger-scale business of making payments to the more deserving who could often afford to wait longer. This resulted in the adoption of administrative systems (such as payments by Giro order and an increase in postal rather than face-to-face contacts) which were ill-suited to dealing with urgent need. On the other hand, it was felt by the authorities that there was a greater awareness of the availability of supplementary benefits, and hence a greater danger that the system would be abused. The counterpart to encouragement for the deserving to see the benefits as theirs by right was greater vigilance against the abuse of privileges by the undeserving, masquerading as the needy. The other side of the poster campaign was the four week rule and the Fisher Report.

It is interesting to contrast the attitudes towards undeservingness under the National Assistance Board with those that have prevailed since 1966. The kind of undeserving behaviour that has always aroused most public outrage has been 'voluntary unemployment' —claims by unemployed people who are seen as 'workshy' or reckless in their attitude to employment. In this, of course, public opinion has been strictly in line with the spirit of the Poor Law with its principle that only those who are quite unable to work should qualify for relief, and that those who are able to work must be prepared to do so on any terms. However, the National Assistance Board adopted a liberal interpretation of this principle, and its reports from 1951 to 1964 contained many references to surveys which indicated that this form of abuse was uncommon. For instance, the 1956 report concluded that 'wilful idleness, unconnected with any ... disability, accounts for lengthy unemployment in only a small number of cases'.[22] Furthermore, people whose claim for unemployment benefit was disallowed (either because they left work voluntarily or were sacked for misconduct), could apply for National Assistance with every confidence that, except in very exceptional circumstances, their claim would be granted. Thus 'undeserving' behaviour was not often penalised under National Assistance, and at the price of the stigma attached to the system, it did operate in the main according to criteria of need.

In 1968, new measures were taken to control voluntary un-employment. Following a Parliamentary debate in which concern was expressed on both sides of the House about 'scroungers' and 'layabouts', administrative procedures were introduced (without a change in the law), under which single men under forty-five who are fit have since been told on claiming supplementary benefit that they will cease to be paid after four weeks if they have not found a job. This has since been extended to include all men and women under forty-five without children. The Child Poverty Action Group found it surprising that 'after so many detailed and carefully pre-pared surveys had found little evidence of abuse ... the Department should have introduced the measures to control voluntary un-employment in 1968'.[23] However, this was just a beginning. The four week rule was defended as 'one of the most effective means of discouraging voluntary unemployment by fit young men' by the Labour Government,[24] and in the 1971 Social Security Act provision was made for the automatic reduction of supplementary benefit of any claimant disqualified for unemployment benefit, and also of all those claimants whose unemployment benefits are sus-pended while insurance officers *investigate* the circumstances of their leaving their jobs or being sacked. In 1972 a procedure was introduced for giving new claimants from outside the area (who had moved to the new area in search of employment), *one* week to find a job before being cut off. The latest variation on this theme was introduced in the spring of 1973, where, if the new area of residence is considered to offer worse employment prospects than their home area (in the opinion of the Supplementary Benefits Commission), claimants are refused benefits altogether, but offered a travel warrant back to where they came from. This effectively reincar-nates the spirit of the Laws of Settlement of 1662, under which for over a century vagrant paupers were returned by the Poor Law authorities to their parish of origin.

Another manifestation of official concern about the dangers of abuse through voluntary unemployment is the continued applica-tion of the wage stop. This is the rule under which unemployed and sick claimants of supplementary allowances are kept at a level of benefit which is no greater than their income would be if they were following their normal occupations. Following criticism of the rule, the official report in 1967, *The Administration of the*

Wage Stop, was at pains to defend the principle behind it. It was not designed, the Report insisted, to reduce people's benefits below the official scale of requirements in order to make them *worse off* than if they were working, but only to ensure they would not be *better off*—what might be described as a 'no-more-eligibility' principle. The Report promised that the Supplementary Benefits Commission would 'ensure that claimants who are subject to the wage stop are dealt with as sympathetically and equitably as possible'.[25] However, a recent survey of the administration of the wage stop concludes that it is being as arbitrarily and carelessly applied as ever.[26] This being so it has been a much more widely used weapon against the poorest group during the recent period of high unemployment than during the full-employment days of the National Assistance Board.

The third area of penalisation of 'undeservingness' is covered by the cohabitation rule. This is the rule that a man living with a woman has to support her and her children whether they are married or not. The resulting 'aggregation of requirements and resources' under which they are all treated as part of the same household, which denies the woman her title to supplementary benefit on her own account, is an example of the Poor Law principle of family responsibility. To allow women to claim for themselves and their children during a cohabitation, however temporary, would be considered to be a penalisation of married claimants, giving special privileges to unmarried parents, and thus weakening the sense of responsibility for the support of children which our system of poor relief has traditionally been dedicated to maintain. Here again, surveys of abuse have not revealed widespread fraud over cohabitation. In 1965 the National Assistance Board studied 152,000 case papers of unsupported mothers in receipt of benefit, and found that fraud had occurred in under seven-and-a-half per cent of cases.[27] In spite of this the number of special investigators, first appointed by the Board in 1956 to check on women suspected of cohabitating, have been steadily increased over the years, and the Fisher Report has recommended a further increase. Furthermore, the methods employed by special investigators have come in for some very severe criticism. 'Sex snooping', intimidation and the confiscation of allowance books on insufficient evidence have all been alleged both in newspaper articles and as a result of Child Poverty Action Group's researches. The latter discovered that 'in 1970 nearly 5,000 claimants were accused of cohabitating and lost either the whole or part of their allowance'.[28] They argue that the small number of appeals against such decisions reflects the fact that:[29]

many mothers feel humiliated by having a cohabitation rule

41

applied to them, and hesitate to go before a tribunal to have their private life discussed by a number of outsiders.... Many of the injustices brought to the notice of CPAG are reversed when local or regional office is contacted. The only cases going to appeal are those thought by the Commission to be most defendable, but the few which CPAG has represented have been won. Unfortunately, only a tiny fraction of claimants have heard of CPAG, and there must be many women who have no one to ask for expert advice.

The relationship between need and deservingness in the administration of supplementary benefits is best illustrated by the example of unsupported mothers. It is generally recognised, even by the Supplementary Benefits Commission itself, that unsupported mothers with young children are the most needy group of claimants in terms of the number of new needs which arise in day-to-day family living which cannot be expected to be supplied out of their weekly supplementary allowance. In their official report on the administration of exceptional needs payments, the Supplementary Benefits Commission stated 'proportionally more ENP's go to women with dependent children than to other recipients of supplementary benefit; the presence of children in the family has a direct relationship with the incidence of ENP's'.[30] However, at the same time, this same group of claimants is the one most subject to special investigation; most frequently suspected of fraud, and most likely to have benefits removed completely through allegations of abuse. The only conclusion one can draw from these facts is that the supplementary benefits system is one whose sensitivity to need is more than balanced by its sensitivity to the danger of abuse. Compared with the National Assistance Board, it operates much more like the old Poor Law, with its emphasis on the deterrence of fraud.

Yet in spite of this penalisation of the most needy minorities of claimants, the supplementary benefits system now operates over a far wider field than was originally intended to be covered by National Assistance.[31]

In 1948, 1,464,880 persons became dependent in part or in whole upon their allowances from the NAB. Twenty-three years later nearly three times as many people draw supplementary benefit. One in thirteen persons has his income, well-being and livelihood governed by the SBC. Far from the service withering away, as Beveridge originally planned, the size and scope of the Commission has grown.

This reflects the decline of the insurance principle as the major strategy for providing social security, and the re-emergence of the older Poor Law principles of poor relief as the dominant ones within our system. The creation of a unified Ministry of Social Security which Beveridge recommended, only served to emphasise this trend. It is very doubtful whether the amalgamation of contributory and supplementary benefits offices has, as was claimed, reduced the stigma and increased the availability of supplementary benefits, but it certainly has blurred the distinction between the two. So many contributory benefits are now having to be supplemented that it is effectively the Supplementary Benefits Commission that determines the level of social security provision in precisely the way that Beveridge sought to avoid. Instead of a national minimum subsistence standard being provided as of right, from which 'individuals may build freely up', there is again imposed a low-level ceiling above which no one who receives supplementary benefits is allowed to rise. It was this inevitable consequence of means-tested poor relief that led Beveridge to opt for universal benefits which were unrelated to income. The failure of his insurance principles to provide these benefits has meant that today, when most people speak of 'social security' (the term which he applied to his scheme), they are referring not to his institutions, but to those derived from the old Poor Law.

However, the story of the triumph of the Poor Law is not completed by tracing the emerging dominance of the Supplementary Benefits Commission. Of perhaps greater significance has been the very rapid advance of old principles of relief in dealing with the 'working poor'.[32] Seldom can a more disastrous label have been attached to a group discovered as a result of a social survey than this one. The Child Poverty Action Group can claim, with some justification, that it was not directly responsible for the proliferation of selective benefits aimed at relieving the needs of the 'working poor' that it had identified. Townsend and Abel-Smith's aberration in suggesting that 'part of the problem could be dealt with at relatively low cost by allowing national assistance to be drawn despite the fact that the breadwinner is receiving full-time earnings'[33] was never followed up by the Group, who advocated the more acceptable alternative of higher Family Allowances. However, their principles were seldom clear or unequivocal. Even in *Poverty and the Labour Government*, where they took a considerable step to the left in making a recommendation for a minimum wage, they were still concerned that 'one of the difficulties about such proposals is that the practical stages by which they might be introduced, and the consequences they would have for the rights people have acquired under existing legislation, have not been specified'.[34] They dismissed the proposal of a guaranteed income for every man, woman and child as of right on purely pragmatic

43

grounds, using figures derived from one particular suggested scheme.[35] Thus,[36]

> This is a cumbersome system to explain to the public and its effects on social insurance benefits (and rights built up previously) is unclear.... Would any political party regard this as realistic, in terms of the amount of public education that would be necessary, the administrative upheaval and the sum effect for ordinary families?

In its obsession with putting forward detailed schemes which might immediately be put into operation by the government of the day, the Group has frequently glossed over the basic principles at stake, hastening on to present the results of its statistical researches and to impress with its detailed knowledge of administrative procedures and how they might be reformed in their particular application. Furthermore, in spite of repeated asides in terms of the wages structure, income policy and the Government's fiscal measures, the problems of the 'working poor' were placed firmly in the context of the methods of poor relief available under the existing structure of the Welfare State. Low wages were discussed alongside the range of social security provisions and the local authority means-tested benefits. The Group reviewed various 'schemes' and came down on the side of the one (containing what the Chancellor of the Exchequer described as a 'civilised and acceptable form of selectivity') which seemed to them to meet the needs of those in low income groups, bearing in mind 'the climate of political and public opinion'.[37]

It would have taken a much greater awareness of the historical precedents for intervention in the lives of the 'working poor' than the Group ever displayed to have predicted the outcome of this pressure. When the Conservatives succeeded in the election, they were already committed to a policy of selectivity and to some kind of income maintenance provision for low-wage earners. With an uncanny sense of political tradition, Sir Keith Joseph produced, in the Family Income Supplement, a replica of the Speenhamland system of allowances which had been a Tory Government's answer to a similar economic dilemma in 1795. In deciding to make up half the difference between a low-wage earner's income and a fixed scale, which has since been adjusted to meet rises in the cost of living, the Conservatives followed the only Poor Law precedent available to them in the history of the past four hundred years. In doing so, of course, they had to flout a great many of Chadwick's principles which had been gaining strength under the Supplementary Benefits Commission's widening powers. Since 1970, the same principles have been equally offended by a whole welter of similar allowances to people in full-time employment—subsidies on everything from rents to butter. Yet, as we have already seen, any system of subsidising low wages undermines the very roots of Poor Law principles. It encourages the lowest income group to 'improvident marriages', 'an excessive growth of population', an irresponsible attitude towards children, a decline in 'habits of industry' and an increase of dependence and apathy, through the disincentive to work. How could the recent Government have made the same mistake as its predecessor, a mistake which was universally recognised in 1834 as having brought the country to the brink of a breakdown in law and order? How in particular could Sir Keith Joseph, with his consciousness of parental responsibility, have done so?

The answer to this question lies outside the scope of the matters discussed in this chapter. The crisis which led to the introduction of the Family Income Supplement was not a crisis in our social services, but in our economy. By 1970 we had reached a point where we could not any longer enjoy prosperity at the expense of a sector of people earning wages of less than subsistence level without a scandal. Some wages were simply not enough to allow those who received them to eat properly. This was not a new phenomenon, but the culmination of a trend. Beveridge's Welfare State was founded on the notion that it was only necessary to provide for the interruption or cessation of earnings. It had now become clear that there had to be some completely different principle to provide a sufficient income for some of the population to live. The choice was not whether to retain the principles of 1834 or to abandon them. It was whether to provide some guarantee of income maintenance for the whole population according to a universal principle, or to follow the precedent of 1795 and create a new class of subsidised paupers. The Government chose the latter course.

4
Wages and the work ethic

I have so far been suggesting that the theory of the 'cycle of deprivation' links poverty with maladjustment, and treats both as manifestations of the 'social problem' of poor families. It then goes on from this to create public welfare services which deal with the poor as a social problem, according to principles derived from the long British tradition of poor relief. But before such a theory could be tenably advanced, it was necessary to show that there is a social problem of poverty.

In the twenty years before 1965, there was no recognised social problem of poverty in this country. There was a problem of social security, which was seen in terms of income maintenance for those whose earnings had ceased or were interrupted. There were also a number of people whose earnings were low. But these two groups of people had very little in common. They did not think of themselves as constituting 'the poor' and official policy did not encourage them to do so. People whose income was low were simply people with a low income.

Take my own case. At the start of 1965 I was a probation officer earning just over £13 weekly. As I had one child, my pay was almost certainly less than my National Assistance requirements. I was badly off. But although I knew I was poor, I had no reason to think of myself as one of *the poor*. Five years later, a similar level of income would have qualified me for a whole series of selective benefits and allowances. The television would have told me that the government recognised my plight, and was constantly introducing new ways of assisting poor families like mine. Indeed, Sir Keith Joseph was making a 'frontal attack' on my problem. Even the trade unions recognised my condition as one of poverty, and encouraged the government to deal with it as a social problem by raising benefits and allowances. I would have seen that I was not, as I had imagined, simply someone with low pay, but part of a whole class of people with a similar social problem.

Social problems have to be defined as social problems before they become social problems. If the Labour Party and the trade unions had taken a different stance in economic affairs, low pay might well have been recognised by them as an economic problem. Instead, poverty was 'discovered' by social researchers like Townsend and Abel-Smith, who had set out on the kind of expedition that could only make a social discovery. Even then, the poor did not exactly rise up like some heathen tribe and attack those intrepid explorers, thus identifying themselves beyond all dispute. For some years there was considerable conflict between the experts and the government about just who 'the poor' were, and just what their social problem was. Now there is no dispute. The poor are clearly identifiable as the people whom the Government has elected to subsidise by the various forms of selective allowances that it has introduced.

If the social problem of the poor was invented by Townsend and the Child Poverty Action Group, the form in which it was created by Sir Keith Joseph was not the one they would have chosen. The Group had preached conversion of the problem by Family Allowances; Sir Keith Joseph chose the course of welfare imperialism in selective benefits. The characteristic of the Conservative approach to the poor was its paternalism. It created a dependent colony of paupers, a separate class, governed by different principles from those which it applied to the rest of the community. Somehow the metaphor of 'lame ducks' which it attached to the victims of its tough economic policies became associated with the beneficiaries of its new social measures.

The Tory principle which underlay the new policies was that of Divide and Rule. The crisis the Conservatives faced was how to arrange for a boom that they knew would benefit only certain sectors of the population. They planned their economic expansion to be based on integration with Europe, but the penalty they knew they would have to pay was that of an increase in the rate of price rises, especially in the prices of essentials like food. Since inflation was bound to be accelerated, they had to deal in advance with the total vulnerability of low-wage earners, whose bargaining position had been made extremely weak by a rapid increase in unemployment. Since the new Government had no intention of allowing their wages to rise enough to catch up with the cost of living (they had already fallen a long way behind it), the best way seemed to be to identify the poor as a needy, disadvantaged group which required a form of special treatment reserved for those who were inadequate to look after themselves.

Sir Keith Joseph offered the poor his *protection*. According to *The Times* report (11.11.70) on the second reading of the Family Income Supplements Bill, he said that

we hope to use it to provide a passport for the poorest to all the remissions available. It will give us contact with the poorest working class households about whom far too little is known, and give us knowledge to ensure these families apply for rent and rate rebates and other benefits.

Another Conservative speaker, Mr Kinsey, reflected the feelings of his party when he said that 'the Bill was a progressive step forward and embodied an entirely new approach. It recognised that the *less able* struggled to help themselves in the first instance. This was what they all wanted to encourage.' The offer was an apparently benevolent one, recalling Pitt's promise in 1795 to 'draw a proper line of distinction between those who are able to provide for themselves by their labour, and those who, having enriched their country with a number of children, have a claim upon its assistance for their support'. But the new Tory benevolence was as deceptive as the old. The double standard which divided the community into two nations (one ruled by the incentives of vigorous competition and rich rewards for merit, the other dependent, passive and subsidised) concealed a deep contempt for the poor. The concept of a whole class of people too inadequate to cope with life in a competitive meritocracy, is based on an assumption that the phenomenon of low wages can be explained as a social problem connected with moral, intellectual and industrial inferiority. The poor require protection by virtue of this inferiority, and it is this inferiority which determines the kind of protection they get. It is also this that determines the level of that protection. Michael Meacher calculated that families with a gross income as low as half the national average wage, would still be between £1·25 and £5 short of the supplementary benefit scale, plus average rent (depending on the number of children in the family) after the introduction of the Family Income Supplement. It was income maintenance for the socially inferior at an inferior level.

It is clear that even as early as 1970 Sir Keith Joseph was already operating according to a 'cycle of deprivation' theory of poverty and maladjustment. He had already formed an impression that there existed in 'the poor' a whole group whose behaviour was characterised by a lack of adequate self-discipline and control, who were often childishly dependent and passive, and whose financial, personal and emotional affairs thus needed to be managed for them by the wisdom of appointed authority. He had apparently been told by one of the new Directors of Social Services in an industrial area that 'we have 20,000 households in this city. Nearly all our problems—delinquency, truancy, deprivation, poverty and the rest—come from about 800 of them. And I think that most of the families have been known to us for five generations.'[1] Armed with this kind of concept of a substratum of society in which all social problems including poverty are concentrated, it followed logically that he should create a new battery of institutions to regulate not only the finances, but also the family life of the bottom five per cent of wage earners.

That this theory cannot be justified from statistics about rates of deprivation and maladjustment has been shown in the first chapter. Deprivation and maladjustment simply do not correlate with poverty in the way suggested by the Director of Social Services who wisely remained anonymous. What is even more alarming about this theory is its economic implications. It assumes that 'the poor', thus defined as the maladjusted and deprived group which is needy by virtue of its personal inadequacies and inferiorities, is a group whose size is limited by its ability to reproduce itself. Hence, presumably, Sir Keith Joseph's emphasis on limiting the size of families of the poor. But of course the size of the group of people who require subsidisation by allowances fixed according to a scale related to the cost of living is not determined by any such thing. It is determined by purely economic factors, such as the rate of increase in prices and the rate of increase of the lowest wages in the economy. Thus the sheer size of the 'social problem of poverty' is governed by economic factors over which Sir Keith Joseph has no control.

This, as Chadwick realised, is what went wrong with the first Speenhamland system. Although part of his justification for the abolition of allowances was the moral deterioration of the poor thus kept in a state of dependency, the other part was the ruinous economic consequences of this policy. This stemmed from the fact that creating a pauper class of subsidised labourers gave rise to a progressive pauperisation of the labouring class. Chadwick argued against allowances for the 'working poor' because 'their effect was to decrease the productivity of labour. They did this by making pauper labour, subsidised out of the rates, compete with independent labour. In the face of this competition, all the free labourers' skill, diligence and good conduct became valueless.'[2] The independent labourer therefore had strong incentives to assume the role of pauper, even if his wages remained sufficiently high to feed him. Thus the productivity of the whole rural working class tended to fall, and rural wages failed to rise during the years after the Napoleonic wars. Furthermore, there was an increase in the numbers of paupers, even though there was a fall in the price of food, which in practice determined the rates of subsidisation. Thus 'the total amount of the money expended for the relief of the poor' in 1831-2 was 'higher than for any year since the year 1820', in spite of the fact that 'the price of corn was lower by about one-third than in 1818, and that of clothes and of the other necessaries of life lower in still greater proportions'.[3]

The price of necessities is not falling at present. It has risen at a rate of between 9 and 10 per cent from 1970 to 1973. Therefore, quite apart from the incentive to pauperism offered by the allowance system (and the disincentives to more work offered by the prospect of a termination in these allowances), the economic factor which will determine whether pauperism will increase (as Chadwick would have predicted) is whether low wages will rise quickly enough to keep pace with rising prices.

It is not easy to produce up-to-date evidence about low incomes. Family expenditure surveys are not published until about a year after they are carried out. What we do know is that in the 1960s the earnings of the lowest paid declined in relation to average-wage earners. 'In 1960 the 10 per cent of male manual workers with lowest earnings averaged 71 per cent of median earnings. But in September 1968 the equivalent group averaged only 67 per cent of median earnings.'[4] In order to keep up therefore, the lowest-paid group will have to reverse the trend of nearly a decade. However, it is extremely unlikely that their position will improve in relation to average earnings, since 'among manual workers the lowest paid tenth earn no more of the average wage than they did in 1886'.[5]

This long-term persistence of inequalities of earnings is a very strong feature of our economy. Between 1913 and 1960, the groups which gained a larger proportional rise in earnings compared with the rest were managers (plus 8 per cent) and foremen (plus 6 per cent). Those who lost ground were clerks (minus 19 per cent), skilled manual workers (minus 6 per cent) and semi-skilled workers (minus 1 per cent). Unskilled workers retained exactly the same relationship to the rest. In 1960 the average unskilled man earned well below one third of the average manager's salary—proportionally less than he had in 1913.[6]

If, therefore, the lowest paid are as badly off in relation to the rest of society as they were at the end of the nineteenth century, it follows that at least they are no worse off than they were then. One might therefore ask why it has been considered necessary at this point in time to treat them so very differently from the rest. Since the low-paid have not conspicuously starved in the streets since the Second World War, it would seem surprising that it should be decided now that they are in urgent need of subsidisation. Since standards of living have obviously risen since the 1880s, it is not clear why this group should suddenly have to be given special allowances to enable them to exist below the official poverty line.

The answers to these mysteries are hidden fairly deeply in the mazes of our advanced capitalist economy. The phenomenon of increasing dependence on public welfare assistance culminating in wage subsidies is not unique to this country. In the USA, there was a 'welfare explosion' in the 1960s, with an increase of 107 per cent of families on assistance in eight years compared with only 17 per cent in the previous ten years. In 1969, President Nixon proposed a reorganisation of public welfare which Piven and Cloward describe as a 'scheme for subsidising paupers in private employ', and conclude 'the general parallel with events surrounding Speenhamland is striking'. They argue that both the increase in volume of assistance and the move towards subsidisation were the result of rising unemployment and a 'response to the civil disorder caused by rapid economic changes'. Extensive migration from southern rural areas to northern cities[7]

> led to a substantial weakening of social controls and wide-spread outbreaks of disorder. For if unemployment and forced migration altered the geography of black poverty, it also created a measure of black power. In the 1960s, the growing mass of black poor in the cities emerged as a political force for the first time.

However, the same type of political explanation does not hold good to the same extent in this country, for although the threat of civil disorder on the American pattern was undoubtedly in the Government's mind in 1970, the poor had not given any evidence of an ability to organise politically to be taken seriously.

The principle of poor relief which forbade the payment of allowances to those in full-time employment was one whose basis in orthodox economic thinking could not be taken lightly. The level of a man's wages was, according to economists, not something arbitrarily reached, but a sum which was a result of the workings of economic mechanisms crucial to the balance of the whole productive system. Because the worker sells his labour on the labour market, his wage is determined by a combination of his scarcity value and his productivity, with the strength of his trade union in processes of collective bargaining introducing a third factor. But this is not the only function of work and wages. These are also the measures of a man's income for consumption. The nature of the productive system is such that workers do not directly consume their own products; instead these are sold to them by their employers as commodities. It has always been considered a necessary part of the whole complex working of the economic system that the market relationships of work leading to wages, leading to income, leading to consumption of commodities, leading to work, should be maintained, and that any interference in these processes was potentially disruptive and reduced the chances of maximising production. While one example of this argument concerns the disincentives to good risk-taking management of a very high rate of taxation, an even stronger case has always been made for retaining the direct work-income connection in the case of wage earners at the bottom of the scale.

However, these arguments, especially those concerning low wages, have tended to lose ground. In part they have lost credibility because of the remarkable stability in relationships between the wages of different sectors and between wages and profits, despite economic fluctuations and changes in the manpower situation. In spite of all the mutations in the productive process and the ups and downs of the trade cycle,

> profits tend to fluctuate more than employment incomes in the short run [and] in 1938 the ratio of gross profits to all employment incomes was 1 to 4·5, in 1962 it was 1 to 4·8 and in 1965 it was 1 to 4·2.[8] Between 1870 and 1950 the share of wages in the national income varied between 36·6 per cent and 42·6 per cent. During the years 1960 to 1962 wages comprised 42 per cent of the national income.[9]

The other reason for the departure from economic orthodoxy is the increased importance of consumption as compared with production. Economic growth has become at least as much a question of ensuring that a wide range of technologically produced gimmicks and gadgets can be sold, worn out and replaced as quickly as possible as of increasing this range and output. Stimulation of demand can be achieved through advertising and through granting status to various forms of consumption, but income for consumption has to come either from work or from some form of state benefit. Since the management of aggregate demand has, since Keynes, become the major focus of Government economic policy, the Government is forced to consider income maintenance in this light. Thus raising social security benefits is one very effective way of putting money into people's pockets which will immediately be spent in the shops—an argument which was used to justify one such rise during the recent recession. But social security benefits did not help the 'working poor' to consume more; at least part of the purpose of selective allowances was to enable low-wage earners, despite inflation, to continue to consume at the required level. Henry Ford is said to have doubled his workers' wages to enable them to buy his cars; the recent Government halved the difference between its low-wage earners' incomes and the poverty line to enable them to buy more essential commodities in an inflationary situation.

This type of explanation also helps account for some of the phenomena of the American 'welfare explosion'. Forced migration of southern families to northern cities as a result of changes in the pattern of agriculture in the south, meant that people were moving from a backward, part-subsistence production economy into an advanced technological system, from one with a lower cost of living into one with a higher. Many of the large city areas to which black families moved had rates of black unemployment which were high in terms of the national average—at 9.3 per cent about three times the national average in slum areas of some cities in 1966.[10] However, these figures do not explain the rise of 217 per cent in families on poor relief in the five most populous major urban counties of the USA between 1960 and 1969.[11] It would seem that public welfare authorities were responding, in part at least, to problems of under-consumption through low income in families which had recently immigrated to the cities from southern rural areas.

Thus there would appear to be some economic justification in the British Government's decision not only to raise social security benefit levels, but also to subsidise some people in work. Indeed, there would almost seem to be a justification for giving people a guaranteed income *as of right*. But the logic of the capitalist economy cannot allow the principle of income maintenance to be taken to this natural conclusion. For the sake of the sanctity of the work-income connection, selective subsidisation of low wages is preferred. As Chadwick recognised, the trouble with this method of poor relief is the effect it has on people who narrowly fail to qualify for subsidisation, and the disincentives to work harder for those who are subsidised. Because of the *selectivity* of allowances, the principle of providing income for consumption has to be denied both in order to get more work out of those being subsidised, and *pour encourager les autres*. Instead of recognising a right to an income for all, it has to be pretended that those being subsidised are some kind of special cases, people who are inherently incapable (through some form of moral or personal inferiority), of earning a living from work alone. Thus the myth that the income-work connection has remained intact can be perpetuated, in spite of these exceptions, so that low-wage earners who are just above the allowance level can be persuaded that they are not being cheated of some kind of right but recognised as superior and virtuous.

The disjunction between the fact of wage subsidisation through selective benefits, and the myth of a necessary connection between work and income, exposes one of the basic contradictions of our present economic stage of development. The fact is that with an advanced technological productive process, there is no 'real' relationship between the work a man does and what he produces. 'Labour no longer appears as an integral element of the productive process. Rather, man acts as supervisor and regulator of the productive process itself.'[12] The 'real' production is done by machines. Even so, man's income is still tied to work.

The contradiction of advanced capitalism is expressed as the necessity for maintenance of the work/income connection. In order to extract a profit, capitalism must maintain both sides of the market mechanism; wages for labour and prices for growth. It is not simply a matter of having to work in order to consume. One must work for wages in order to have the money to buy goods at a price which yields profit.[13]

Capitalism is its own contradiction in process, for its rule is to reduce labour time to a minimum, while at the same time it maintains that labour time is the only measure and source of wealth.[14]

The present combination of benefits and allowances in this country is the perfect expression of this contradiction. It implicitly admits that the process of automation has gone too far to require the labour of part of the workforce, for in competition with machines they cannot earn enough to feed themselves. On the other hand, having made them effectively redundant, it cannot allow them not to work. If they resort to supplementary benefit, it hounds them back on to the labour market, only to provide them with filthy jobs, at wages so low that they have to be subsidised by the State out of taxes.

It is this aspect of enforcement of low-wage work which gives the whole situation its peculiarly repulsive character. It is not unique to this country.[15]

The structure of the American public welfare system meshes with and enforces the work system, not least by excluding potential workers from aid. Furthermore, harsh relief practices also maintain work norms by evoking the image of the shamed pauper for all, especially the able-bodied poor, to see and shun. And so it is that if the justification given for welfare restrictions is usually moral, the functions these restrictions serve are typically economic. Those who exploit the cheap labour guaranteed by these practices can take comfort not only in their Godliness, but in their profits as well.

In this country, low-wage work enforcement takes the various forms of the restrictions on supplementary benefit mentioned in the last chapter. The four week rule, the one week rule and the new 'Law of Settlement' ensure that men and women without children do not become dependent on supplementary benefit when there are jobs available (and when there are not), no matter how badly paid or menial those jobs may be. The wage stop ensures that families with children are given an incentive to accept low-wage work by keeping their benefits well below the officially defined poverty level. Throughout the long period of high unemployment that is just coming to an end, the poor relief authorities ensured that the unemployed took no comfort in their redundancy, and they are now using these regulations to harass them back into the labour market.

But if the regulations are themselves punitive, their actual administration is more so. 'Relief practice is always more restrictive than relief law.'[16] The Child Poverty Action Group found that 'the SBC local office does "put pressure" on family men without evoking the four-week rule procedure. Claimants call it the "roughing up treatment".'[17] Similarly, the wage stop is often used more harshly than official reports would suggest. The 1967 report stated that, in calculating the wage stop figure 'the estimation of future earnings must take account not only of the basic wages payable to men in their usual occupations, but also of the possibility of overtime, bonus payments, etc.'.[18] However, the *Sunday Times'* investigation made it known that the 'A' code under which calculations were carried out gave instructions that officers must 'never add for overtime'.[19] The Child Poverty Action Group also found that there was seldom any discussion with the claimant about his normal earnings, in spite of the report's requirement of this, and 'in few of the cases looked at did the wage stop figure reflect any serious attempt to come to a reasoned decision on the man's potential earnings in his "normal" occupation.' The real purpose of the wage stop is revealed in the cases they quote of[20]

> Mr. J. of Oxford, who had eight 'O' Levels and four 'A' Levels, had been earning between £30 and £25 per week in his previous occupation, and yet was being wage stopped, without his knowledge, as a temporary clerk at £15.75 [and] Mr. K. also of Oxford, who held a degree in Chemistry and a diploma in Engineering from a Pakistan university, was being wage stopped as a labourer at £12.90 without any discussion.

The administration of the wage stop is designed to provide employers with an adequate supply of temporary clerks and £12.90 a week Pakistani labourers.

Another set of administrative practices which enforce low-wage work are those of the Department of Employment. During the period of high unemployment, the device of 'alternative classification' was freely used to 'guide' redundant men with skills into unskilled low-paid occupations. Very often seasonal, short-term or temporary employment in such occupations was sufficient justification for the Department then to reclassify such men when they became unemployed again, either resulting in a wage stop or, where seasonal work was taken for three years running, a total loss of unemployment benefits. In one case known to me personally, a redundant coppersmith from a nationalised industry volunteered to be reclassified as a storeman after a year's unemployment, on condition that he was not sent to a particular factory, which had a bad record of industrial relations and redundancy. The *next day* he was offered a job as a storeman at this factory and, when he refused the job, his unemployment benefit was disallowed. Another Department of Employment device is the non-registration of claimants. New applicants for unemployment benefit in one country office known to myself are frequently given several low-paid job vacancies, and told to try these before they register as unemployed. If they do not accept one of these they are told that they cannot register, as they are not eligible for benefit. Because of this procedure, one claimant took a month to sign on as unemployed, and became destitute in the process.

The contradiction which is embodied in the relationships between work and wages and benefits and selective allowances is expressed in these regulations and their administration. The Government is anxious to claim that it is being generous on an unprecedented scale in its provisions for those who cannot work. But in order to give these new and more liberal 'rights' to the 'deserving' who are too old, severely disabled or sick to take part in the productive process, it has to make things all the more tough for anybody who could be suspected of malingering or of masquerading as unfit, and for those who use unemployment statistics as a cloak for 'work-shyness'. In the case of selective allowances for those in work, the balance is still more complex. Since they are working, they are by definition neither unfit nor incapable. Therefore there has to be some other justification for their subsidisation. Poverty alone will not do, because there is too much room for dispute about the arbitrary line dividing those who are subsidised from those who are not. Therefore there has to be invented some new kind of inadequacy, moral and personal, which requires this special treatment. Thus those who escape from the brutalities of those regulations designed to punish 'undeservingness' which they suffered while they are in receipt of supplementary benefit, find that many of the same rationing rituals (delays, means-test forms, the necessity publicly to parade their poverty, etc.) are carried over from that 'less eligible' situation into the next only slightly more eligible one of being in low-paid work. What the whole system of poor relief is designed to imply is that only those who can support themselves from income from work are to be treated as worthy of the respect accorded to fully-independent citizens. If the 'deserving' cases (the old, severely disabled and the sick), are permitted to feel that they have some right to support, the 'working poor' are part of a continuum with the 'undeserving', whose inferior status is reinforced by the treatment they receive from the public welfare authorities.

The way in which the stigma of poor relief gets attached to all forms of selective benefits can be seen in the very low take-up rates of all the allowances available to the 'working poor'. This applies to the various systems of rate and rent rebates, free school meals and prescriptions, but especially to the Family Income Supplement (which in spite of advertising programmes is estimated at 52 per cent of those eligible). Here again the experience is the same as in the USA.[21]

> During 1968 in New York City for example, approximately 150,000 families were eligible for wage subsidies (according to the Welfare Department's own estimates), but only about 15,000 families were claiming them. That few people know the welfare regulations only partly explains this peculiar situation, for even when poor families are informed of the funds available to them, they usually refuse to claim the payments. That the working poor are ready to forfeit such substantial sums is powerful testimony to the force with which the ideology of work and success, together with abhorrence of the dole, has been driven home to those who gain least from their labor.

So clearly is the message given that those claiming subsidies are part of the inferior pauper class, that even those living well below the poverty line prefer to do without selective allowances to retain their self-image as independent citizens.

Given the very low level of many men's wages, one way in which this can be done is by the wife taking a job. Without the addition of a wife's earnings, the numbers qualifying for subsidisation would be much higher. Hughes estimated that in mid 1970 (just before the introduction of the Family Income Supplement), there were one million men earning under £17 gross per week.[22] The proportion of married women in work has increased dramatically since the war. 'In 1931 married women constituted 16% of all women at work, while in 1961 the proportion was 51·4%. Looked at from a different angle, the proportion of married women occupied was 13% in 1931 and 30% in 1961.'[23] In a survey of working mothers and their children in 1963, Yudkin and Holme found that nearly half of their sample gave financial reasons for working. Of those whose motive was 'genuine necessity' (12% of those with financial motives), there were three times as many women who were sole supporters of their children as women with husbands. However, of the rest who said that their reason for working was to 'improve their standard of living', such items as 'to help out' or 'for clothes for the children' indicated that the improved standard was not necessarily luxurious. The authors concluded that an important factor in the decision of a mother to take a job was often 'financial pressures, usually very real, often directly related to housing shortage or to the desire to give children higher material and educational standards'.[24]

Married women are a further source of cheap labour to employers. 'Nearly four out of five women receive only a poverty wage for a full week's work, using the same measure as for men.'[25] In fact, about half of married women with children in Yudkin and Holme's survey worked only part-time, another factor contributing to low wage rates. The popularity of women as workers is reflected in their low unemployment figures. Many firms go to development areas and qualify for investment grants ostensibly because they are potential relievers of male unemployment, only subsequently to employ women workers at low rates of pay.

The paradoxical aspect of this situation is that many married women have come to regard work as an outlet and an escape from household drudgery, even where they do not have strong financial motives for working. Even among those who have least to gain in terms of wage rates, the work ethic seems to have been accepted as the way to self-respect as well as higher income. In the USA[26]

some AFDC mothers, with four or five young children, who picket welfare departments for MORE MONEY NOW! also carry signs proclaiming WE WANT JOBS! Among most welfare recipients, in short, the moral imperative to work—often no matter what work, the wage, or the child rearing obligations of the women who presume themselves to be employable—remains deeply felt.

This attitude gives rise to the extraordinary phenomenon of a popularised version of the movement for women's liberation which consists in nothing more than a fight for women to compete on equal terms with men for the right to spend long hours away from their families in adverse conditions of employment, in the worst paid jobs—disputing the opportunity to be exploited.

Working mothers have long been under suspicion as a possible cause of social problems in their children. This suspicion has never been justified in older children, but there is evidence that 'pre-school children whose mothers are at work are more often admitted to hospital, and are likely to stay there longer'.[27] Furthermore, 'where a mother sees little of her children from an early age, even if stable arrangements are made, the normal close relationship may fail to develop between them and conflicts of loyalty may arise for the child'.[28] These facts have not led the authorities to provide adequate incomes as of right to widowed, divorced or separated mothers of young children who are often, as we saw in the last chapter, the subject of the most intimidating and arbitrary treatment by supplementary benefits officers—tactics which frequently result in their attempting to support themselves out of full-time earnings, to the detriment of their children's development.

The officially sponsored preservation of the work ethic can thus be seen as one of the most divisive and destructive forces in our system of poor relief. In order to retain the exaggerated respect demanded for work (at any wage) which is considered an essential element in the market economy, the authorities devise procedures which stigmatise, ration and harass both those who are not working and those who cannot afford to live on what they earn. Yet, instead of instilling hatred for exploiting employers or their official accomplices, this policy only causes the independent poor to work harder and to despise those who require relief. Indeed, it was the fear of the workhouse and the shame of pauperism that more than anything else gave the deserving poor their industrious and thrifty traditions. The price paid in human misery for these prudent virtues has been a heavy one. Within a whole class of our society, it is accepted that work is inevitably heavy, exhausting, unsatisfying and merely a means to the end of having enough to live on. It is assumed to be inevitable that more money can only be respectably obtained by working longer hours or by working harder so as to do more during those hours. The whole basis of 'productivity deals' in manual occupations has been that people should have to work harder in order to earn more, in spite of the fact that labour-saving machines were all the time replacing men as the chief productive means. Taking orders, lacking all control over their work, doing dirty and degrading tasks, it is hardly surprising if, at the end of the working day, such people have little energy to devote to their children and see their leisure, such as it is, as an opportunity to escape into some form of relaxation that contrasts with the daily grind of their work.[29]

Of all the principles of poor relief upon which our present 'Welfare State' rests, the one that people should be prepared to work at any price to qualify for benefits, is probably the most brutal in its consequences. It is also likely to be the most difficult to maintain. Only by increasing the repressiveness of the penal measures against the undeserving and whipping up more conflict between the subsidised and the unsubsidised poor are the authorities likely to preserve the tattered work ethic in an utterly contradictory situation. The Speenhamland selective allowance system has once brought this country to the brink of a breakdown in law and order and could do so again. Eventually, it may come to a choice between the artificial preservation of the work ethic, at the price of organised conflict between resentful tax-paying workers and a dependent pauper class, or the overt abandoning of the work-income connection.[30] Perhaps only such a drastic situation could lead to the recognition of a new principle for income maintenance, based not on selection of the morally inferior, but on the recognition of a universal right to a guaranteed income.

5
Rationing, conflict and the Claimants' Unions

In the last chapter, I suggested that the notion of a 'social problem of poverty', which included deprivation and maladjustment, gained acceptance among other groups in society largely through the workings of the poor relief machinery used to administer selective benefits. It is largely through the stigma attached to these benefits that the poor acquire their reputation of inferiority, and attract the hostility not only of the officials who administer the system, but also of those who do not qualify for subsidisation. No account of the processes leading to a 'cycle of deprivation' theory would be complete without a more detailed examination of how this is achieved.

One of the political attractions of selectivity as a principle of social administration is that it gives rise to an impression among the many who do not qualify for benefits that the poor are being well (indeed too well) looked after by the government. It was a frequent theme of party political broadcasts by the recent Government that they have introduced new and unprecedented benefits to help special groups not previously covered by the Welfare State. The implication is, of course, that each of these minorities is a deserving one, characterised by a particular form of incapacity which requires relief. However, this does nothing to offset the general impression that the mass of the poor are being treated with a generosity they do not really deserve.

This impression is sustained by periodic references to abuse, or the danger of it. The setting up of the Fisher Committee to investigate abuse was an early act of the Conservative Government. The timing of its report was extremely fortunate from the Government's point of view. It came just at the moment when job vacancies were increasing, and the unemployed were needing to be forced back into the labour market. Even the relatively mild tone of the report was seized upon as evidence for long cherished prejudices. Newspapers which only months previously had run stories about social security bullies and sex snoopers, now carried editorials denouncing scroungers and layabouts. The resentment of unsubsidised workers became a tool in the hands of the Government, a means of threatening claimants into a socially acceptable pattern, and especially of enforcing the work ethic.

The advantage of selectivity is that Government boasts of generosity cannot be refuted by the actual experiences of many of the electorate. Since the majority do not qualify, they do not know what it feels like to be on the receiving end of the Government's largesse. This gives rise to the phenomenon so frequently encountered in social security offices of people making their first claim experiencing a shock in finding out how difficult it is to obtain benefits. But instead of causing identification with fellow claimants, this often provokes the reaction of resentment that 'those who don't want to work seem to get everything with no trouble at all'. The discovery that claiming is difficult for someone as virtuous as themselves merely confirms that the undeserving who are 'on it all the time' are having things too easy by half. Complaints from long-term claimants themselves about what happens to them are treated with some scepticism by the majority, since 'there must have been some reason for them to be like that in the first place'.

In addition to this, the very low level of many benefits and the consequent very small advantage to be gained from them is seldom recognised by those who do not qualify. The psychological reaction of the unsubsidised is characteristically, 'They're lucky to get anything at all—I have to manage without it.' The caricature of selectivity is found in the 'butter subsidy'. The Government were caught in a politically compromising situation over the European butter surplus, and the revelation that butter was being exported at a very low price to the Soviet Union. In a flash of inspiration entirely consistent with their social philosophy, they decided to provide the surplus butter as a selective benefit to the poor. Significantly they included those receiving Family Income Supplement with recipients of supplementary benefit. The level of the butter allowance is 10p per month, or less than 2½p per week. The administration of the new benefit involves vouchers issued at the post office and produced at the shop, the latter being an unprecedented advertisement of poverty not required by any previous selective measure. The administrative costs will almost certainly exceed the saving to the consumer, and in addition to this small shopkeepers are being forced to add to the prices of other items to compensate themselves for time spent reclaiming butter coupons from the Government. All this ignored the fact that many poor people had dropped butter from their diet as too expensive several years ago, so although most claimants see the butter subsidy as an insult, most non-claimants see it as a welcome gesture by the Government to those in need.

Yet it would be misleading to describe the feelings of the unsubsidised working class for claimants of selective benefits as 'envy'. Nineteenth-century labourers knew that the diet of paupers in the workhouse was better than their own, but they did not envy them. Mixed with resentment at the generosity of the authorities' treatment of the poor, are feelings of contempt and pity that anyone could sink so low as to require such treatment. These feelings in turn stem from the kind of assistance which is given to the poor. If they were simply provided with an income, as of right, without strings, then it would indeed be a source of envy. But an allowance that has to be claimed as a privilege, for which the qualification is destitution, which can be removed at an official's whim, and to which conditions of total dependency are attached, constitute a state of 'less eligibility' which is to be despised more than envied. In order to preserve the independence and the resentment of the unsubsidised therefore, it is necessary for the Government that relief authorities should maintain these unpleasant aspects of selective benefits to preserve their less eligible status.

The manner in which this is done varies between the different types of benefit. I have already described in chapter 3 how supplementary benefits are made less eligible, particularly for the most needy, by various administrative procedures introduced since 1968 to 'control abuse'. However, a mere description of these measures cannot do justice to the state of near warfare that exists in some offices between sectors of claimants and the staff. It may be significant that in the days of National Assistance, the notion of a union for claimants was never canvassed. The first signs of such an organisation coming into existence coincided almost exactly with the introduction of the first control procedures. It was in Birmingham in 1969 that the first Claimants' Union was formed, and since then they have sprung up in about eighty different areas all over the country. Claimants' Unions have adopted militant collective tactics in an attempt to combat the restrictive procedures of the supplementary benefits staff, and to protect rights which they saw being steadily eroded by changes in the administrative system under which payments were made.

One factor in this war has undoubtedly been the deteriorating financial situation of the supplementary benefits staff themselves. As benefits have been raised, their pay has virtually stood still, and their resentment has been expressed as much in their treatment of claimants as in their protests to the Government.[1]

The only significant change in earnings has been the downward trend of pay in public administration, very largely since the war. The 'Welfare State' has become the major low-payer, rewarding many of its own workers with less than it regards as adequate for an average family's needs on supplementary benefits.

This has not led to a mutual identification of interests (except during the CPSA strike), and supplementary benefits officers, far from making a common cause with Claimants' Unions, have tended to condemn their activities as disruptive and dangerous. Their attitude towards the stigma which their own procedures induce can be gauged from the fact that they insisted on having a separate department to deal with their claims for Family Income Supplements.

The war between the 'deserving' section of the working poor (as represented by social security clerks), and the 'undeserving' section of claimants (as represented by the Claimants' Unions), gives melodramatic expression to the social consequences of government policies. While the better-off sections of society get on with their daily business, these two factions battle it out, cancelling each other out in the fury of their confrontation. It is perhaps partly the small-scale and highly ideological conflicts between these two groups that enables the *status quo* to persist for the rest, in spite of the contradictions inherent in our present system. Pinker suggests that:[2]

> investigations into the welfare expectations and evaluations of the general public indicate complacency, and a general disposition to be easily satisfied with relatively modest levels of social provision. It seems possible, therefore, that most of those groups in the community who are diagnosed as 'under-privileged' or 'deprived' are far less aware of their condition, and far less ideologically motivated by it than those who undertake the diagnoses.

Pinker's analysis is hardly borne out in the writings and the activities of Claimants' Unions. The ideological commitment which he suggests is confined to 'minorities in the universities' is clearly identifiable in Claimants' Union literature.

> We do not intend participating in our poverty, we intend organising to abolish it. We want the power to destroy the Means Test system and the values attached to it such as the work ethic which we deplore. Nobody is going to offer us this power. We have to take it and run our own lives. And when we demand a say in our own lives we don't mean 'participation'. What we mean is CLAIMANTS' SELF-MANAGEMENT OF THE WELFARE STATE, and a GUARANTEED INCOME FOR ALL PEOPLE WITHOUT A MEANS TEST.[3]

'Supplementary Benefits are payable as a *right* to a person whose income is below the level of requirements approved by

Parliament' (DHSS). But to us Claimants this is all some joke —and a pretty sick one at that. At some time or other most of us have had our supplementary benefit refused, withheld or reduced. We know from bitter experience that the actual legislation contained in the 1966 Social Security Act makes a mockery of these lies. Paragraph 4(i) (b) of the 1966 give the Supplementary Benefits Commission absolute power to withhold or reduce benefit.[4]

The campaign for a guaranteed income[5]

lends to all our daily struggles as claimants against the S.S. and other arms of the State, a clear vision of an alternative form of society. As soon as the demand is considered in any detail, it will raise for everyone further possibilities and concrete ideas of movement towards a Socialist society which is based on production geared to NEED.

In practice, these 'daily struggles' have often been violent and have involved a much wider section of claimants than the articulate minority who write Claimants' Union pamphlets.

On Thursday, February 17th, about ten Claimants' Union members joined 60-80 other claimants at the H—— Social Security office. The anger was high. Most people had been waiting hours by half past two when the Union first arrived. When people started making their claims TOGETHER, backing each other up, the S.S. staff walked off. Some of the claimants had been there the previous days with no luck. Others had been promised Giros that had never come. And were told yet again: 'It'll be in the post'. Shortly after the Office was closed, one S.S. clerk punched a claimant who was taking pictures and smashed his camera. This was too much for those who were waiting. Claimants poured into the interview rooms and after the S.S. clerks had locked themselves in the back office, proceeded to smash up the interview rooms. Two cubicles were destroyed and there was a lot of other damage. The door between the waiting area and the room where the staff had run to was locked. This was smashed open by claimants who then crowded into their room. The staff couldn't escape. Standing there frozen with terror. The terror they are so used to inflicting upon the claimants. They were forced to listen to the claimants' demands. When the police arrived, three members of the Claimants' Union were selected by the S.S. staff to be arrested ... the state of H—— is notorious. Most days there are fifty to a hundred people waiting and waiting in their dingy, stinking waiting room.

The barricades have been put up to protect the S.S. staff at interviews. The clerks' hostility to claimants shows no sign of decreasing. They close the office whenever they feel like a break—and the money is getting further away.[6]

On Monday, March 6th, local Claimants' Unions marched from the Gazette offices, where we protested at their violent disregard of claimants' grievances, to S—— Social Security office. There were about 40 Claimants' Union members at the S.S. office, and with us we returned the stinky, mouldy WRVS furniture they had tried to dump on one claimant. We don't accept second hand goods. We arrived peacefully and waited our turn to be called for interview. As it became apparent that we would not leave without the S.S. staff taking down our claims, more police arrived. Within an hour there were about 40 police from about 3 divisions. It only needed a wave from the Manager's wrist for the police to forcibly and brutally eject most of the claimants. . . . Children were thrown on to the streets while their mothers were kept inside. Three women, two of them having children, and a man were arrested and eventually charged with threatening behaviour or obstruction.[7]

The right to representation has been one of the hotly contested issues.[8]

On Tuesday, Feb. 22nd, myself and another rep were asked to rep three strikers from Salversons, at H—— S.S. office at 2.0 pm. When we arrived we collected the number cards and went into the waiting room. Just after we sat down a S.S. officer came and said to the other rep. 'B——, I've had a complaint about you from one of our customers, you will have to leave the building, if you don't I will have to call the police.' A few minutes later the S.S. officer returned and said, 'B—— I'm going to call the police now, you're a nuisance. It's time you found a job instead of coming here and telling me how to do my job.' The rep replied, 'If you were doing your job properly there would be no need for us to be here.' The strikers backed us up at this point, and the S.S. officer stormed out of the room. Several minutes later a copper arrived.

Invasions of privacy are another area of conflict, particularly affecting unsupported mothers. The most obvious examples concern the activities of the special investigators. Here the isolation of claimants usually prevents effective action in countering espionage, harassment and the removal of order books. However, some claimants have adopted equally undercover methods to hit back at their tormentors. One unsupported mother succeeded in obtaining her social security file, and published the results of her own investigations.[9]

> I've had the usual experiences that claimants have had—unnotified visits, people barging into the house and asking all sorts of rude questions, having to wait for weeks on end for any money to come through, having to wait for long periods when my order book expires, but really this is commonplace with all claimants. So a few weeks ago I decided it would be fairly interesting to get hold of my file. What I expected it to contain was lots of information about myself as a member of the Claimants' Union because a friend's file, in fact, had a statement on it saying 'This woman is likely to be accompanied by Carol Parris, who is a well-known pest and agitator, and always spells trouble and must be treated with caution at all costs.' And so when I managed to get hold of my file I was amazed to find transcripts of my interrogations, with amazing details of their interpretations of my character and my sex life, etc. I'll quote some of the things that are in the file. It says, 'A very neurotic girl indeed ... in need of psychiatric treatment ... a rather self-centred person (who lives) in a twilight area of Brixton in some sort of community centre.' In the file there's a description of this male friend who went along to the office with me one day saying 'Claimant was seen at office window accompanied by a man five feet eight or nine inches, long brown hair, eyes blue (?), wearing glasses; he did not speak, but I gained the impression that he was from the Claimants' Union.' As a matter of fact, he wasn't from the Claimants' Union.

Other claimants who have 'obtained' their files have found similar detailed reports and speculations about their private lives by social security officers; hence the call for 'counter espionage' by Claimants' Unions following the publication of the Fisher Report.

While most of the erosion of claimants' rights since 1966 has taken the form of controls on 'abuse', administered by counter clerks in the offices, another whole strategy has been the changes in office procedures (such as the appointments system), and the centralisation of the social security system involving the closure of small local offices. These changes added to the difficulty of getting emergency payments for those in urgent need. At Newton Abbot, in Devon, the Claimants' Union decided to mount a campaign against the closure of its office, which would have meant a journey to Torquay, seven miles away, for urgent needs payments over the counter. The Union succeeded in mobilising not only claimants throughout this small community, but also a cross-section of the rest of the town and the surrounding area. In spite of the lack of precedents for demonstrations in Newton Abbot, the Union organised a march, depending for support as much on offended local pride as on the militancy of its own members. A dinner for pensioners and a concert in the park by the town band gave the occasion an almost carnival atmosphere. The Union relied on ridicule as much as rhetoric in its attack on the proposed changes. A street-sweeper's cart was trundled through the streets as 'Free Transport to Torquay provided by the Social Security', and a group of claimants took part in the procession as 'The Redundant Social Security Officers' Dance Team'.[10]

> Most of the marchers were old-age pensioners who make up five-sixths of the claimants. Other delegations included the Blind Federation and Orthopaedic Association. Other protesters were social workers and members of churches and trade unions. The only incident during the good-humoured protest occurred when a loud explosion and shattering glass was heard from a shop in the main street. An astonished shop assistant, seeing Newton Abbot's first recorded demonstration, had dropped a large bottle of boiled sweets.

This protest, followed up by an intensive campaign locally and a national sit-in by other Claimants' Unions, succeeded in persuading the Department to keep open an emergency service in Newton Abbot which provides over-the-counter payments for cases of urgent need. The volume of payments made (up to fifty per week) indicates the sort of hardship that occurs when centralisation leaves behind no local facilities for emergency needs.

Another of the battlegrounds between Claimants' Unions and supplementary benefits staff has been Section 7 of the Ministry of Social Security Act. This states that 'Where it appears to the Commission reasonable in all the circumstances they may determine that benefit shall be paid to a person by way of a single payment to meet exceptional need.' Claimants' Unions have argued that this gives the Commission very wide powers to relieve the needs of those living in poverty. There is no statutory limit on the amount of an exceptional needs payment or on the purpose for which it can be used. By implication, therefore, it makes the Commission responsible for the relief of any exceptionally needy claimant in such a manner as to bring his standard of living (in terms of household equipment, furniture, clothing or any other need) up to an acceptable standard. Thus, according to Claimants' Unions, any claimant living in conditions of extreme poverty represents a reproach to the Commission, and evidence of its failure to exercise its powers under Section 7 of the Act.

The Commission's own interpretation of this Section is, in fact, very restrictive. It is determined by the fear of appearing to reward the spendthrift 'undeserving' behaviour of those who fail to make proper provision for all the necessities of life, either when they are in work or out of it, and thus of penalising the provident and the thrifty. The official report on the administration of exceptional needs payments states that although the scale rates of supplementary benefit are supposed to cover the cost of the repair and replacement of clothing and footwear, over 50 per cent of all Section 7 payments were made for such items.[11]

> To the extent that the Commission make such double payments, they are treating those who, for whatever reason, have not made proper provision for their foreseeable expenses more favourably than those who, though not less in need, have succeeded in doing so.... Against the risk of hardship in individual cases must be set the risks of unfairness, as well as those of encouraging a small minority of claimants deliberately to mis-spend their income, or more commonly to fail to manage it properly, in the confidence that the Commission will always bail them out at the end of the day.[12]

The bogey of abuse is thus invoked once more to justify rationing policies, which are plainly aimed not only at ensuring that 'undeservingness' is not made more eligible than deserving behaviour, but also at preserving incentives to thriftiness by those in work. Even though the Commission's own investigations found only '42 cases of misuse or mis-spending ... out of 1,429 cases examined',[13] there was clearly anxiety that too much generosity would have a demoralising effect. Here, of course, what is meant by 'mismanagement' is failure to provide for such large-scale outlays as are involved in purchasing winter clothes, or in redecorating a house. In order not to penalise people who are expected to do this out of incomes from work which are well below supplementary benefit levels, the Commission withholds exceptional needs payments from long-term claimants whose situation might otherwise seem too comfortable by comparison.

This same fearfulness of the consequences of a more liberal interpretation of Section 7 is seen in the Commission's attitude to the suggestion that 'rights' to these payments should be advertised. It is feared that no kind of advertisement could clarify the delicate mechanisms involved in the decision whether or not to make such payments.[14]

> In general, when meeting exceptional needs, the Commission believe that the right principle is to meet those needs that are felt and expressed by claimants themselves.... The Commission do not regard it as their function to bring all supplemen-

tary benefit households all over the country up to some pre-determined minimum level of stock in clothing, bedding and household equipment.

For these reasons, the Report concludes that 'The Commission fear that an "advertising campaign" would do more harm than good' by stimulating 'a flood of unsuccessful claims'.[15] What this means in practice is that many claimants who have no idea of the existence of exceptional needs payments are left with the onus for making claims for things they do not know they can get. Still others who do not regard appalling conditions of poverty and chronic want as unusual features of their lives, are encouraged to accept their lot; they should not, says this policy, be misled by rash promises to become discontented with things as they are. Such poverty, after all, is not really exceptional, but more or less in the everyday run of things.

The effectiveness in rationing exceptional needs payments of this policy is reflected in the fact that they made up only 0·7 per cent of expenditure on supplementary benefits in 1971.[16] Yet it is widely known in Claimants' Unions that the supplementary benefits staff *do* have a list of clothing, bedding and household equipment which is regarded as constituting an acceptable standard of living, and that there are very few long-term claimants who could not qualify for some kind of exceptional needs payment at once if they were aware that these are available. The hypocrisy of Government statements about wishing to relieve poverty has infuriated Unions who are aware of the enormous powers available to the Commission under Section 7 which are not being used to meet known needs as a result of deliberately restrictive policies. As a result, a running battle over claims for exceptional needs payments has taken place between some Unions and staff, focused on trying to get such needs met by over-the-counter payments.

These tactics have been adopted in the face of a further move away from reasonably accessible exceptional needs payment through reductions in the visiting services of the department. In addition, the office appointments system helps keeping waiting rooms empty, both by telling those who can afford to wait when they can be seen, and by telling those in urgent need who cannot afford to wait that they cannot be seen without an appointment. The Claimants' Union have seen this as another sinister development.[17]

> *Most worrying* is that the new systems (on top of the three-type classifications of claimants into 'non-problem', 'potential problem' and 'active problem' which came in earlier this year), are going to make it easier for the S.S. to cut down the number of claimants making *demands* on the system, and make

oppressive treatment of a small minority that much easier. For example, those claimants who are getting a better deal from the appointments system are not going to have so much sympathy for those who lose out.

Here again, the Claimants' Unions have tried to break through barriers by the use of Section 13 claims, stressing the department's responsibility to pay *immediately* for urgent needs. In one case, a claimant who was asked to prove that she was starving bit the clerk's hand. In another case, a man waiting for a visit for a clothing grant went to the office to claim an immediate payment because his trousers had a large split in the seat. He and a group of others with similar claims were told they would be visited. When they insisted on being interviewed, the police were called, and the claimants were forcibly evicted from the office in a scuffle that caused injury to women and a baby. In this case, a waiting queue of claimants intervened to protect a representative who was being manhandled by the police.

For those who are aware of the existence of exceptional needs payments, and who make claims for appropriate needs as they arise, such grants can form a much more important source of extra income than the 0·7 per cent average proportion of supplementary benefits would suggest. Any knowledgeable claimant counts his eligibility for these as worth a good deal more than the halfpenny in the pound that the Report's figure would imply. Indeed, qualification for Section 7 payment is one of the many factors which operates in the so-called 'poverty trap', under which those who do claim all the selective benefits for which they are eligible are placed in the invidious position of having to give up all of them simultaneously if they get work at a wage above their supplementary benefit entitlement.

The 'poverty trap' is the other side of the coin of less eligibility. While the majority of claimants are deterred by the stigma or rationed by the administrative procedures attached to selective benefits, there are some who make it their business to get every penny they can out of the system—the philosophy of the Claimants' Unions. But unless this is combined with a rejection of the work ethic, and a determination not to accept low-paid work on any conditions, the result is that within a broad band of incomes above supplementary benefits they lose a pound for each extra pound they earn. This applies increasingly with rent rebates, as the cost of housing is rising more rapidly than any other cost.

What is not generally recognised is that some 'poverty traps' operate even within the system of state benefits. For instance, invalidity benefit is a type of higher-rate sickness benefit paid to people who are sick for over seven weeks. It is devised so as to put some claimants' income just above their supplementary benefit entitlement. This means that they immediately lose their entitlement to exceptional needs payments, their free school meals, exemption from prescription charges, their milk tokens, and in some cases part of their rent and rate rebates. It is significant that invalidity benefit allows the wife of a sick man to earn a much larger sum at £9·50 than supplementary benefit disregards (£2), thus giving a broad hint at where the extra money is expected to come from. One member of the Newton Abbot Claimants' Union was so much worse off on invalidity benefit by the working of this mechanism that he fought a long battle with the local social security office, arguing strongly that he had paid insufficient contributions to qualify, while they insisted that he had.

The poverty trap is one of two features of selective allowances which help explain why the take-up rate for such benefits as rent and rate rebates and Family Income Supplement are estimated to be about 50 per cent. People on low incomes do not want to believe that their situation is a long-term one, and do not want to claim these allowances just to lose them again if their wages improve. The other reason lies in the very complicated claims procedures attached to these allowances, and the long delays involved. Such claims involve filling in a complex form (giving incomprehensible scales of qualifying income), sending wage slips covering several weeks, and waiting several more weeks for determination of the claim. The sheer proliferation of these allowances and the forms that accompany them is also a factor. Even where people are competent to understand and complete applications, they are overwhelmed by the volume of them. In Newton Abbot (population 20,000), only *one* tenant made representations to the local authority against its determination of the levels of 'fair' rents for council houses. Effective as this method of rationing by form filling and delays may be, it is not as stigmatising and deterrent as the control procedures on supplementary benefits. Allowances for people in work such as rebates and Family Income Supplement are not actively accompanied by the same level of unpleasantness because they do not involve direct contact with relieving authorities. Like benefits paid in weekly order books, they remain impersonal in their insulting character. This factor helps to make allowances for the working poor, and consequently low-wage work itself, marginally preferable for many to the indignities of unemployment.

It would be a distortion of the changes that have taken place in our social security system since 1966 to suggest that supplementary benefits staff *enjoy* or welcome the kind of conflict with claimants which I have described in this chapter. While it is an inevitable consequence of the sort of controls on 'undeservingness' which have been introduced by those who decide on how benefits are to be administered, the violence and unpleasantness which has taken place in many social security offices is deplored by most of the staff. Simultaneously, a number of changes have been made in the system of administering supplementary benefits which are intended to reduce stigma and conflict. These include Giro order payments, postal review and the appointments system in office waiting rooms. All these changes have probably benefited the majority of claimants, except when they have found themselves in urgent need. They constitute a move in the direction of supplementary benefits offices operating more like contributory benefits offices, conducting most of their business through the post, and minimising face-to-face contact with claimants.

However, as we have seen, these procedures are hopelessly ill-suited to deal with urgent need. Where this arises, it inevitably causes clashes between staff whose priority is checking entitlements against claims and the issuing of Giro orders through the post, and claimants in immediate need of money. The strategy of the Supplementary Benefits Commission, therefore, has been to export the conflict and turmoil surrounding its most needy claimants to an agency which already deals with turbulent and stigmatised people. This policy serves several ends. It gets rid of a nasty violent problem; it allows the Supplementary Benefits Commission to get on with their nice clean postal jobs, and it fulfils the needs of the less eligibility principle by handing over the 'undeserving' sector of claimants to an agency which already carries greater stigma in the eyes of the public than the social security itself. That agency is the local authority social services department.

Stevenson has argued that such a change follows inevitably from the attempt to make supplementary allowances serve as a substitute for the subsistence social insurance benefits which were the original basis of the Welfare State.[18]

> One aspect of the movement to reduce stigma was a concern to establish a principle of 'entitlement' to benefit. The word, which came into use after the formation of the SBC in 1966, but whose implications were already evident in the NAB, carried an implication of 'a right' rather than 'a need', thus shifting somewhat the formal power relation between claimant and official. With this, however, went the expectation that entitlement would be precisely defined by legislation, so as to reduce the extent of individual discretion and decision-making by officials in particular cases.

She points out that this emphasis on 'proportional justice' (i.e. the equitable distribution of benefits according to criteria of fairness as between individuals in society), demands a shift away from the provision of 'creative justice', which is 'concerned with the uniqueness and therefore the differential need of individuals'.[19] 'However ... neither the NAB nor the SBC have eliminated discretionary powers which represent an element of creative justice in the system.'[20] Stevenson goes on to say:[21]

It appears to the writer to be unarguable that a means-tested scheme that is, in effect, a safety net into which people fall when other forms of benefit are not available or have been exhausted, must be flexible or it is a contradiction in terms. This flexibility implies a capacity to respond sensitively to a diversity of financial needs, to the unique circumstances of individuals.

There remains, of course, the question of how this flexibility of response can best be provided. If it is admitted that *any* scheme for benefits as of right will require some such underpinning, it is quite another question whether this should be done by the same agency which dispenses these other benefits, by a separate residual income maintenance service (like the National Assistance Board was intended to be under the Beveridge scheme), or by a social work service like the local authority social services department. Stevenson herself gives some strong arguments against the latter pattern, based on American experience of public welfare agencies.[22]

Whether from philosophical yearnings or from a need to rationalise the status quo, the role of social work in public assistance in the U.S.A. was justified on the grounds of the indivisibility of need—material, social and psychological. Those who criticise the idea ... fear the intrusiveness of the social workers, who may ask questions irrelevant to the material need and who may, in actuality, or in the perception of the client, offer assistance in return for certain kinds of 'improvement' in behaviour. There is no doubt that what has been described as 'the psychiatric deluge' that swept American social work in the 1940's played a significant part in all this. ... Such influences filtered into public assistance agencies, affecting workers, many of whom were untrained and professionally insecure, and resulted in an inappropriate application of Freudian theory in which practical requests were believed to require examination at a 'deep level' to uncover their underlying significance.

Stevenson's analysis of the origins of the American public assistance workers' theoretical framework is questionable, and she goes on to conclude that we should not be hasty in applying conclusions from American experience to our own system. However, in these few sentences at the beginning of a book giving a detailed and largely approving analysis of recent developments in supplementary benefits and social work, she clearly demonstrates the relevance of the American public welfare agency as a model to compare with our own. In particular, we should consider the likely effects on the lives of the most needy group of claimants on having their cases exported by the Supplementary Benefits Commission to local authority social services departments.

What has happened to our social security system is that supplementary benefits have been expected to do too many things at once, and consequently have come to satisfy no one. Since 1966, there has been a huge increase in claims from retirement pensioners, who have become eligible under revised scale rates. This very 'deserving' group deeply resents the means test, and the stigma of even the modified supplementary pension. This helps to explain the recent Government's tax credit proposals, which will remove several hundreds of thousands of the most 'deserving' old age pensioners out of the supplementary benefits scheme, and prevent many more joining it.[23] However, at the other end of the scale, supplementary benefits have increasingly failed to meet the needs of the younger poor, and especially of parents of young children. Criticisms and conflict have led to the gradual transfer of emergency and exceptional need provision for poor parents to the local authority social services departments. This transfer means that the younger poor are being dealt with by a very different kind of service, and this has very important implications for the kind of treatment their poverty is likely to receive.

But equally importantly, we should consider the effects on the services provided by local authorities of this influx of income maintenance obligations. Our services for children and families have been built up with immense care and massive endeavour out of the shambles of the Poor Law, and the crisis and scandal of the era of Dennis O'Neill and the Curtis Report. We should think of what is being done to these services by making them take on the role of underpinning to the Supplementary Benefits Commission. We should consider what is involved in making a public welfare agency.

6
The making of
a public welfare agency

So far I have suggested that the development of the income maintenance services since the war has been in the direction of reaffirming the principles of the old Poor Law in relation to the 'undeserving' poor, the dangers of abuse, and the necessity for using punitive methods to uphold the work ethic. In the last chapter I indicated the consequences of this development in the sometimes violent conflict between supplementary benefits staff and groups of organised claimants. I have argued that this conflict can be traced to an erosion of claimants' rights to immediate payments for urgent needs, which have followed from the authorities' attempts to make supplementary benefits an acceptable form of income maintenance for the majority of the five million people who now rely on them.

This attempt to use supplementary benefits as the basis of an overall income maintenance provision for a broad section of the population has resulted from the failure of the principle of social insurance to establish itself as a firm foundation for subsistence provision for the worst-off members of the community. However, in attempting to replace the contributory principle with a means-tested system for this broad section of largely respectable and 'deserving' people, the Supplementary Benefits Commission has converted itself into an agency which is ill-suited to meet the needs of the most needy group, and to deal with emergency situations. It has therefore required underpinning by a public welfare agency which, on the American model, dispenses a restricted form of special payments along with control and supervision, and a social work service for those families whose failure to provide can be seen as resulting from personal inadequacies.

In this chapter, I shall suggest that such an agency is being created in the local authority social services departments. The direct ancestors of these new departments were the local authority social work services which came into existence in 1948. However, I shall suggest that by a slow and subtle process, they are coming to take on many characteristics of their more remote forebears, the Public Assistance Committees of the period immediately preceding the Second World War. This is happening not so much as a result of direct Government intervention or conscious planning, as in response to needs created by changes in the income maintenance services.

The Public Assistance Committees, which were created in 1929 when local authorities last underwent a major reorganisation of their boundaries and powers, represented both the first step in the break-up of the old Poor Law, and the final pre-war expression of the principles of 1834. Throughout their brief existence, they co-existed with the Unemployment Assistance Board, a centrally administered agency, funded out of taxation, which dispensed a rather more liberal type of means-tested outdoor relief to the able-bodied poor. The work of the local authority Public Assistance Committees, therefore, was confined to financial and institutional provision for the old, the sick, the disabled, the homeless, the mentally ill and subnormal, and children deprived of normal family life.

Not much scholarly attention has been given to the work of the Public Assistance Committees, perhaps because they are generally seen as an intermediate stage between the old Poor Law (which is generally studied as both the origin of our present social services and a contrast with them), and the more enlightened provisions of the Welfare State. In fact, they are of considerable interest because both in structure and in function they closely resemble our newly-created unified local authority Social Services Departments. An exception to the rule of academic neglect of their work is Nigel Middleton's book *When Family Failed*. In it, he documents the extent to which the principles of 1834 still governed the work of the Public Assistance Committees, and particularly their approach to children in their care.[1]

> Although there was no public repudiation of the Poor Law principles, they were generally assumed to have died with the abolition of the Boards of Guardians in 1929. Nevertheless, they can be seen to form the basis of the treatment for children in community care, especially the aspects of it which deprived them of full citizenship.

In particular, the practice of segregation of the sexes in the workhouse, and the separating of parents from children, continued to be ruthlessly pursued.[2]

> The policy of ignoring family ties was so widespread that even a cursory investigation shows how it largely repeated the procedures of the nineteenth century. Immediately on arrival in Poor Law care, the segregation of the sexes began, and consequently the breakup of the family unit. Complete families taken into the workhouse, after the usual reception routine,

were compelled to live a separate existence. In the 1930s, a high wire netting divided the workhouse grounds into sections. Through this, wives conversed with husbands and children with fathers. . . . Little tots pressed their lips to the wire in awkward kisses for their fathers stooped low on the other side of the netting. The fathers only saw their children for an hour or so each evening, and only in this way. . . . After a time, the children were taken to separate children's institutions, where the general rule was still to allow a monthly visit from the parents, who usually had to walk the several miles between the two establishments clad in pauper uniform and under the escort of officials.

Middleton leaves no room for doubt about the motivation behind this punitive treatment. It was the need to preserve the principle of 'less eligibility' for those in need of poor relief.

The Poor Law could consider but one category of inmate—the pauper; the person who ought not to be there; the semi-delinquent who ought to be grateful for being kept alive, whose condition, far from being improved, is supposed to be kept less eligible than that of the lowest grade of labourer.[3]

The social services acceptable to this situation were those based on the Poor Law, since the costs were known to be easily met, and any tendency to lavish expenditure could be eliminated.[4]

Thus, the quality of the service for all categories of people dependent on the Public Assistance Committee was regulated by the need to ensure that no class of pauper should be seen to be treated better than the poorest independent citizen. The work of the local authorities continued to be the same as the work of the Boards of Guardians.

When the National Assistance Board was created in 1948, it took away all responsibilities for outdoor relief (i.e. financial assistance to non-institutionalised people) from the local authorities, leaving only the institutional side of the old Poor Law to be administered by the new local authority agencies, set up to deal separately with the problems of old age and homelessness, deprived children and the mentally ill. The task of the Welfare, Children's and Mental Health Services was to build up a new tradition in their approach to helping the families and individuals who depended on their care. They inherited an appalling legacy. 'Whatever faults were inherent in the Poor Law, and there were many, the consequential destruction of the family must rank as probably the most damaging; not only did it strike at the very unit of society, but the resulting damage to individual personalities was often irreparable.'[5]

In creating a new ethos of respect for individuals and families, the local authorities had to attempt to build a social work service out of what had been an instrument of repression. In this they were greatly helped by having had their duties for poor relief, and consequently all the punitive implications of public assistance, taken away from them and assumed by the National Assistance Board. It was only thus that they could establish services which were not weighed down by considerations of 'less eligibility'.

In the search for antecedents for the ethos and the methods of the new local authority social work departments, it is tempting to look for 'founding fathers' (and mothers) among earlier generations of social workers in different settings. However, it is difficult to discover strong direct links between the first local authority caseworkers and any previous tradition of British social work. The influence of family casework, derived from the Charity Organisation Society and its successor, the Family Welfare Association, is usually cited as the most formative one. However, for some time after the setting up of the local authority departments, family casework was still confined to voluntary agencies. In the 1950s it was still possible to write an article *contrasting* family casework with the kind of work done by local authorities, and stating that 'the agencies set up to deal with family problems have, with few exceptions, been voluntary organisations, called into being by citizens of different towns to meet a definite need'.[6] Family casework, in the tradition of the Charity Organisation Society, flourished in this voluntary setting, and family caseworkers were not employed in local authority departments until several years after the 1948 Act. Indeed, the appointment of such general purpose workers would not have seemed appropriate to the specialised tasks for which the new departments were created. For instance, the Curtis Committee saw the work of Children's Departments in terms of the needs of children in care, and the role of social work within it as the personal relationship between the Children's officer and the children. Family casework played no part in their plans, and although they recognised the need to support the family unit, they saw this as outside their terms of reference.[7]

The other main tradition of British social work before the war was the newer one of psychiatric social work, derived mainly from American training and practice. A group of British social workers had gone to study in the USA, and returned with much prestige to spread their knowledge among colleagues in the psychiatric setting. However, the approach which they brought back— understanding the problems and methods of casework in terms of psychological theories which had swept over American social work in the 1920s as a 'psychiatric deluge'[8]—had only a very limited influence in this country both before the war and immediately after it. Similarly, the work of the British Child Guidance Clinics, though itself important, was not adopted as a method or as a theoretical model by the new local authority agencies. Psychiatric social workers, who continued to be the most highly trained group in the country throughout the twenty years after the war,[9] were still largely employed in psychiatric hospitals and clinics rather than in the local authority services, and their training remained largely separate in high-prestige courses like the London School of Economics Mental Health course.

British social work, on the eve of the creation of the new local authority departments, therefore consisted mainly of two traditions, one residing predominantly in voluntary family casework agencies like the Family Welfare Association, and the other, derived partly from American voluntary organisations, concentrated in the psychiatric field. Neither of these traditions had influenced the work of the Public Assistance Committees up to this time, and when the new local authority services replaced them, neither was recognised as providing the kind of caseworker suited to the new departments' tasks. Yet, within a few years of the recognition of the need to provide a public social work service for the old, the homeless, deprived children and the mentally ill, a whole new breed of local authority social workers had been created. The assumption of responsibility for such services by local authorities had given rise to a completely new kind of *public* social work, which was different in a great many ways from the varieties which had developed both here and abroad, where these tasks were seen as properly done by voluntary bodies. Furthermore, these new local authority social workers not only developed new methods and traditions, but also, within a decade or so, successfully integrated their professional organisation and training with those of the longer established family and psychiatric social work groups, so as to produce a massive and unified social work profession. It was the achievement of this new breed of social workers that they consolidated the position of the *public* social worker in the local authority service, as the *predominant* professional role (as compared with the USA where social workers in voluntary agencies control and define the professional identity). By the time the British Association of Social Workers was established in 1970 it was clearly recognised that local authority social workers had the right to characterise professional social work in terms of their functions, and as fitting that its first General Secretary should be a former Children's Officer, Kenneth Brill. It is therefore to the history of the local authority services themselves that we should look to understand how this process of integration and assimilation between the very different traditions of social work and the local authority services which grew out of the Poor Law was accomplished.

In tracing this development, it is natural for several reasons to concentrate on the history of the Children's Departments. The break-up of the Poor Law was accompanied by a ferment of new ideas, of public outrage and protest about the old regime, and this centred on the treatment of children under the Public Assistance Committees. Middleton summarised the way in which children in their care were deprived in every sector of their lives.[10]

> In plans for their future careers, the consideration was not of their ability, but of the standard applicable to the lowest labourer. The work to which they were directed, both in the institution and later when they started work, were tasks which everyone could do but no one wanted to do; this was the criteria of Poor Law test work. The children were also deprived of their civil rights in that they did not become part of the local children's community, and share in the services provided. . . . The institutional child also suffered loss of liberty, while belonging to an institution carried a stigma, sometimes made obvious by wearing a uniform. All these items added up to the complete battery of Poor Law sanctions, i.e. loss of citizenship, loss of liberty, the stigma of community dependence, and committal to distasteful low-status work. Moreover, it can be seen that there was confusion of roles on the part of those controlling children's institutions, for although they had assumed the place of parents, they had not assumed their responsibilities or duties. Instead they played the part of workhouse overseers, treating the children in their charge according to a formula that had been evolved for deterring the feckless and the workshy from sponging on the community.

To a great extent, therefore, the growth of the new services represented a quite specific reaction against revelations about the conditions under which *children* had been kept by the Public Assistance Committees. Thus the new ideas and new methods that were evolved after 1948 tended to be concentrated in the Children's Departments, which had the very clear and comprehensible task of brushing away the gloomy relics of the long history of repression of pauper children. But even in the Children's Departments, as Jean Packman has shown, the development of the new services was far from evenly spread throughout the country, and many local authorities continued to provide so minimally for deprived children, that one could readily recognise the persistence of principles of deterrence and less eligibility in their approach. This was even more clearly evident in the standards of the Welfare Departments. While provisions were equally unevenly developed,[11] the emphasis on institutional care and services for old people allowed structures and functions to retain more continuity with Poor Law traditions. Welfare Departments employed fewer trained social workers than Children's Departments; gave their workers larger caseloads, and defined their roles more narrowly.[12] It was therefore in the traditions, structures and functions of the Welfare Departments that the Poor Law was able to retain its foothold, and since the creation of the unified social services departments, it has been the welfare tradition which has exerted the dominant influence in defining social work's newest role. Significantly, more Welfare Officers than Children's Officers became heads of new social services departments from 1970 onwards.

Meanwhile, it is important to try to analyse just what was new about the work of the Children's Departments after 1948, and the origins of these innovations. Most writers agree that the war played a crucial role in the official acknowledgment of the need for a public social work service for children. 'It was during the war that social case-work won final recognition.'[13] In particular, the evacuation of children gave rise to a more widespread understanding of the needs of those deprived of a normal family life. 'Most children separated from parents showed distress, many were severely disturbed, and through efforts made to help them a new understanding of the problems of homeless children was gained by thousands of ordinary people.'[14] Both the sufferings of ordinary children, and the dispersion (and consequent contact with a wider public) of institutional children contributed to the lively and informed public debate which was triggered off by Lady Allen of Hurtwood's letter to *The Times* in July 1944. The researches of Dr John Bowlby and the death of Dennis O'Neill thus contributed to what was already a strong climate of opinion against the barbarisms of the Poor Law. Thus Chadwick's dictum that it was not the business of the State to ensure 'that the children shall not suffer for the misconduct of their parents' was ripe for official repudiation, and the stage was set for the assumption of official responsibility for a service intended to provide children deprived of family life with conditions as similar as possible to those enjoyed by other children. The aims of the new service were defined by the 1948 Act as to care for each child in 'such a way as to further his best interests and to afford him the opportunity for the proper development of his character and ability'.[15]

In this process, it was recognised that social work had a vital part to play, but it was a particular kind of social work, closely related to the particular shortcomings of the Public Assistance Committees and the scandals and tragedies of that era. It was the notion of a personal relationship between a representative of the local authority and the child in care that was considered crucial.

This followed the recommendation of the Curtis Committee that:[16]

> we have been impressed by the need for the personal element in the care of children.... No office staff dealing with them as case-papers can do the work we want done—work which is in part administrative, but also in large part field work involving many personal contacts and the solution of problems by direct methods, in particular the method of interview rather than official correspondence.

Thus it can be seen that when one writer stated that 'The Children Act, 1948, could well be described as the attempt to ensure that the principles of social casework should be extended and applied to the whole child-care field',[17] what was implied was not so much a new *technique* of caring for children, as a new and more personal approach to the provision of services, based partly on an attempt to avoid, wherever possible, the rigours of institutional care, but also in large measure on a much more individualised method of selecting foster homes, and the retention of a personal relationship with the boarded-out child. By the end of 1947 there were already sixty-five students training to be child care officers in preparation for the tasks which the Curtis Committee had defined for them.

In contrast with the very specific recommendations of the Curtis Report, the 'principles of social casework' which formed part of their training were abstract and generalised.

> If the basic human fact in social work is a person in some need which he cannot meet unaided, and the basic activity of the case-worker is to give the individual in need individual treatment, it could quite fairly be maintained that, broadly speaking, the case-worker does no more than to try to act as a well informed and sensible family friend.... The essential difference is that the case-worker has to study to equip herself to offer this relationship to a great many more people than would normally fall to her share; to a large number of people indeed who would, in the normal course of things, be strangers to her.[18]

> The fundamental basis of all case-work is the belief that the individual matters. He matters in himself ... because every man has the right and duty to work out his own salvation, and therefore, within the limits of his society, must be allowed the chance to do so.[19]

> Any sound system of comprehensive general social service will need to be supplemented by a more intensive, selective case-work provision.[20]

It can be seen that this 'more intensive and selective provision' was based on a kind of universalism that accorded well with the principles of the Beveridge Welfare State. It was selective according to the individual's social problem, and not according to his means. Middleton points out that throughout the inter-war years, there was a potential conflict and contradiction between the community services for family support which were gradually developing in the wake of the Liberal Reforms of 1905 to 1914, and the old institutions of the Poor Law.[21]

> The adherents of individualism and the Poor Law insisted in interpreting the evolution of community support as the administration of doles, which must be hedged about by a safety margin of 'less eligibility', and kept under local administrative control, denying help as long as possible and then not offering it at a national scale. Wherever possible no aid was to be allowed to develop into a service, but treated as emergency relief, the arrangements being withdrawn as early as possible. ... The older regime used its powers to shackle and mar the institutional child, while the newer system gave the family-based child a new dimension in life. The contrast centred largely on the acceptance of the value of family to a developing child. The sum of the experience in the last half-century has, therefore, gradually focussed increasing attention on the importance of the family in providing a setting for the full development of children. Other solutions are possible, but family support is the most economical and the most natural; once its importance to the child is realised, to maintain the family as a viable unit seems worth almost any sacrifice; this is the application of the Freudian principles to social policies.

If social casework went further than the Curtis Report in its emphasis on the importance of the family, it was in line with the Beveridge approach both in this and its respect for each member of the community, whatever his economic situation. Just as Beveridge prescribed a universal 'National Minimum' for income maintenance, so social casework principles laid down a kind of charter of irreducible individual rights, which should be granted to those even with the most disruptive social difficulties. Whereas provisions for pauper children and adults under the Poor Law were constantly dogged by the fear of making their condition 'more eligible' than those of the working poor, the new local authority services could seek to provide the best possible treatment for anyone suffering from the particular problems for which they were appointed, without fear of offending principles of poor relief. While there were many inadequacies in these services, as in those for income maintenance, they were not the result of intentionally deterrent policies. Like any services financed out of local rates, they were short of resources, but their aims and intentions were lofty. Social workers were trained to believe that their work consisted of 'giving such attention and study to an individual and his environment as will enable him and the caseworker to work together, using all the resources available in the whole situation, to supply some need which is more than he could deal with by himself'.[22]

Inevitably, the very vagueness and loftiness of such principles attracted criticism from those who were sceptical about the tangible benefits that clients of these services got from their relationships with their social workers. Barbara Wootton was particularly withering in her attack on casework concepts, and proposed an alternative definition of social work which stressed its integration with the other social services, and the necessity for the worker to guide her client through the mazes of Welfare State provisions.[23]

> The complexity of relevant rules and regulations has become so great, that the social worker who has mastered these intricacies and is prepared to place knowledge at the disposal of the public, and when necessary to initiate appropriate action, has no need to pose as a miniature psychoanalyst or psychiatrist: her professional standing is secured by the value of her own contribution.

This theme has been taken up periodically in the evolution of local authority social work, and appears to be the stance adopted by Child Poverty Action Group towards social services departments. 'The special appointment in social service departments of a person to deal solely with welfare rights issues'[24] was advocated by the Deputy Director of the Group in 1972, and the recommendation has already been followed in several departments. However, this kind of criticism did not suggest that social workers should become directly involved in the *dispensing* of material benefits. Ironically, this development stemmed from the Family Casework School within the local authority services, and was related to the recognition of the importance of supporting the family as a unit.

Very early in the history of the post 1948 services, social workers began to express concern about the ability of the National Assistance Board, which had taken over all the responsibilities for financial provisions of the Public Assistance Committees, to deal sufficiently sensitively with the needs of those suffering emotional stress. As long ago as 1950 it was argued 'that a kind of diluted case-work should be the basic operation round which the statutory social services should be organised'.[25] For example, a National Assistance Board visiting officer had to consider special needs, taking into account particular circumstances.[26]

If the liberty of the individual is to be respected, case-work principles must be embodied in the structure of the services. The content of any service ... is important.... The quality of the social services, and in particular their impact on the individual citizen, is in the long run quite as important and cannot be left to chance or to the personal predilection of individual officials.

This theme has recurred, with variations, ever since, culminating in the recent appointment of social work officers within the Supplementary Benefits Commission to try to instil some of this spirit into the work of providing supplementary benefits. Recently, Olive Stevenson, a former social work adviser to the Commission wrote,[27]

an increase, however small, in the numbers of social workers within the Supplementary Benefits system may help to provide a better balance between proportional and creative justice within the administration.... In those cases ... in which the *problem itself* is compounded of social, psychological and practical elements, the skills of the social worker, as yet uncertain and immature, seem to offer the best chance of justice. Their use *within* the SBC to communicate *within and across* systems seems worth trying.

Meanwhile, however, events in the local authority services had not waited on this development. Dissatisfaction with the approach of the National Assistance Board came most strongly from those who saw their responsibilities towards families with young children at risk as having been too narrowly defined by the 1948 Act. 'The intimate relation between parents and their children, even their neglected children, seems to have been overlooked until the experience of the first few years brought home the difficulty of offering a service to children without having to deal also with parental reactions.'[28] Accordingly,[29]

some local authorities have recognised the imperative need for a family case-work service at an earlier stage. At the risk of going beyond the scope of a too narrowly conceived Children's Act, they sometimes arrange for their officers to visit the disintegrating home and try to give such help and understanding as will prevent complete breakdown.

Encouraged by Ministry circulars and by the example of the Family Service Units, many authorities appointed family caseworkers to do preventive work with a small caseload of families whose children were considered to be in danger of having to be received into care. Very often, these were 'multi-problem families', in which there was material deprivation as well as emotional stress. It was with these families that the Children's Departments came face to face with the inflexibility of the National Assistance Board's officers, and their basic lack of sympathy with the fecklessness which they saw as characteristic of a very 'undeserving' group of people. It was largely out of this experience that there developed the movement towards investing local authority departments with limited powers to give outdoor poor relief to those families to which it was already heavily committed in terms of casework resources.

The desire to provide financial assistance was thus secondary to the movement to do preventive family casework. This movement was gathering momentum, and was to be the major contributory factor on the professional side to the unification of local authority social work departments. It was based on casework principles, which required that the family, like the individual, should be seen as a whole, with all its strengths and weaknesses and not simply in terms of its destructive effects or its inadequacies. In practical terms, this meant that the principle that wherever possible families should be kept together, had to be reinforced by sensitivity to the possible consequences in mismanagement and bad budgeting of emotional stress. This sensitivity was lacking in the National Assistance Board; therefore some provision had to be available within the local authority services if all their caseworkers' endeavours were not to be thrown away, with a family breaking up over an unpaid bill or a rent in arrears.

It was therefore those local authority departments which had taken their preventive responsibilities most seriously, that were most anxious to recommend the inclusion of limited financial powers with the statutory encouragement for family casework provided by the Children and Young Persons Act of 1963. Following the recommendation of the Ingleby Committee in 1960, Section 1 of the new Act stated that

> it shall be the duty of every local authority to make available such advice, guidance and assistance as may promote the welfare of children by diminishing the need to receive children into, or keep them in, care under the Children Act 1948 ... or to bring children before a Juvenile Court, and any provision made by a local authority under this Subsection may, if the local authority think fit, include provision for giving assistance in kind or, in exceptional circumstances, in cash.

The fact that the financial powers were contained within the same section of the Act as the clauses which enabled preventive family casework indicates that the former were intended to be strictly limited to serving the needs of the latter. However, this is not how things worked out in practice. First, the National Assistance Board and later the Supplementary Benefits Commission interpreted this section as giving the local authority services powers to make payments to families with children along the lines of their own exceptional needs payments—as poor relief provided to meet particular circumstances, wherever the alternative would be a danger of eviction or the break-up of a family. Instead of being confined to those families who were already subject to casework supervision and support by social workers, Section 1 became a prime source of new referrals of families in need of urgent financial assistance, frequently referred by the Supplementary Benefits Commission itself.

The growth in the numbers of applications for the various kinds of help available under Section 1 of the Children and Young Persons Act 1963 can be judged from the annual child care statistics. The numbers of children in families actually advised or assisted under this Section in England and Wales increased from 133,687 in 1967 to 182,478 in 1969, and 220,743 in 1970. In 1972, the figure for *England alone* (for some reason the Welsh statistics were not included) was 247,556. The number of *families* thus assisted almost exactly doubled in that period of five years (54,458 to 109,981). The percentage of all referrals and applications to Children's Departments represented by those assisted under Section 1 of the 1963 Act was 57 per cent in 1967 and 62 per cent in 1970. It is important to note that there was a large increase in all kinds of referrals and applications concerning children in the period 1967 to 1972, but no increase in the annual number of children received into care. In 1967, the total number of children about whom applications and referrals under the 1948 and 1963 Acts were made was 234,736, and the number of children received into care was 53,381. In 1970, there were 354,849 children subject to applications and referrals, but only 51,542 received into care. The 1972 figures are confused both by the exclusion of Wales and by a change in the method of recording of receptions into care. However, total applications and referrals of children in *England alone* were 422,462, of whom only 37,374 were received into care under the 1948 Act, and 3,066 brought before the court as in need of care, protection and control. As the Welsh figures for 1970 were only 1,786 children received into care, this suggests that there were many *fewer* children admitted to care in 1972 than in 1967, but in spite of the fact that total numbers of applications and referrals had almost doubled.[30]

It is not possible to specify exactly how many of this enormous number of referrals and applications were dealt with by means of financial assistance, either with or without accompanying supervision or guidance. However, a Manchester University research project gives some very significant indications.[31] Taking the total of *all* cases involving preventive work, under the 1963 Act, on social workers' caseloads in two boroughs and two county areas in north-west England, they classified these into three groups. The first group contained clients who had received *financial* help (in the form of grants, loans or rent guarantees). The second group was of clients who had received *material* aid (second-hand clothes, bedding and furniture, etc.), at no direct cost to the departments. The third group was of clients who had received casework advice and guidance without financial or material help. The proportions of cases in each group varied quite widely between the four areas, but in no area did the group receiving casework alone outnumber those receiving financial and material help. Over all, the total numbers in each group were almost exactly equal, so those receiving either financial or material help were twice as numerous as those receiving casework alone. In one of the authorities, the number receiving financial help was over 40 per cent of the total.

Again, it was significant that the actual sums of money devoted to financial assistance by these departments was very small. One borough had for several years allotted funds of only £50 per annum for Section 1 payments, and limited social workers' discretion to £2 and under without committee approval. In spite of these very stringent limits, this borough had the highest proportion of clients who were financially assisted out of the total 1963 Act caseload, an indication of the very small sums involved, and the necessity for very strict rationing principles to be applied by social workers. The other borough, in which financially assisted cases formed under a third of all 1963 Act clients, had an original budget of £200 which had risen to £500 by 1968. These figures help to explain why, even as late as 1970, there was still a very uneven distribution of expenditure on financial assistance under Section 1 among local authorities in England and Wales. Only twenty-three authorities spent more than £3,000 on cash payments, and the highest recorded was a London borough which spent £8,000. Against this, twenty-two spent less than £100, and eleven spent nothing at all.[32] The Manchester research shows that these low totals often conceal a large volume of work, both in the form of making small grants, and also in refusing them to applicants who do not meet the rationing criteria. Furthermore, the size of funds allotted for this purpose has been increasing very rapidly. In the four areas studied by the Manchester research, there was a 200 per cent increase in cash assistance in the period between 1966 and 1969. This trend has continued under social services departments since 1971. Table 1 gives amounts paid in direct assistance to families by five West Country local authorities, with estimates for this expenditure in their ten-year plans. All these authorities were low down in the original 'league table' of expenditure on Section 1 payments.

TABLE I : *Expenditure on Section I payments*

	1971–2 £	1972–3 £	Estimate 1982 £
Devon	4,923	4,875	7,500
Torbay	840	1,050	2,700
Exeter	389	900	1,200
Plymouth	6,257	5,600	7,268
Somerset	4,515	8,900	—

No estimates for 1982 are available for Somerset, but indications are that expenditure in 1973-4 will be at least £10,000.

Small as these totals may seem, they are by no means insignificant when compared with expenditure by the Supplementary Benefits Commission on exceptional needs payments. In 1971, this totalled £4,726,000 (including Scotland) which means an average of only £20,000 approximately for each local authority area in England and Wales; bearing in mind the range of needs covered by exceptional needs payments and the five million claimants of supplementary benefits, the local authority figures for areas without conspicuous social deprivation seem quite substantial by comparison. In Warwickshire the combined estimates for direct assistance to families and rent guarantees for 1973-4 are already over £20,000, and the estimate for 1982-3 is £63,000.

Thus, even areas which originally made little provision for these payments have rapidly increased their estimates with the overall trend towards making local authorities undertake assistance duties. It is also important to recognise the extent to which local authorities have used material provisions (second-hand goods) as a substitute for cash payments and grants.

That these new duties are a form of poor relief for the group in most desperate need is clearly shown by the Manchester research. In each area, they found that the group which received the financial assistance contained the highest proportion of large families living in poverty, either on or below the supplementary benefits subsistence level (68 per cent over all in this group). These families contained the highest proportion of wage stop cases, of families dependent on supplementary benefits, and of single parent families. The group which received material help tended to be not quite so desperately badly off as the first group, but still poor. They tended on average to be more stable unions in which the father was usually a manual worker, living in privately rented accommodation. The third group which received casework help alone had lower proportions of families living on or below supplementary benefits' levels (36 per cent), and fewer families dependent on benefits. The families had fewer children. The picture of the financial provisions under Section 1 which emerges is of a form of very limited public assistance which is confined to short-term emergency situations (between 40 and 50 per cent of payments were for *food*), and concentrated on the poorest sector of families, both in work and out of it. However, the research team's questionnaires revealed that the *social workers* perceived what they were doing as *preventive casework* rather than poor relief, and were confused about the financial and material aspects of their work. They were aware that even when they could justifiably claim that their long-term aims were to do with maintaining family stability and parental performance, they were making decisions about giving or withholding money in the short run according to different criteria.[33]

> Grants, loans or guarantees were given where there were large families; where there was a possibility of collecting a loan back because the client was responsive to social work help; where there was no alternative accommodation; where families had severe physical or mental handicaps; where there was no other means of preventing children coming into care; where the cost of children coming into care would be saved; where families were really trying to help themselves; where the family was in a crisis, in imminent danger of disintegration; where the parents were good managers.... Workers were clearly haunted and troubled by the old spectre of the 'deserving' and the 'undeserving' poor, and their insecurity really came from being faced with clients in desperate need. Workers wanted to help them all financially but were unable to justify doing so, particularly in the long run because they knew that financial help *by itself* would not guarantee that they would achieve the goal.

Casework the aim, poverty the need, destitution the cause of referral; what the research describes is a classic case of the consequences of employing a social work agency to dispense strictly limited funds to a group of people whose main distinguishing characteristic is their extreme poverty.

In Scotland, the wider financial powers possessed by social work departments, and the earlier unification of the services have both contributed to making that country an advance guide to future developments in England and Wales. A letter in *Social Work Today* from Ian Mathie, a Glasgow social worker, gives a flavour of the new-style social work[34]

> Perhaps we have suffered this somewhat longer in Scotland, as the Social Work (Scotland) Act has been in force since 17

November 1969. The major feature of the Act is Section 12 which makes it a duty on the local authority to 'promote social welfare' and goes on to describe the financial powers through which this will be done. This has served to accelerate the process already begun by Section 1 of the Children's Act of 1963. Claimants presenting at DHSS offices, with rent arrears or urgent destitution, are summarily directed down the road to 'the Welfare' ... increasingly large proportions of social work man hours and resources are being directed into boosting clients up to a basic foundation of social security, before the *real* social work problem can be contemplated. This shift in emphasis in role at a time of staff shortage, has led to a hidden cost in other services being ignored, particularly the disabled and the elderly.

In retrospect, it is possible to recognise that very much too little account was taken of the extent to which the earlier development of preventive family casework in local authority departments was enabled by the separation of the social work from poor relief. While it is true that many families with emotional problems get into financial difficulties, it is equally true that the best services for those with emotional problems cannot be provided by a department which has blanket responsibilities for the financial needs of the many who are in urgent need, simply by virtue of their poverty. The systematic referral of people who are in a state of financial crisis, which frequently bears no relation to emotional stress of the kind helpfully dealt with by social work, has reduced claimants' rights to exceptional needs grants from the Supplementary Benefits Commission, while at the same time, undermining the confidence of social workers in the usefulness of their skills.

Even after the event, social workers have been slow to recognise the effects of the change, and to combat the very effective methods of the Supplementary Benefits Commission in shedding their tiresome duties in respect of emergencies threatening needy claimants. Commenting on provisions for social workers to pay cash benefits, Stevenson says:[35]

> their existence undoubtedly complicates the relationship between the SBC and local authority social work services.... The plain fact is ... that the vagueness of the powers on both sides means that, in the last resort, many decisions must be taken at local levels on a judgement of an individual situation, and that local relationships will affect such judgements. Thus, for example, the occasions on which the SBC rather than a Social Service Department will clear a rent or fuel debt to prevent eviction, continue at times to be a source of dispute.

However, this approach ignores the fact that the changes which have taken place since 1963 are all in the direction of local authority taking on more responsibility for payments which previously would only have been made by the National Assistance Board. The Supplementary Benefits Commission mention in their paper on exceptional needs payments that 'local authority social services departments ... have powers to make cash grants in certain circumstances',[36] and their own attitude towards the convenience of this provision in dealing with their more awkward customers is shown where they add:[37]

> There are a number of cases in which fuel debts and rent arrears are the result of mismanagement, and there are signs that the number, though still small, may be tending to increase. In such cases, the Commission consider that since the taxpayer's responsibility to the claimants has already been discharged, they should not meet claimants' debts, and should certainly not meet them repeatedly except in the very last resort where no other sort of help is available and severe hardship would result. In a high proportion of such cases there are children in the family, and the local office would normally consult the social services department of the local authority who may be able, as part of social work help for the family, to advise the claimant about budgeting, and may exceptionally be able to use their powers under the Children and Young Persons Act 1963 to pay off the debt.

In practice, ever since the 1963 Act, Children's Departments have been besieged by parents seeking payment of electricity and gas bills and rent arrears, and what was meant to be an exceptional provision has become standard procedure.[38]

> The Supplementary Benefit Officer has a duty to advise the claimant of the appropriate social service agency in those cases in which the need becomes apparent in the course of his financial investigation. (Where the claimant is not capable of acting on advice, the official is instructed to get in touch with the agency himself.)

Since social security officers are trained to regard cases of unpaid electricity and gas bills and rent arrears as evidence of mismanagement, these all serve as a ready justification for social work supervision, and for the referral of claimants who have never previously heard of local authority departments.

This development has been accelerated by the changes in the local authority services carried out as a result of the Seebohm Report. Here again, the pressure from professional social workers for the amalgamation of the Welfare, Children's and Mental Health

Services, was based on a belief that a family casework service could best be provided by one department rather than several, whose functions were defined by their focus on specific problems. The debate which led up to Seebohm had been focused mainly on the work of the Children's Departments with juvenile delinquents, which produced overlaps and conflicts of aims between them and the probation service. Pressure for change in the juvenile courts' system had come from the Labour Party in opposition and had been expressed in the Longford Report, *Crime, a Challenge to us All*. The new Government in 1965 published a White Paper about delinquency which foreshadowed the Seebohm proposals by adopting Longford's recommendation that a local authority family service should deal with the problems of juveniles as family rather than criminal problems. The evidence of social workers to the Seebohm Committee stressed fragmentation and inter-departmental rivalries, leading to a failure to develop adequate services for those whose problems were undifferentiated or difficult to fit into administrative categories. The Seebohm Report envisaged that 'our conception of an effective family service assumes the provision of general family guidance in much of the day-to-day work of social service departments'.[39] Local authority family casework for parents and children, the deprived and the delinquent had, it seemed, arrived. The establishment of the social services departments seemed to many the culmination of twenty years of effort to give shape to the best kind of public social work agency.

However, even while the Seebohm Committee was sitting, others already had a different notion of how the unified local authority department might function. Professor Titmuss, who was deputy chairman of the Supplementary Benefits Commission, argued that the emphasis should be on the provision of *services* rather than on support for the family or any other pattern of relationships.[40] His point of view was reflected in the eventual choice of name for the new departments—*social services* rather than family welfare. New legislation tended in the same direction. I have already indicated the significance of the Social Work (Scotland) Act of 1968 (Section 12), which extended the financial provisions of Section 1 of the Children and Young Persons Act of 1963 to include all persons (not just children), 'where (it) would avoid the local authority being caused greater expense in the giving of assistance in another form or where probable aggravation of the person's need would cause greater expense to the local authority on a later occasion'. In 1970, the Chronically Sick and Disabled Persons Act was passed which, as Stevenson notes,[41]

strengthens the evidence of a trend to take back into local authority aspects of financial welfare which have hitherto been the responsibility, in the main, of the SBC. Although the Act does not empower any form of direct cash assistance, there are a number of duties placed on local authorities which would in the past have been regarded as potentially within the scope of the exceptional needs grants of the Commission. For example, local authorities must consider the provision of telephones and of the 'adaptation of the home and additional facilities to secure his greater safety, comfort or convenience' (Chronically Sick and Disabled Persons Act, 1970, Para 2 (i)).

True to their past form in the matter of gas and electricity bills and rent arrears, the Supplementary Benefits Commission lost no time in clarifying the apparent duplication of functions. Writing in the first edition of *Social Work Service*, the former Assistant Secretary to the Supplementary Benefits Commission reported that an agreement had been reached about telephones between the two departments that 'all requests for such help should be investigated by the local authority first. . . . A person needing a telephone would thus have to approach only the local authority, and the financial responsibility would then be agreed between the local authority and the social security office.'[42] Local authority social workers are still reeling under the impact of this massive source of referrals of new clients, most of whom require nothing more than the specific aid in question. While applications for telephones, bath rails, wheelchairs and ramps roll in, families with emotional problems must wait their turn. Casework has become a luxury.

That a supplementary benefits system which was trying to develop a notion of the 'rights' of deserving claimants required such an underpinning of special services was suggested in the last chapter, and will be developed further in the next. Meanwhile, it is important to recognise the characteristics of the new public welfare agency which has been created. It is essentially a service which dispenses various forms of benefits according to the old established principles of poor relief. But it does this not merely through the various tests of means and deservingness which exist within the supplementary benefits system, but also through a much more complex rationing system. It is operated by social workers, on a shoestring budget, restricted to contributions from the local rates. Limitations on the funds available mean that benefits are dispensed according to 'welfare criteria', which are totally beyond the ken of those who claim them. There are no rights to appeal. Social workers, trained in the assessment of their clients' personalities as a tool in the process of helping them with complex emotional problems, are being required to use these assessments as justification for the refusal of benefits. The principles of casework are being perverted by the abuses of poor relief.

This type of public welfare provision has already been made notorious by American experience. It is no coincidence that one of the most bitter critics of the American system of relief is also the author of the most sensitive account of casework in the public service.[43] Alan Keith-Lucas's analysis of the decision-making process in American public assistance agencies documents the way in which what claims to be a professional social work service (but in which 'only 4 per cent of workers primarily engaged in public assistance are "fully trained" in the eyes of the profession') is used to apply pseudo-psychiatric justifications for the practice of relief restriction and social control. He shows how 'workers did not use the highly technical science of psychiatry or of individualized diagnosis to shape their decisions, but rather a mixture of ethical presuppositions and more or less popular "science" of a sociological nature'.[44] The result is that 'the recipient may find himself subject to a more or less pervasive control of his life as a condition of receiving assistance'. So far from enjoying a 'right' to benefits, he gets these only as a privilege, conditional upon his fulfilling requirements such as supervision by social workers who have the power to withdraw assistance if their expectations are not put into practice. As another American commentator put it, 'the otherwise objective process of dispensing a material subsidy is mixed with and confused by a theoretical commitment to personalised emotional therapy supposedly demanded by the neurotic character of the caseload'.[45] Or, as expressed by Piven and Cloward, 'Casework prescribes modern procedures of psychological diagnosis, "individualization", and counselling, as if by being poor the client proves his personality weakness and his need for professional treatment.'[46]

These statements (and particularly those of Keith-Lucas), are not intended as criticisms of casework *per se*. They are intended to indicate the arbitrary, insulting and insidious effects of employing casework as a method of rationing and controlling the dispensing of public assistance. Neither are they meant to imply that caseworkers should never be involved in the giving of services; indeed, Keith-Lucas's definition of casework is, 'the way in which the agency, through its workers—or the worker, in the name of the agency—makes available a service which the agency is empowered to give'.[47] The point is not so much which services are offered, but the way in which they are offered.[48]

There is no particular reason for us to try to establish which of these many services is the most important or requires the greatest amount of knowledge and experience to administer. The point is that we have, or may have, responsibility to make any or all of them available to a client who may see in them some hope of a solution, or some step towards a solution, of whatever it is that has made him so uncomfortable that he has asked for our help. Our job is to help him find out whether indeed the service we offer is, in fact, helpful to him, and to help him use it if he can. We can do this badly or well. If we offer him the service casually, or impulsively, indulgently, or hatefully or thoughtlessly—if, by the way in which the service is offered or given, he remains as confused, as fearful, as unable to care for himself or to make his own decisions as he was before (or, as sometimes happens, even more so)— then the probability is that we have not done very good casework.

The local authority social work services, and particularly the Children's Departments, had succeeded in building up a tradition of providing services for children and their parents according to this spirit of casework. They had done so mainly because they had been set free from the shackles of public assistance which had limited their progress by considerations of 'less eligibility' in the period before the war. Since 1963, there has been a steady trend towards returning a number of these public assistance functions to the local authority services. The Seebohm Report, which social workers saw as giving rise to a family casework service, has instead recreated first in structure, and now increasingly in function, the Public Assistance Committee of the 1930s. Referrals to the new departments are more and more concerned with poor relief, and social workers who are swamped with decisions to make about these applications for benefits, are less and less able to provide the other services with the sensitivity which is required.

One of the primary principles of casework is the client's right to self-determination. For social workers in the public services, this individual right always has to be balanced against the community's right to require its citizens to respect each other's safety, security and peace of mind. Social workers have always been concerned with providing services for the 'maladjusted', which attempt to restore them to a mode of behaviour which is in line with the standards of the rest of the community. There are circumstances in which this type of work can be reconciled with the principle of self-determination.[49]

There can be no objection, for instance, to the attempt to produce 'adjustment' in persons who are aware of a lack of this somewhat undefined quality in themselves. There can similarly be no objection, it would seem, to the use of some such concept in relation to persons who have demonstrated a lack of 'adjustment' through their breaking the law, or their legally determined inability to care for their own affairs, although in the first case perhaps something more—a recognition of personal responsibility—is needed. What does appear antithetical to the kind of society that would preserve those values generally associated with the Western Christian culture, is to attempt to induce this 'adjustment' in a class of people whose primary relationship to their government is based on their need to be provided with the necessities of life. To do this involves a classification of people which is essentially undemocratic. It suggests that there is a large class of people, distinguishable only by their economic condition, who are in need of 'adjustment' which the State should induce. Even if it be admitted that all people would be better off if they were permitted this opportunity to adjust, the selection of this particular group would be unwarranted.

The public welfare agency which is being created on the American model is well suited to carrying out the policies which stem from Sir Keith Joseph's theory of the 'cycle of deprivation'. It invites people to apply to it by virtue of their poverty, and then treats them as maladjusted. It is more controlling and intrusive than any bureaucratically administered system of benefits. Starting from an assumption about the moral inferiority of the poor, it proceeds logically to the conclusion that the benefits made available to them should be conditional upon supervision by authorities concerned with moral improvement. It mops up an untidy problem from the income maintenance services in a way which is consistent with the principles of 'less eligibility'. One of the results has been a very painful dilemma for social workers.[50]

It was the absence of precise eligibility rules, the apparent arbitrariness of decisions, the responsible nature of public accountability, the stigma imposed by society upon their particular clients, the history of charity as opposed to rights, and additional feelings about giving or withholding money, which made the problem so acute for the workers.

Some further aspects of this problem, for clients as well as social workers, will be considered in the next chapter.

7
'Front line troops in the war against poverty'

The Seebohm Report expressed the hope that the new unified local authority social work department would reduce the distinctions between those who pay for social work services (the ratepayers) and those who consume them (the clients).[1]

> At many points in this Report we have stressed that we see our proposals not simply in terms of organisation, but as embodying a wider conception of social service, directed to the well-being of the whole of the community and not only of social casualties, and seeing the community it serves as the basis of its authority, resources and effectiveness. Such a conception spells, we hope, the death-knell of the Poor Law legacy, and the socially divisive attitudes and practices which stemmed from it. Above all, the development of citizen participation should reduce the rigid distinction between givers and takers of social services, and the stigma which being a client has involved in the past.

In effect, this is an argument for a universalistic concept of social work, with both the 'strongest' and the 'weakest' participating in a community-based service. Sir Keith Joseph's theory of the 'cycle of deprivation' leads social work in the opposite direction, to a selective type of provision, but it is selective in a different way from traditional casework services. Instead of dealing with referrals of certain specialised problems (relating to child care, for instance, or mental health), it invites applications from the lowest income group for various forms of assistance, and then concentrates its attention on this group. Sir Keith Joseph justifies this selectivity on the grounds that the poorest sector contains people (and especially children) who are 'most vulnerable'. 'It is where there is a combination of bad factors—problems associated with poverty, poor housing, and large family size, for example—that children are most at risk.'[2] By providing various kinds of benefits, social service departments are enabled to control and regulate the family lives of the poor, to supervise them, to impose conditions upon their receipt

of assistance, and to treat them as the social problem which the
Government regards them as being.

Obviously, because of their other statutory functions, social service departments still receive referrals for particular kinds of social
work help from all sectors of society. However, the sheer volume of
work with families, the sick and disabled, and the elderly, who
require financial and other material assistance has meant that the
provision of services requiring casework alone has tended to appear
of secondary importance. Furthermore, the structure and the ethos
of the service has come to take on a form which is determined by
the public assistance function of the agency. Administratively,
social services departments are now geared to the provision of
benefits and specific services like clothing grants, bath rails and
wheelchairs; philosophically, they are geared to the rationing of
these benefits according to the principles of 'less eligibility' which
underlie all poor relief. The ethos of public assistance inevitably
spills over from this sphere of the work into the services provided
for children and families, and into the way in which they are
provided.

The consequences of this type of selective provision for a group
distinguished from others by their need for public assistance were
well illustrated by a recent BBC documentary programme about
social work called *The Person from the Welfare*. The programme
started by describing social workers as 'front line troops in the
war against poverty', a description which was not challenged by
any of the workers who took part. Towards the end of the programme, a group of non-clients were interviewed about their
view of the social work clients who formed about half the inhabitants of one street. Though obviously poor themselves, the non-
clients spoke of the clients with the same kind of mixture of pity,
contempt and envious resentment that non-claimants use to
describe claimants of social security. Social work clients were
getting special privileges, extra material assistance and support as
a result of their dependence and fecklessness. They therefore could
be identified as a super-stigmatised group apart, distinguishable not
by their exotic social problems so much as by the type of material
help they were getting from social workers. The social workers,
too, seemed to accept this notion of a special group of people who
'couldn't function properly', and therefore required a special kind
of individualised public assistance. The whole programme seemed
to illustrate Pinker's dictum that 'the most personal forms of
social service are likely to be the most humiliating for the benefi-
ciary'.[3]

The changes which have brought about this new focus for local
authority social work have caused a deep malaise among professional social workers, amounting almost to a crisis of identity.

While the storm was looming for some time before it finally broke, the start of this can be dated to coincide with the more or less simultaneous events of the election of the recent government, the creation of the social services departments, the publication of the *Sunday Times* Supplement article 'What are social workers doing about poverty?', and the first issue of the broadsheet *Case Con*.[4] Much of the hostility aroused by changes in the structure and function of social work has been displaced into 'casework'. As the new duties of poor relief have proliferated, social workers have come to recognise that they are more and more often dealing with people who are clients solely by virtue of their poverty. But instead of questioning the processes by which poor people are referred to an agency with very limited financial resources, but a staff of workers skilled in human relationships, angry social workers have instead attacked the basis of their training, suggesting that they have been given the wrong skills. Instead of criticising the shift of poor relief responsibilities into local authority departments, and resisting its effect on existing local authority services, they have belaboured the casework approach for its inadequacy to provide tangible benefits for the poor. The standard *Case Con* cartoon, repeated in many different forms in successive issues, is of a social worker interviewing a woman with young children who is living in conditions of appalling squalor, and asking her 'Well Mrs Bloggs, how do you feel about your rats?'

As a result, casework has been slated as the root of all social work evils.

> Casework is part of bourgeois ideology, the purpose of which is to maintain the institution of the family, and to police the 'deviants' of society and reinforce the Capitalist system.... Given the confusion, irrelevance, conflict, sheer nonsense and attempts to mystify and *deliberately* divert from the real problems facing both social workers and clients, it is impossible to consider casework in any way seriously.[5]

> Since the Human Growth and Development course and case discussions based on this perspective is really the core of professional training, the social worker is *motivated* to classify clients in these terms ... to select features stressed as central in the models of development, because the use of this framework confirms the professionalism of the social worker. The 'presenting problem' for example, of delinquency, overspending, bad housing is transformed into an 'underlying problem', for example of sexual difficulties or emotional relationships with which the social worker feels competent to work, and from the discovery of which he will gain considerable satisfaction. Thinking on the socio-economic level tends

to be unsophisticated, and statements about political forma-
tions are usually based on individual psychology.[6]

What these criticisms imply is that many (indeed most) of
social work's clients require immediate financial assistance more
than they require Freudian-based insights into their personalities or
family dynamics. However, so the argument goes, casework can
serve as a block to the social worker recognising the very obvious
material needs the clients present, by assuming that there is some
deeper meaning to the request for help.[7]

> Not only may this mean that the practical help demanded is
> seen as being a symptom of the underlying emotional diffi-
> culties, but also that the suitability of practical help at all is
> questioned. Social workers tend to raise the objection that
> what a client sees as a suitable goal or need for himself is not
> *realistic*. Being realistic appears to mean that you ask for no
> more than is offered—so clear pressures are put on clients not
> to demand their full rights.

It therefore follows from these criticisms that social workers should
have *more* powers to give material and financial aid, and should
use the powers they possess more generously. This can be achieved
by abandoning casework as an agency goal.[8]

> The basic question here is what *motivates* the social worker
> when he deals with a client. Why does he discount the overt
> 'presenting' problem and substitute quite a different frame-
> work to explain the client's past and present behaviour, and
> avoid giving quick material aid which is often all that is
> demanded in the first place? I suggest that the basic of the
> social worker's motivation lies in the professionalisation of
> social work.

Without this misleading and mystifying ideology, it is argued,
social work would give more people more help, and shed many of
its odious implications of social control.

Such attacks seem, to me, to put much too much emphasis on the
role played by casework theory in determining social work's function, and to underestimate grossly the damaging effects of the Poor
Law principles which inevitably accompany any obligations to
provide poor relief out of the local rates. The criticisms of the casework ethos arise largely out of a failure to recognise the full
implications of recent administrative developments in the social
services. It is perfectly fair to ask what social workers are doing
about poverty, but it is unfair to blame them for their inadequacy
in the face of responsibilities for dealing with it in the absence
of resources. Above all, it is unfair to blame a training for a job,

which until recently was concerned mainly with personal relationships, for its failure to equip social workers to perform the tasks
of pre-war relieving officers of the Public Assistance Committees.

Casework is an approach to a helping relationship which is based
on compassion for people in trouble, sorrow, need, sickness and
various other adversities. Properly applied, casework is a necessary
condition for the humane and decent provision of certain services
for people in various kinds of emotional distress, in crisis, suffering
bereavement, trauma or despair. The best illustration of this is the
development of the Children's Departments in the twenty years
after the war. One only has to compare the revelations of the
Curtis and Monkton Reports with what one knows about the child
care services which had been developed by the time of the unification of local authority social work to see that Curtis was perfectly right to require that there should be 'a personal element in
the care of children ... involving many personal contacts and the
solution of problems by direct methods, in particular the method of
interview rather than official correspondence'. Casework in this
sense (which if not its original sense is at least one established use
of the term), has very little to do with social control or the class
war. The specialised service which was established with the break-
up of the Poor Law, was able to give priority to the individualised
treatment of children largely because it was no longer fettered
by considerations of public assistance.

Since then, local authority departments have taken on many
other more ambiguous roles, concerned with delinquency, homelessness and poverty, which raise much more directly issues like
the one about social control. It is probable that the Curtis Committee would have disapproved of these developments, because it saw
the task of caring for deprived children as a very specialised and
important one which should exclude all other considerations. However, in other ways, there were many anomalous things about the
narrow duties of the original Children's Departments, especially the
lack of encouragement to do preventive work with parents, and
to tackle delinquency in its early stages. The problems raised by the
extension of local authorities' powers to include these responsibilities are only just beginning to be recognised as theoretical
issues in the training of social workers.[9]

Much of the thinking about the functions of social work and
the role of the social worker has rested on an acceptance of
a particular model of society and of social organisation which
suggests a fundamental consensus about social values underlying the social system, and which allows for an interpretation
of the social work task as one of helping to hand on accepted
values to individuals and groups who have been insufficiently

socialized into society and its value system; thus social work clients are seen in terms of 'failure' or 'deviance' or 'maladjustment' to which the answer is resocialization of the individual in the direction of accepted social values.

Heraud goes on to suggest that 'one of the ways of interpreting the functions of social work and the welfare institutions is in terms of regulation of group or class conflict, and the establishment and maintenance of a form of consensus'.[10] Radical social workers have argued that this gives social work, and especially casework, an essentially conservative role in preserving the *status quo*.[11]

The identification of social work with individual casework in the fifties coincides with a new optimism in the affluence of society under capitalism, and people who remained poor or homeless or unemployed were seen as individual failures in a society that offered opportunities of prosperity to everyone.... But this personal emphasis serves to obscure the fact that social and economic anomalies continue to exist. It blinds the social worker to the situation of clients as viewed *collectively*, and the simple recognition of poverty as a *structural* phenomenon, rather than as an individual misfortune. In this way, the practice of casework also serves to prevent the full exploitation by clients of what is available under the Welfare State, as it redirects the client's and social worker's attention to the client's personality, even his childhood, and away from his economic and social rights.

It is clear that these perceptions of social work are, to some extent, justified in the work done by official agencies with the 'maladjusted', and particularly with school truants and delinquent children, or with parents who neglect or ill-treat their offspring. There are inevitable overtones of 'social control' in the work of the probation service, for instance, and the same is true of local authority departments since they have taken on a similar range of problems. However, while there is certainly an element of conflict regulation in work which assumes a consensus in society about the need to control and modify some forms of 'anti-social' behaviour, it is misleading to identify this function with casework, and to contrast it with income maintenance as Cannan does in the article quoted above. Handler's study of the work of three London Children's Departments in 1968 showed that the chief method employed for controlling clients' behaviour was the way in which a social worker dispensed rewards and benefits that families needed.[12] The power to give cash under Section 1 of the 1963 Act was often used as a way of getting families to adopt standards which were considered to be more acceptable to the rest of the community, an exact parallel with Keith-Lucas's findings in American public welfare agencies. It was this power to give material assistance, rather than the threat of court proceedings, that was the first and most widely employed device in conflict regulation and social control. Bearing in mind the high proportion of referrals of children to social services departments that come from parents themselves, and the fact that the Manchester research already referred to suggests that more than half of all referrals require financial assistance or material aid, the power to give poor relief becomes quite evidently the most important weapon of authority in the social worker's armoury, and the shortage of resources for the purpose of relief becomes his most important motivation for exerting this control.

The notion that casework is an instrument of class oppression, 'part of the bourgeois ideology' and used to 'reinforce the Capitalist system' is therefore based largely on a misinterpretation of the evidence from social services departments which have been increasingly used for tasks of income maintenance, which have perverted the original purpose of social work training. Obviously there has always been some casework which was defensively professional rather than genuinely caring. But, there is no inherent reason why good casework, any more than any other form of compassionate behaviour, should be associated with the repression by wealthier members of society of the poorer. Love and compassion are always open to exploitation. If those who are anxious to protect their privileges use social work as the instrument for reinforcing existing advantages, then social workers can be blamed for failing to recognise the ways in which they are serving evil ends. However, the effective resistance to this exploitation is not to abandon their compassionate principles, but to refuse to do the dirty work of their masters. In the present case, the dirty work is public assistance.

Halmos has shown the extent to which love and compassion, rather than any particular scientific theory or therapeutic commitment, underlies all social work practice. While social workers 'are likely to continue to believe that they are appliers of socio-psychological knowledge and skill, much as medical men are appliers of biological and physiological knowledge', his careful analysis of the literature of psychiatry and social work reveals that they 'profess, openly or by implication, that they consider their warm personal attachment to the help-seeker as a vital instrument of helping'. Writers about counselling professions 'have been in the habit of characterising their professional relationship with their clients as "sympathetic", "accepting" and "supportive", and from time to time some counsellors would comprehensively refer to the relationship as *loving*'.[13] Halmos goes so far as to suggest that there is within this ideology a well disguised faith in the efficacy of love to overcome hate, and thus a quasi-religious belief in the power of good to triumph over evil.

Halmos has also shown that there has been an international expansion of the counselling professions which partake of this ideology, and that this expansion has gone hand in hand with prosperity and the increase in affluence. In another book, *The Personal Service Society*, he argues that the expansion of *the professions* generally is being accompanied by an increasing influence of the counselling ideology over professional people, even in the 'impersonal' service professions. 'The moral and ideological influence of the personal service professions envelop the training and cultural context of these professions who have been trained for impersonal service.'[14] He goes on from here to conclude,[15]

I believe that the professionalisation in the Capitalist west inevitably introduces more and more collectivistic and other-regarding considerations into the social functioning of individuals, and weakens the *laissez-faire* licence of a free enterprise, the *rapacity* of penal justice, the *harshness* of educational discipline, and the *mercenariness* of 'marketable' doctoring. At the same time, the increasing efficiency and affluence of the Communist countries will extend their capacity to pay for more and more personal social services in their communities, and multiply the numbers of leading intellectuals whose concern will be with personal services and personal ministrations of help, and not with the grand strategies and actuarial realities of the state or party.

Because he fails to take account of the way in which economic changes, and especially changes in income maintenance provisions, are related to this expansion of the personal social services, Halmos's analyses are sometimes naïve.[16]

In a way, to provide the wherewithal of material comfort—from washing machines to television sets, and from family cars to modern housing—we already require no new technology of materials, of construction or of organisation. We require only good sense and some decades of peace to equip all the homes from China to Ghana, and to let people be persuaded by their new comforts and knowledge of their value to resist a strangulating procreative excess. But to attend to those whose marital, parental, or filial relationships or other human ties are harrowingly disturbed, and to those who are in fear or pain as a result, we do require a *new* know-how or, at least, a rapid refinement and expansion of existing techniques. As our standards of physical amenities 'grow beyond the dreams of avarice', more and more honour and prestige, more and more recognition and love, will go to those who will be able to supply the vital non-material amenities and comforts of existence.

This kind of optimism grossly underestimates the in-built compulsion of the capitalist economy to create scarcities and bottlenecks, to concentrate on producing more and more expensive luxuries, while allowing shortages of necessities, and to widen differentials between rich and poor. It also fails to recognise how social work and the other counselling professions may come to be employed to reinforce inequalities and deprivations rather than to deal with residual problems in overall conditions of prosperity. While it is true that these professions have expanded as affluence has increased, they have served different ends in different countries. In France, for instance, training for social work is under the strictest state control, and *assistantes sociales* are employed mainly in roles similar to English Health Visitors, giving very direct advice and assistance as part of a programme of raising standards of hygiene and medical care, of 'improving' dietary and budgeting provisions of poorer families, and bringing about more up-to-date and uniform standards of family life both in backward rural communities and impoverished urban neighbourhoods. Similarly, no doubt, the 'counselling' services of Eastern European countries are designed to serve very directly the aims of government social programmes. Finally, and most importantly in Britain and the USA, an expansion in social work provision may simply betoken a change in the method of dispensing public assistance.

However, Halmos is right to emphasise that there is one tradition of official social work—in this country especially in local authority social work—which has strong links with the ethos of counselling based on the notion of a loving and compassionate relationship as the most effective therapeutic method. Furthermore, the existence of private social work agencies in the USA and in Britain makes it clear that casework does not necessarily serve any particular economic or political interest. Halmos calculated that around 1960 there were about 2,700 trained social caseworkers in this country, the vast majority of whom were employed in official agencies, mainly in local authorities. At the same time, he estimated that there were in the USA some 45,000 social workers. This estimate was based on Gordon Hamilton's figures for 1940, when she totalled 'between one hundred thousand and one hundred and seventy-five thousand persons in social work positions',[17] of whom Halmos's figure represented the trained proportion. It is reasonable to assume that the vast majority of the untrained group (which formed more than half of the total), were employed in public welfare agencies, but this leaves most of the remainder as caseworkers employed by voluntary agencies of various kinds. Most of the theoretical literature of American casework emanates from these agencies, which normally charge their clients fees for their counselling services, and which therefore inevitably cater mainly for better-off members of the community.

This phenomenon is not unknown in this country. The influential Institute of Marital Studies (formerly the Family Discussion Bureau) which is part of the Tavistock Clinic, operates on a similar basis, giving casework to couples with marital problems at an hourly fee. It is no coincidence that this type of provision should have developed in a psychiatric setting. The 'purest' forms of casework have always been associated with problems of mental health which are less influenced by economic conditions and social class, and where better-off people may indeed be more vulnerable than worse-off people to certain kinds of stresses. The Child Guidance Clinics represent a public service for parents and children which illustrate this point. The clinics' methods are 'pure' in a way which takes no account at all of the social origins of patients, to the extent that they have been accused of favouring the middle-classes, by following procedures which poorer patients find difficult to understand. Furthermore, because of the relatively clinical setting, and the nature of the referral process, child guidance has remained relatively protected from the pressure of 'raw' social problems. 'Among many parents all living ... within relatively easy reach of the child guidance clinics, there was a surprising ignorance of the function of these clinics.'[18] However, there can be very little argument that the clinics produced a service of a high standard, and that they tended to attract the best-qualified social workers.

All these facts suggest that casework can, and does, flourish in the service of its clients' needs both as a public provision and as a private enterprise, virtually unrelated to the economic demands of the productive system, provided that certain conditions are realised. I have suggested that one important set of conditions is connected with the purposes of those who employ caseworkers, and that one particular purpose (public assistance) is particularly fatal to good casework as it is generally understood. The other set of conditions is organisational and administrative. Social work is an arduous task, and the best caseworkers doing the most sensitive work require support and reinforcement if they are to go on doing good work for any length of time. This kind of support is built into the organisation of high-powered American casework agencies, and also into much British psychiatric work and its derivatives. For instance, the Institute of Marital Studies' caseworkers have regular psychiatric consultations both on an individual and a group basis, and consider that a large proportion of the working week spent in such back-up activities, is time well spent in terms of the efficient performance of their therapeutic task. This luxurious provision is quite impossible in local authority settings but, even so, the need for casework consultations and supervisory support was clearly recognised in the structure of the original Children's Departments. The Curtis Committee had envisaged that Children's Officers (i.e. the chief executives of local authority departments), would have personal responsibility for each child in care; indeed, she would either have a personal *relationship* with each child, or would employ only a small staff.[19] The sheer size of the child care problem soon made nonsense of this concept, but the Curtis Committee was undoubtedly giving recognition to an important principle in the administration of the personal social services. The individualised care of clients depends in large measure on the extent to which social workers themselves feel valued as persons within their own departments, and thus a large, impersonal, administrative machine is unlikely to produce a sensitive and caring response to its clients' individual needs.

This principle has been recognised in the American literature of 'organisation theory'. Etzioni has developed a general typology of organisations according to the way in which those in charge get 'lower participants' to carry out the goals of the organisation.[20] The methods used in his three categories of organisations are respectively 'coercive' (as in prisons), 'utilitarian' (as in businesses), and 'normative' (as in churches and political parties). The last type of organisation requires a positive commitment on the part of subordinates to the goals of the agency, for effective accomplishment of these goals, since without the motivating force of a subjective endorsement of the agency's values, the task cannot be adequately performed. Etzioni and his associates have made a special study of social work agencies as one example of normative organisations, and have analysed the special problems of instilling and reinforcing the values necessary for the performance of effective casework.[21] Studies of social work agencies have highlighted the key role of supervision, both because of the difficult, painful and uncertain nature of the casework process, and because of the 'semi-professional' nature of much social work, in which those actually working with clients enjoy something less than full professional status. This last point is especially relevant in public agencies, where there is accountability to an elected committee through the head of the department, and where not all social workers are necessarily fully trained.[22]

Claudine Spencer has applied these theories very usefully to the problems posed by the creation of the new unified local authority social services departments after the Seebohm Report.[23] One of the key problems is that of the 'professional in a bureaucracy'. Although social workers are the members of the agency who have direct contact with the public, they do not necessarily determine the values or the functions of the department. This is particularly relevant when trained social workers from one agency (e.g. the Children's Department) find themselves working within the structure of an agency with an administrative hierarchy not necessarily committed to the same professional goals (e.g. the old Welfare Department). 'This is a problem of organisational restraint on the professional employee. The principal sources of these constraints are the statutory obligations of the social work department, its accountability and the problem of resources scarcity.'[24] She gives the example of Section 1 of the 1963 Children and Young Persons Act to illustrate possible conflict between professional workers and bureaucrats. Because this section is vague, but mentions both casework and financial provision,[25]

> the extent to which policy expresses professional commitment then depends on those in power. A persistent and wide disparity between professional objectives and agency practice ultimately means that social workers cease to be social workers in any meaningful sense of the word.

Spencer also anticipated that the provision of material assistance would be 'subject to bureaucratic control'.[26] She concluded that 'both theory and research findings point to the importance of delegating decisions to the professional on the job ... attempts to programme the field worker's decisions for him are only likely to weaken his commitment to the job'.[27]

In practice, these problems have proved every bit as thorny as Spencer's article anticipated. The widespread promotion of qualified social workers into positions of 'middle management' in social services departments denuded area teams of trained staff to work with clients, but it did not strengthen the relative position of the professional vis-à-vis the bureaucrat. On the contrary, the proliferation of material benefits, especially under the Chronically Sick and Disabled Persons Act, the need to create new unified administrative structures, and the sheer weight of new referrals demanding material help all combined to give the bureaucrats a field day. Indeed, the efficient dispensing of all these benefits demanded a more hierarchical structure, more forms to be completed, more administrative checks and double checks. All these procedures were particularly offensive to ex-child care officers who already were experiencing the difficulties of adapting to their new generic duties. Partly as a result of this, the turnover rate of social workers in area teams became phenomenally rapid. Within a year of the Seebohm changeover, many offices, even in stable rural areas, had not a single social worker left from the original teams. The notion of a long-standing personal relationship between worker and client, which is fundamental to many kinds of casework, became immediately unrealistic. The Curtis Committee's expectation of a single social worker providing continuity throughout the whole of a childhood in care was as obsolete as the horse-drawn tram.

As one would expect in an organisation with such a high turnover of staff, and with a wide variety of often unfamiliar functions, the commitment of staff to agency goals has become very much weaker than in the days of the separate departments and this, in turn, has further increased the need for tight control and detailed supervision by those in charge. The resultant picture of a characteristic social services department is of a large organisation (described in *Case Con* as a 'Seebohm factory') staffed by young, disaffected and relatively inexperienced workers, under the close administrative control of a large hierarchy of well-organised bureaucrats and confused, alienated, senior professionals, bemoaning their lack of contact with clients.

One not unsurprising phenomenon associated with these developments has been the emergence of a 'trade union' type of resistance to administrative control by basic grade social workers. It is significant that this resistance should take the form characteristic of workers in what Etzioni would call 'utilitarian' organisations (in which employees' main motivating force is financial gain) rather than the 'normative' type of resistance that one would anticipate in organisations where lower participants expected to share in the values of the agency. The main area of conflict between social workers and their employers since Seebohm has been the question of payment for standby duties—the obligation to remain on call to clients in the evenings and at weekends. It is interesting to trace the connection between pressure on standby duties and the transfer of income maintenance responsibilities from Supplementary Benefits to local authority social services departments.

Under the Ministry of Social Security Act, 1966, the Supplementary Benefits Commission have a clear responsibility not only to provide benefits to claimants on specified dates when they are eligible to receive them, but also to meet urgent need as it arises throughout the community. Section 13 of the Act makes it clear that any person in an emergency situation should get this help, and the Supplementary Benefits Handbook confirms that this includes people in full-time employment who encounter some exceptional circumstance that leaves them destitute. There is no similar provision in any of the statutes governing local authority social work, though the Children and Young Persons Act 1963 has been interpreted as applying in this way to families with young children. Thus, the Supplementary Benefits Commission *should* provide a twenty-four hour, seven day a week emergency service to meet urgent financial need, while the social services departments are obliged to provide such a service only to meet their obligations under the 1959 Mental Health Act and the 1948 Children Act. The social services standby officer should, therefore, perform only casework functions in relation to admissions to mental hospitals and to care; it is for the Supplementary Benefits Commission to meet evening and weekend financial emergencies.

However, what has evolved in recent years is quite a different picture. The Supplementary Benefits Commission have consistently and successfully shifted the onus for emergency payments on to social services social workers in almost every area of the country. It has suited them to do so for a large number of reasons. In the first place, they have never had a proper emergency system of their own. Their own standby officers are volunteers, and it is no part of their contract of service to work out of office hours. They have to pay claimants out of their own pockets, and cannot claim travelling expenses if they stray outside their area. Their telephone number is not available to the public, but only to the police and social services departments. As a result of all these totally unsatisfactory features, the emergency officer of the Supplementary Benefits Commission very often simply does not exist or, if he does, is unobtainable. Social services standby officers, frustrated by repeated failures to get hold of social security officers for emergency payments at weekends, have got into the habit of making payments themselves, and reclaiming from their own department or from the social security the following week. In many areas, this arrangement has been given the blessing of the hierarchies of both departments.

However, the arrangement has not stopped at a service for outside office hours. The Supplementary Benefits Commission have been following a policy of centralisation of their offices. Small local offices, which were seen as the basis of the administration of the National Assistance Board, are being rapidly closed or reduced in status to 'caller points' (advice centres, with no power to make payments). In rural areas, this has meant that claimants may be as much as thirty miles away from the nearest social security office. This is part of the movement in the direction of creating a more anonymous, impersonal postal service to claimants, a move which includes changes like payment by Giro orders and a reduction in the number of visiting officers. But it is also a move away from flexibility and responsiveness to urgent need. The postal system is slow and cumbersome, and it takes several days to meet even the simplest of claims, simply because of the bureaucratic processes involved. (Eight different officers are required for the business of despatching one giro.) Thus, immediate needs cannot well be met by post, and if the nearest office is many miles away, the destitute claimant cannot even afford to go there in search of a payment. Even if he does manage the journey, the new system does not readily allow payments over the counter, so he is likely to have to return home empty handed to await the morning postman. This difficulty in getting emergency payment was responsible for a lot of the conflict between claimants and social security staff described in chapter 5. It is precisely this kind of noisy, violent problem of urgent need that the Supplementary Benefits Commission is anxious to export to the social services departments.

In many areas, the Commission has already succeeded in doing so. Even during office hours, many financial emergencies are being dealt with by social workers rather than social security officers. In rural areas, the pretext is the difficulty of travelling; a local social services office makes payments in order to save the claimant having to travel a considerable distance to the nearest social security office. In urban areas, the policy of transferring responsibility to social workers has been more systematically pursued. In the Midlands, several local authorities (including Birmingham), have made arrangements for their social workers to carry form WM/SB 624/3, which allows them to make payments for emergency *and* exceptional needs, and to reclaim these from the Supplementary Benefits Commission. The point about these payments is that although they are made by social workers, they are not made under any legislation which governs their own department's functions. They are social security payments, made under social security regulations, by local authority social workers, acting as social security officers. Those who receive payments do so simply by virtue of their social security requirements, and not as clients of social services. Indeed, most of them are not clients at all, but pensioners whose order books have got lost in the post, or sick people whose benefits have been delayed by administrative hold-ups. In all these cases, social workers are doing work solely concerned with income maintenance, for which they have no statutory obligations, simply because of the non-availability of social security provision. The difference from the claimant's point of view is that if a social worker refuses him a payment, he has no right of appeal. Incidentally, if the social worker *overpays* a claimant by failing to observe the social security regulations, he may be refused reimbursement by the Supplementary Benefits Commission, and *he* then has no right of appeal.

The consequences of this assumption of responsibility for financial emergencies have been as monumental in many areas as the new duties under the Children and Young Persons Act and the Chronically Sick and Disabled Persons Act. In one area of Liverpool, social workers besieged by claimants referred to them by the social security office formed an 'intake team' specifically to refer such claimants back to the Supplementary Benefits Commission again. In most areas, however, social workers have simply soaked up these responsibilities unquestioningly. They have preferred to be overworked rather than risk the hardship to poor people that they see as an inevitable alternative, given the rigidity of the new social security arrangements and the absence of an adequate emergency benefits' system. Their frustrations were expressed, not in organised resistance to pressures from Supplementary Benefits, but in resistance to their own employers, expressed in the demands for standby payments for the heavy work involved—often by way of dispensing payments—in evening and weekend duties. The 'trade union' element in social workers' recent activities is therefore directly related to their new public assistance role.

Administratively, these changes have reinforced trends already evident since the formation of the social services departments. Because of the weight of referrals, many departments have introduced new grades of unqualified workers to deal with applications for benefits, and to make financial assessments. Sometimes they have been appointed as welfare assistants; elsewhere they have been given temporary social worker status. The Central Council for Education and Training in Social Work is currently canvassing the notion of a new grade of intermediate, semi-qualified 'welfare officers' for such tasks. The existence of such non-professional staff, and the large amount of face-to-face contact they have with clients, serves as a further justification for tight administrative control and a form of supervision based on detailed regulation of tasks, rather than casework support. The professional and 'normative' elements of the hierarchy of social services departments are reduced with each increase in public assistance responsibilities, and the 'instrumental' and 'managerial' functions increased. These developments all have consequences for trained professional workers.[28]

> Bureaucratic constraints ... lead to bureaucratic controls which can reduce the professional's satisfaction with his work and with his agency. This means a reduction in commitment which, in turn, may be postulated to affect the quality of the service given. Bureaucratic controls are largely irrelevant to the orientation of social workers to the job, although they may safeguard some minimal standards of service.

One argument for a new grade of 'welfare officers' is that the allocation of routine tasks to this level of staff would set social workers free to practise truly professional tasks, and make maximum use of their skills. In fact, however, where this kind of system has been adopted, the change of function and priorities in the agency, and the consequent rigidification of the administrative structure all work against any progress in this direction. For instance, in one West Country county, where the old Children's Department had one of the highest ratios of trained staff in the country, the appointment of temporary social workers has not reduced the number of routine assessments which the relatively few remaining trained staff at basic grade level are required to undertake. It has, however, led to a suspicion among professional workers that the hierarchy has seen in temporary workers a cheaper instrument for providing the essentially service-orientated provisions which it defines as characteristic of the new department's role. Thus, more and more temporary appointments have been made, while trained applicants for permanent posts have been rejected on the grounds that they are unlikely to 'fit in' with the agency.

Professional standards are affected, not simply indirectly through the morale of trained workers, but also directly, through the infiltration of the public assistance ideology into the practice of face-to-face work with clients. The obligation to provide poor relief has not only altered the whole structure and ethos of local authority departments; it has created a new kind of relationship between social workers and their clients, based not on principles of casework, but on principles of public assistance. Services which were once provided as best they could be, within the limited resources of local authorities as personal services, are now rationed according to the means-tested ideology of the supplementary benefits system, with all the humiliation of the recipient that this entails. The following examples both concern elderly clients, but similar ones could well be given which apply to families with children.

To illustrate the callous disregard for an individual's needs and feelings which becomes possible once responsibilities (which should be exercised by an income maintenance service, providing proper rights of representation and appeal) are taken over by a local authority public welfare agency, I shall quote in full a letter to the editor of *Social Work Today* from Mrs Helen Slater, of Bishopsteignton, Devon, who is a social worker in a hospital setting.[29]

My attention has been drawn to the plight of a 70 year old lady who has been living happily in a registered home for the elderly for two years. Until December last, she received a supplementary allowance which covered the modest weekly charges and allowed her pocket money. In January, the DHSS sent for the book, and when it came back the amount had been reduced from £10·50 to £6·75—there was no explanation for this action. When an enquiry was made, the DHSS stated that the Exeter City Council had assumed responsibility for supplementing the incomes of people in registered homes. Weeks went by and the amount remained at £6·75. Many calls were put through to the department of social services; the director was 'not available', and a member of the department made the staggering statement, 'we have no money, and I do not know when we shall have, but I will get her into one of our Part III homes as soon as possible'. The claimant does not wish to move from her present home.

After waiting eight weeks, during which time this 70 year-old lady did not receive sufficient to meet the weekly charges, and had no allowance for pocket money, she was feeling her security severely threatened. At this point, when after waiting over a week no reply had been received to a letter addressed to the DHSS, I contacted the Manager and was asked to get in touch with the Exeter Department of Social Services. I pointed out that the subject under discussion was a supplementary allowance which had been reduced. I informed the Manager that the matter was being referred to the Claimants' Union, and because of the important principles involved, a letter was being sent to a professional journal to draw the attention of social workers to the implications of the situation. Within a few hours of this conversation, a message was received from the DHSS that the supplementary allowance was immediately being made up, together with back payments; an apology was made for the inconvenience caused. I was also informed that other people in similar circumstances in the City had also come to light, and these were being promptly put in order by the DHSS.

Clearly, many questions need to be asked.

(1) By what authority are decisions made about accommodation and income of a happily settled old lady of 70 by two authorities without the courtesy even of information?

(2) This old lady is not mentally disordered and does not need after-care, but, if she was needing some after-care, is she not a free citizen?

(3) Why did the Exeter Department of Social Services assume this considerable responsibility, knowing that they did not have the necessary financial resources?

(4) Has the Department of Social Services the right to put someone on their waiting list for Part III accommodation when no application has been made?

(5) Quite apart from the discourtesy and insensitivity shown by the Exeter Department of Social Services to a 70 year-old lady, and the considerable number of telephone calls made on this matter which were ignored, it appears that the DHSS, at any rate at senior level, may not have been fully aware of the plight and the stress suffered by the people involved. The responsibility of the Supplementary Benefits Commission, is, and has been for years, to deal direct with citizens of this

country and allow them sufficient income for their needs. Is it not dangerous to tamper with this direct responsibility?

The Supplementary Benefits Commission is structured to help people in need, including a built-in appeals procedure. It is one of our clients' fundamental rights, and social workers should do everything to help them and the Supplementary Benefits Commission to develop and strengthen this.

P.S. On the evening of 7 March, I received a phone call from this 70 year-old lady seeking assurance that she could stay in her present home. On pursuing the matter further, I was informed that a message had been received at the Home during the afternoon from the Department of Social Services, to say that as they could not supplement payments they were, at 4 p.m. today (8 March) collecting her and another elderly resident to take them to Part III homes.

At 8 a.m. today, I phoned the director at his home to check the facts and seek an assurance that this elderly lady would not be collected from her home and moved to Part III. He was unable to give this assurance as he was unaware of the situation, but he agreed to look into the matter and ask the responsible member of his staff to ring me back at 9 a.m. At 9.30 a.m. I received a message from the department to say that the 'move of two or three people had been postponed until Mr "X" can look into the position'. A social worker also called at the home at about 9 a.m. to say that the two ladies would not be collected today as 'Mr "X" is reviewing the situation'.

The second example is of a means-test procedure. Old people accommodated in local authority homes are assessed as to their ability to contribute towards the authority's cost in maintaining them there. Traditionally, those who agree to pay the full rate of contribution were not required to declare their total means, either savings or income, as they were requiring no subsidisation. However, in one county area, the administration of the social services department now requires social workers to complete assessments on *all* applicants, including those who pay the full contribution. The reason is so that the department can keep a check on the way applicants and residents dispose of their resources, so as to ensure that they spend their money in a 'reasonable way'. This attempt to control 'undeserving' behaviour in the form of spendthrift expenditure by elderly people goes beyond the means-test procedures of the Supplementary Benefits Commission, for they have no powers to impose their assessments on those who have not even applied to them for assistance. But the position of dependence of elderly people on social services departments enables them to take intrusiveness and lack of respect for privacy to this new depth.

The means-test mentality of public assistance that has taken over the administration of social services departments, destroys the respect for persons which has traditionally been associated with social work services.

What these two examples illustrate is the way in which public assistance provisions by social services departments are *less* respectful of clients' rights than are the income maintenance services. Thus, every assumption of an income maintenance responsibility by a social services department is, as Mrs Slater's example clearly shows, an infringement of the rights of citizens (such as they are) to supplementary benefits. At least the supplementary benefits system contains some safeguards in appeals' procedures. At least the Supplementary Benefits Commission cannot physically shift a claimant from his home. At least claimants are not so totally dependent on supplementary benefits that they look to the Commission for the provision of a roof over their heads. Social work's clients often are just so dependent, and this makes the responsibility on social workers to respect them as persons such an important one. These examples show that this responsibility is not being lived up to.

Social workers have allowed public assistance duties to be shifted on to them because they have been unhappy about the inflexibility of the income maintenance services. It all started with the 1963 Act because Children's Departments were dissatisfied with the National Assistance Board's sensitivity to family needs. Since local authorities assumed these powers, the income maintenance services have been getting steadily less flexible. They have increasingly relied on local authorities to underpin their rigid and unresponsive system of dispensing benefits, and they have shifted the burden of emergency and exceptional need, and much of their disputed area of discretion, onto social services departments. The sheer size of the problem left over after social security 'rationalisation' and centralisation is illustrated by the case of Newton Abbot. When the Claimants' Union succeeded in retaining a local emergency social security 'pay point' in the town, the DHSS argued that it would only have to deal with a handful of claims each week. In fact, an average of between thirty and fifty over-the-counter payments were made every week during the six months after the main office was shifted to Torquay. This represents the volume of emergencies (excluding weekends and evenings which would swell the number yet again), most of which arise simply from delays in paying supplementary benefits by way of the centralised postal system that has been adopted. The population of the area served by the Newton Abbot office was under 60,000, and the total number of claimants about 6,000. This gives some indication of the amount of hardship caused to the most needy group of claimants as a result of the centralisation policy, and of the potential source of referrals to social services departments of people in emergency need.

In this type of situation, social workers are inclined to believe that they bring to the task of relieving urgent need a kind of flexibility and humanity that the Supplementary Benefits Commission lacks. This is not the way claimants see it. They are all too well aware of the diminution of their rights under provisions from 'the Welfare'. They experience the need to request help from social workers as like asking for charity. What social workers consider to be flexibility, they see as partiality. They recognise in procedures like supervision and the repayment of loans (both of which are characteristic of local authority payments but not of supplementary benefits), the 'strings' which are attached to this kind of poor relief. They see the significance of the limited social work budget as compared with the notionally unlimited funds available for supplementary benefits.[30]

> The local authority social services department (the Welfare), are supposed to give you grants if otherwise your kids would have to be taken into care. But the Welfare are worse than the S.S. (Social Security). They ask you questions about your private life and, if they refuse you money, there is no right of appeal.

What I have tried to show in this chapter is that social work's crisis of identity, which has been focused on the relevance, efficacy and moral justifiability of casework, can be better understood in terms of the shift of public assistance responsibilities onto social workers. It has always been true that poor people used local authority social work services more than better-off people. Jean Packman found that 'the lower social classes, and particularly manual workers, were heavily over-represented' among the parents of children in care, and that 'by far the greatest number of fathers were to be found in the lower social classes, and mostly as manual workers'.[31]

However, these groups used the service more mainly because, for various reasons, they required the kind of help with family emergencies (for instance caring for young children during the mother's illness or confinement), which better-off families could cope with by other means.[32]

> This pattern does not mean that families in the higher social classes and families of black-coated workers do not break down, nor that their children escape deprivation. What it does suggest is that they rarely approach the local authority in times of trouble, but find other means of coping with their

difficulties, for instance, boarding schools or private foster homes.

Thus, poorer people applied for these services because they needed the services, not because they were poor. The services were not, in themselves, any kind of poor relief. The services were based on that need and not on the applicants' social and economic attributes, such as their poverty. Increasingly, during the past five years or more, local authority social services have attracted applications for forms of public assistance, *some quite unconnected with their statutory functions*. This has inevitably affected the structure and ethos of the departments, and the role of social workers.

Casework only becomes an instrument for class oppression when it is used selectively on the poor, as the means of providing a form of highly stigmatised, individualised poor relief, accompanied by rationing devices based on an assumption of the moral inferiority or emotional inadequacy of the applicants. The bad image that casework has increasingly obtained, both inside and outside social work, is directly connected with the growing volume of public assistance responsibilities of local authority social services departments. In exporting their violent and turbulent problem-claimants to the local authorities, social security has indeed succeeded in making social workers into 'front line troops in the war against poverty'. From the point of view of the claimant, this often seems like a war on the poor. Social workers, as front line troops, must expect that the conflict, which has become part of the everyday experience of many social security offices, will soon invade their own corridors and waiting rooms.

8
The social services and the culture of poverty

It is time now to return to the original problem posed in the first chapter of the relationship between poverty and maladjustment. Sir Keith Joseph's theory of the 'cycle of deprivation' suggests that poor parents bring up their children in such a way as to create a new generation of families which are both poor and maladjusted. Using 'deprivation' as a term which describes both emotional and material impoverishment, he suggests that this is something which is thus transmitted from one generation to the next. One of the experiences from which he is said to have derived this theory was being told by a local authority director of social services that, 'We have 20,000 households in this city. Nearly all our problems—delinquency, truancy, deprivation, poverty and the rest—come from about 800 of them. And I think that most of the families have been known to us for five generations.'[1]

The reasons why social workers' testimony on the subject of the social distribution of deprivation and maladjustment is unlikely to be entirely reliable have been indicated in the last two chapters. In the first place, public services for deprivation and maladjustment have always tended to be used more by the lower classes and less by the better-off, who dealt with similar problems by other means. Second, recent changes in legislation and in the administration of the income maintenance services have resulted in local authority social services departments being involved increasingly with the poorest sector of the community, and in social workers being encouraged to see its poverty as a symptom of maladjustment. Research findings tend to contradict social workers' perceptions, both by indicating the high incidence of various forms of 'deviant' behaviour among better-off members of society, and by showing that emotional deprivation and maladjustment do not correlate with poverty to any significant extent, at least in Britain.[2]

However, at least in a commonsense fashion, social workers are obviously right to draw attention to the extent to which the poor are 'at risk' in ways that better-off members of the community are not. Above all, there is the problem that the poor face when they are forced to adopt a style of family life which, though in origin a defence against the uncertainties and insecurities of their existence, comes to be defined by better-off people as deviant or maladjusted. Their efforts to adapt to the conditions of their poverty, and to evolve ways of dealing with the crises in their day-to-day life, are thus treated as evidence of their psychological and emotional immaturity, and of a need for social work or psychiatric supervision. Social workers who point out that the poor are often deemed maladjusted, or their children adjudged to be deprived, as a result of patterns of family life arising directly from their poverty, are rightly drawing attention to the inevitable interaction between economic factors and social adaptations, in which the former frequently give rise to the latter.

Even here, however, social workers may tend to assume that particular economic conditions are *the* cause of a form of deprivation or maladjustment, and account for what they take to be a high incidence of these phenomena. For instance, social workers in old working-class areas with low average incomes and high rates of unemployment often blame these economic conditions for the plight of their emotionally deprived clients. However, research findings indicate that these factors are not associated, for instance, with high rates of deprived children, and that areas of higher wages and better employment prospects, but with high rates of homelessness and a great deal of immigration from both inside and outside the country, are more commonly associated with high rates of children in various forms of non-family care.[3] This suggests the existence of many 'bad' factors which affect the family patterns of the poor in different ways, some of which may contribute to one form of 'deviant' behaviour, and others of which may be associated with quite other socially unpopular patterns. The notion of a particular group of people living in the worst possible conditions is misleading, because many 'bad' factors seldom co-exist. Thus, 'the picture of "maximum need" is confused, like a double-exposure, with one set of circumstances overlaying another',[4] some of which (like high unemployment and heavy immigration) are virtually inconsistent with each other. Furthermore, there is no obvious direct and straightforward link between any one 'bad' factor, or any combination of them, and any one form of 'bad' or antisocial behaviour.

This leads on to what is said to have been another influence on Sir Keith Joseph's thinking about the 'cycle of deprivation'. A theory of 'the culture of poverty' has grown out of the work of the American anthropologist, Oscar Lewis, who studied the way of life of the poorest classes in Mexico, Puerto Rico and New York. In *La Vida* he sets out in summary the basis of his theory of a culture of poverty, which is intended to account for a pattern that[5] transcends regional, rural-urban and national differences, and shows remarkable similarities in family structure, interpersonal relations, time orientation, value systems and spending patterns. These cross-national similarities are examples of independent invention and convergence. They are common adaptations to common problems.

Lewis lists the factors which give rise to the problems which produce a culture of poverty:

it tends to grow and flourish in societies with the following set of conditions: (1) a cash economy, wage labor and production for profit; (2) a persistently high rate of unemployment and under-employment for unskilled labor; (3) low wages; (4) the failure to provide social, political and economic organisations, either on a voluntary basis or by government imposition, for the low-income population; (5) the existence of a bilateral kinship system rather than a unilateral one; and finally (6) the existence of a set of values in the dominant class which stresses the accumulation of wealth and property, the possibility of upward mobility and thrift, and explains low economic status as the result of personal inadequacy or inferiority.[6]

The most likely candidates for the culture of poverty are the people who come from the lower strata of a rapidly changing society and are already partially alienated from it.[7]

The lack of effective participation and integration of the poor in the major institutions of the larger society is one of the crucial characteristics of the culture of poverty. This is a complex matter and results from a variety of factors which may include lack of economic resources, segregation and discrimination, fear, suspicion or apathy.... In the case of a relief system which barely keeps people alive, both the basic poverty and the sense of hopelessness are perpetuated rather than eliminated.[8]

These are the social and economic preconditions for a culture of poverty, but Lewis stresses that the culture of poverty requires other factors than poverty itself for its creation.[9]

The economic traits which I have listed for the culture of poverty are necessary but not sufficient to define the phenomena I have in mind. There are a number of historical examples of very poor segments of the population which do not have a way of life that I would describe as a subculture of poverty.

Lewis gives the examples of primitive peoples with a relatively integrated, satisfying and self-sufficient culture; of the Indian lower castes, which are integrated into the larger society and have their own organisations; of the Jews of eastern Europe with their organised communities; and of the position of the poor in socialist countries, and especially in post-revolutionary Cuba. He concludes,[10]

> in effect, we find that in primitive societies and in caste societies, the culture of poverty does not develop. In socialist, fascist and in highly developed capitalist societies with a welfare state, the culture of poverty tends to decline. I suspect that the culture of poverty flourishes in, and is generic to, the early free-enterprise stage of capitalism and that it is also endemic in colonialism.

He estimates that the culture of poverty is much less extensive in the USA than is poverty itself.[11]

> My rough guess would be that only about 20 per cent of the population below the poverty line (between six and ten million people) in the United States have characteristics which would justify classifying their way of life as that of a culture of poverty.... The relatively small number of people in the United States with a culture of poverty is a positive factor because it is much more difficult to eliminate the culture of poverty than to eliminate poverty *per se*.

It is the processes by which the culture of poverty perpetuates itself that link this theory with Sir Keith Joseph's notion of a 'cycle of deprivation'.[12]

> The culture of poverty is both an adaptation to and a reaction of the poor to their marginal position in a class-stratified, highly individuated, capitalistic society. It represents an effort to cope with feelings of hopelessness and despair which develop from the realisation of the improbability of achieving success in terms of the values and goals of the larger society.... Once it comes into existence it tends to perpetuate itself from generation to generation because of its effect on the children. By the time slum children are age six or seven they have usually absorbed the basic values and attitudes of their sub-culture and are not psychologically geared to take full advantage of changing conditions or increased opportunities which may occur in their lifetime.

This process of transmission of a way of life which justifies hedonistic living in the present, an absence of planning and responsibility and an almost total mistrust of official institutions, in terms of a fatalistic view of the inevitability of failure, seems to be almost exactly what Sir Keith Joseph is describing in his theory which attributes deprivation and maladjustment to the family patterns of the poor.

However, if this part of Lewis's theory fits well with Sir Keith Joseph's own, the social and economic bases of it are not so readily reconcilable with the views one would expect to be held by a Secretary of State for Health and Social Security. Lewis suggests that a culture of poverty would not be expected to flourish in an advanced capitalist society with an adequate welfare state. Presumably Sir Keith Joseph would argue that the present-day manifestations of a culture of poverty in this country are residual phenomena carried over from an earlier period of our history; from the era of the social and economic conditions associated with the unrestrained, competitive free-enterprise capitalism. Unless Sir Keith Joseph uses this kind of argument, he would seem, according to Lewis's theory, to be drawing attention either to the inadequacies of the welfare state, or else to the consequences of a more unbridled form of free-enterprise capitalism than even the recent Government was accustomed to claim to represent.

It would certainly be difficult to test the hypothesis that there are fewer people living in a culture of poverty now than there were at an earlier period of our history, and equally difficult to verify a statement that there are more. What it is possible to say is that, as has been shown in chapter 1, sociologists have not discovered the same concentration of social deviance in our slums as they found in the slums of American cities. Researches like those of Sainsbury in the 1930s did not find that forms of deviance other than crime and psychotic mental illness correlated with poverty, and more recently Jean Packman's study of deprived children showed that high rates of these correlated negatively with indices of poverty, and positively with indices of affluence. If these facts have any bearing on the question of a culture of poverty, they suggest that any such culture that has been passed down from earlier generations of the poor in this country was not associated (in the 1930s) with behaviour patterns leading to alcoholism, drug addiction, neurosis or suicide, or (in the 1960s) with family break-up, illegitimacy or child neglect. Thus, if Sir Keith Joseph wishes to claim the present existence of a culture which does contain such elements (and his speech to the Pre-School Playgroups Association suggests that he does), then he has to account for it in terms of very recent developments in social and economic policy, rather than as residual features of patterns derived from earlier slum conditions.

A more testable and perhaps more constructive question to ask about Sir Keith Joseph's theory is whether recent changes in our welfare state, and particularly changes in the period since the recent Government took office, can be seen as likely to have militated against the growth of a culture of poverty, or, if one exists, to have reduced its extent by breaking into the cyclical processes by which it maintains itself. If we recognise in the culture of poverty a far more persistent and stubborn feature of the social life of the poor than poverty itself, then we should see it as a primary aim of social policy to check and limit its growth. Lewis's theory suggests reassuringly that it is possible for an advanced capitalist economy to do this effectively, so long as it develops the right kind of social services. He even mentions the combination of income maintenance and social work as one possible method of achieving this.[13]

> In the United States, the major solution proposed by planners and social workers in dealing with multi-problem families and the so-called hard core of poverty has been to attempt slowly to raise their level of living and to incorporate them into the middle class.

Presumably, therefore, one important criterion in judging the effectiveness of social services is whether they reduce or reinforce the patterns of family life which can be identified as associated with the culture of poverty, and thus with the transmission of deprivation from one generation to the next.

It is instructive, therefore, to consider first the list of behaviour patterns and personality traits which Lewis gives as characteristic of the culture of poverty.[14]

> On the family level the major traits of the culture of poverty are the absence of childhood as a specially prolonged and protected stage in the life cycle, early initiation into sex, free unions or consensual marriages, a relatively high incidence of the abandonment of wives and children, a trend towards female—or mother—centred families and consequently a much greater knowledge of maternal relatives, a strong predisposition to authoritarianism, lack of privacy, verbal emphasis on family solidarity which is only rarely achieved because of sibling rivalry, and competition for limited goods and maternal affection. On the level of the individual, the major characteristics are a strong feeling of marginality, of helplessness, of dependence and inferiority.... Other traits include a high incidence of maternal deprivation, of orality, of weak ego structure, confusion of sexual identification, a lack of impulse control, a strong present-time orientation with relatively little ability to defer gratification and to plan for the future, a sense of resignation and fatalism, a widespread belief in male superiority, and a high tolerance for psychological pathology of all sorts.

If these characteristics are transmitted in the course of family life, it is important to analyse the impact of the intervention and activity of the various social services which deal with the poor, and how this affects family patterns.

As soon as we attempt to do this, we shall be struck by a paradox which is inherent in the whole system of poor relief which has been described in this book. Public assistance in the Poor Law tradition has been dedicated to the preservation of certain social institutions (the family, the work ethic and law and order), but in its attempts to support these it has always had its eye on those who are *not* receiving relief. It attempts to uphold the virtues of the majority, and the institutions upon which these virtues are based, by treating the minority in ways which illustrate the penalities of lapsing from virtuous principles. Thus the way to uphold the work ethic is to penalise the workshy; the way to maintain law and order is to punish the disorderly; and the way to uphold the family is to make life tough for those whose husbands or parents have not provided for them. The penal regulations are not designed for the edification of the unprincipled minority so much as for the re-inforcement of the principles of the marginal members of the majority.

The unfortunate side of these measures is that the actual application of the policy of less eligibility to those who require relief very often has the effect of reinforcing in them the very short-comings which it is designed to stamp out in the majority. The regime which deters the marginally virtuous merely confirms the identity of the marginal failure. The obvious example is of prison, which makes criminals out of many chance offenders in the process of deterring many non-offenders. The same was true of most of the Poor Law institutions which, as has often been remarked, were based on similar principles. The total institutions of the work-house induced dependence in those who were forced to accept its offer of support, just as it forced independence on many who preferred to starve. While it encouraged more families to care for their own, under threat of what it would do to their members if they were admitted, it damaged beyond repair the links between members of those unfortunate families that were admitted. Middleton says that the Poor Law regulations[15]

> were in many instances framed so as to destroy directly the family unit as a feature of the deterrent system. In fact the only time the Poor Law was concerned with the family was when a relative was sought out to support someone who had applied for relief.

It is undoubtedly the intention of our present-day social services to support the institution of the family, and to help bring about a society consisting of the maximum possible number of stable, responsible marriages, with a father in work, supporting his children (preferably not more than two) out of his earnings. However, not all families are able to achieve this ideal, and in order to encourage those who are attempting to do so against considerable odds, it is necessary, so it seems, to deal with those who have failed in such a way as to make them no better off than those who are still trying. This is the origin of so many of the regulations governing public assistance that it is worth looking in more detail at how they affect people who are already dependent in one way or another on the social services, with particular reference to the characteristics of the culture of poverty.

Perhaps the most important trait on Lewis's list is the tendency towards female- or mother-centred families, and to families headed by a mother. It is not difficult to recognise one strong reason why there should be a tendency towards this pattern among the poor. A man in low-wage employment, without prospects of an improvement in his income, and without security of earnings, is in a weak position to sustain the role of head of his family. His struggle to provide for his wife and children out of his unsatisfying and exhausting labour is hardly a rewarding one for him, and it is therefore not surprising that he seeks his satisfactions and his status in other interests and activities. While higher incomes have been associated with the development of nuclear family structures, a joint conjugal role relationship, companionate, shared interests and activities between husband and wife and an emphasis on family-based leisure pursuits, Lewis's study of the culture of poverty illustrates how it gives rise to segregated marital roles, supported by extended family and kinship networks, and for the men an emphasis on leisure activities which prove their manliness and courage through their daring and physical prowess, or else provide the excitement lacking in their working life, as for instance in gambling. Thus, within the family group, security is often represented not by an ambitious dependable father figure, who gains solidity through his work role and his prospects of a still higher income to come, but by the ever-present network of female kin and neighbours who support the mother, constituting an informal lending and borrowing service, a baby-sitting or short-term fostering resource group, a nursery class, a nursing corps and even sometimes, in relation to the men, a bodyguard.

The object of poor relief has always been to encourage men in low-wage employment (often working for wages below public assistance rates), to be responsible about the business of providing an adequate income to feed and clothe their children, to spend their earnings prudently and to maximise the family side of their expenditure and minimise their self-indulgence. However, while wage levels are in many cases below scale rates for assistance, this can only be achieved, so it is argued, by the mechanism of the wage stop; for if one man is working all day to keep his family and unable to afford such luxuries as tobacco or a drink, it is wrong to reward another who is not working, and who if working could command no greater wage, by giving him assistance at a rate which will allow him to provide as well as the former for his family, and still have enough left over for a drink and a smoke.

However, this principle has never been applied to the unsupported wives of low-wage earners, or to those who desert their husbands because of their low earning power. The National Assistance Board and, subsequently, the Supplementary Benefits Commission, have invariably paid full scale rates to a woman bringing up children on her own; thus, if her husband cannot earn enough to bring the family income up to supplementary benefit level, a wife is quite literally better off without him. This situation has a considerable influence on the stability of marriages in the poorest sector of the community. In *Abuse and the Abused*, the Child Poverty Action Group gives one example of the way in which a husband was so undermined by the implications of his inability to provide for his wife and seven children that he finally left the family.

The father is a man of low intelligence who has never been able to read or write. He is physically strong, but the only work he can undertake which will bring in a large enough wage to keep the family is road-work. There are more men after this type of work in Bradford than there are vacancies, and the father has been unemployed for a number of years. When the claimant was first married, and up to the point where he had only two children, he was able to take a lower-paid job and manage. It has been since the growth of his family that the unemployment problems have become acute.

He was subjected to various kinds of pressure by the Department of Health and Social Security office—keeping him waiting for payments, leaving the family without money over the weekends and leaning on him to take work at £13 or £14 a week.[16]

Allowing for stoppages and travelling expenses, this would have meant that he would have been worse off than they were on the wage stop benefit of £13 a week. Anxiety built up until finally the claimant left home in February 1970 saying he would try to get a job away from Bradford. He was away about a month, and during that time his wife received no communication at all, which is not surprising considering that he was unable to read or write. He then came home for a week-end and said that he had been working on casual jobs in the Midlands. As soon as he had left home the D.H.S.S. paid his wife full benefit. The claimant remained away until the beginning of May 1970, during which time he made about three week-end visits home. By this time his wife was having great difficulty in coping and her health was deteriorating. The claimant, finding her in this state, decided that his place was at home with her. But the D.H.S.S. reverted to wage-stopping the family. Finally, under this pressure, the claimant disappeared last October and has only been seen a couple of times since. It would appear that the enthusiasm of the local officers and the S.B.C. to get this man back into work, combined with the operating of the wage-stop ruling, has been successful in creating a one-parent family.

Even where there is no wage stop in operation, the existence of an unemployed man in the family can lead to penalisation of his family through the application of Poor Law principles to the administration of exceptional needs payments. The fact that pro-portionately the greatest amount of these payments goes to un-supported women with dependent children indicates that wives with unemployed husbands get a lower proportion, undoubtedly because the generous provision of grants to such families would be considered a disincentive for the husbands to seek low-wage employment. The application of principles intended to support the work ethic thus has the effect of putting married women claimants and their children in a worse position than women bringing up their children alone, a fact which does not escape the notice of claimants. It is well known among women claimants that 'if you're on your own, they *have* to give you grants'.

The cohabitation rule also had paradoxical effects in appearing, to claimants at least, to encourage single parent families. Ostensibly, it is intended to ensure that married people should not be at a disadvantage compared with cohabiting couples. In a paper on cohabitation, the Commission says that the relaxation of the rule 'would certainly be attacked as a discouragement to marriage, as indeed in many cases it would be, since the couple would be better off on supplementary benefit than if they were married.'[17] Steven-son supports this view with the statement that 'within the frame-work of existing social and moral conventions, the case as pre-sented by the Commission seems unarguable'.[18] However, it is a deceptive argument that is employed, for it rests on the fact that, under the system of 'aggregation of resources and requirements', a married couple's entitlement is *lower* than that of two people who are not living together. Thus, the basis of the Commission's case lies not in the fact that without the rule cohabiting couples are potentially better off than married couples, but in the fact that married couples are already *worse* off than people living singly. The allowance for a woman bringing up children alone is £6·55, while if she is with her husband, their requirements are aggregated at £10·65. Married claimants are not assessed as individuals in their own right, and the principle of family responsibility, defended for its moral and social implications for non-claimants has precisely the opposite effect for claimants of giving an incentive for couples to live separately and make separate claims.

Equally, the cohabitation rule itself has the effect of discouraging relationships (short-term or long-term, stable or unstable) between a woman bringing up children on her own and any man who might support her. In a very obvious way this is done by 'sex-snooping', which makes many women claimants afraid of embarking on a relationship at all. But more subtly, it discourages not only non-claimants from taking on the full responsibility of a number of dependents, but also fellow-claimants, who would be penalised under the aggregation of requirements. Thus, if a man and woman who are both claimants form a relationship, it is in their economic interests not to live together, and to avoid giving the impression that he is taking any responsibility for her or her children. This is why the Claimants' Unions have asked, tongue in cheek,[19]

Did you realise that the S.S. actually encourage homosexuality and lesbianism? A man and a woman living together are assessed as man and wife and so get a married person's allowance.... A man and a man, or a woman and a woman, living in the same accommodation and who are probably also sharing a common purse are each assessed as single people so that each will get a full allowance.

These regulations thus have the effect of producing in claimants (and undoubtedly in the children of families growing up on supplementary benefits), a strong reinforcement of the feeling that there is greater economic security (and indeed often actually greater prosperity), in situations where the family is headed by a woman than where it is headed by a man. Feelings such as these could certainly be transmitted from a mother to her children, who would in any case observe the kind of pattern of relationships between parents caused by the wage stop, or the reactions of a mother who was anxious about the cohabitation rule. Among the claiming class, therefore, a culture inevitably develops in which those family patterns which already associate security with the female line are reinforced by Poor Law principles; and in which the weakness and unreliability of males is constantly revealed and exaggerated by their disadvantages in relation to low-wage work and benefits. These are crucial features of Lewis's culture of poverty.

There has been, as Stevenson notes, a 'dramatic increase in the number of women claiming benefit', a fact which had created 'mounting anxiety among staff that abuse among "unsupported mothers" is on the increase'.[20] The increase of special investigators and the tactics of removing order books described in earlier chapters represent the response of the Commission to a phenomenon that they have not linked with their own policies, but which seems to be explainable at least in part by official principles for regulating the poor. The phenomenon is not unique to this country (indeed Moynihan tried to attribute the *whole* of the American welfare explosion to it), and it seems to betoken the creation of a class of claimants whose cultural patterns are being adapted to the conditions under which they receive their poor relief.

The other crucial feature in Lewis's list is the short duration of childhood as a stage of dependence on parents, and the insecurity of the child's position in the family. Here again, there are obvious links with the situation of the father's low earning power in work; the necessity for the mother to undertake employment, insecurity of accommodation and the perceived need to learn to fend for oneself at an early age, to acquire the necessary ruggedness of character for survival in the tough world of the poorest class. However, many of the official principles of poor relief play into this insecurity for children. For those families for whom life is very much a hand-to-mouth business, financial crises are not uncommon, and thus the Supplementary Benefits Commission's chosen way of dealing with emergency situations is an important factor determining how family members will be affected by a sudden onset of urgent need. We have already seen that the Commission's recent administrative policy changes have made it very much more difficult for families to get emergency payments, and how claimants have been forced to adopt drastic means to obtain them. Even in the days of National Assistance, it was not unknown for claimants to abandon their children in the local office as a way of proving their need, and showing the authorities that they just could not afford to feed them. But recently the Claimants' Unions have used tactics of *collective* abandonment of children in offices as a way to force emergency payments when these were being systematically refused. Most people who have not experienced the type of extreme situation encountered by many claimants in desperate financial straits would deplore the use of children in this way, and draw attention to the damaging effects on them of this type of traumatic separation. However, for those experiencing the effects of the Supplementary Benefits Commission's policies which are designed to encourage family responsibility, there often seems no other way open to them;

if they leave the office unpaid they are going to have to deprive their children anyway. Official policy allows claimants no other way of getting money needed to support children, and children thus become bargaining counters in a grim battle for survival, in which they are all the time learning the rules of the poverty game.

If this kind of situation is exceptional in social security claims, it is absolutely general in dealings between social services departments and their clients. The 1963 Act makes financial help *dependent* on a danger of children coming into care. Of course, it was intended as a provision enabling preventive family casework, and as such is unobjectionable. Without the threat of family break-up, such work would have no focus, and without this danger as a precondition, the Act would serve as an unwarrantably broad licence for social work intervention in people's lives. However, as things have worked out, a very large proportion of work under the Act is, as the Manchester research showed, simply emergency poor relief.

Social services departments are providing a service for the poorest sector, to deal with their most immediate needs by small payments, but all this is done under the threat of children having to come into care. Thus, the very moment a parent applies to the social services department for a payment, she is of necessity having herself assessed as to her ability to bring up her children. Having once embarked on a career as a social work client, she is in constant jeopardy as a mother, for her every action is being observed and judged not only (as in social security) for its deservingness, but also for its parental quality. She is thus undertaking a dangerously open-ended commitment in using the threat of having to put her children in care, a threat which is the *only* one which should carry any weight in applications for financial help for social services departments. Indeed, the very act of applying is seen as a form of inadequacy, for it specifically implies inability to provide for children in a way that application for social security does not. Thus, social workers, because of the statutory mixture of casework and financial responsibilities, are dealing with claims for emergency payments on the basis that anyone who makes such claims should be seen as a potentially inadequate type of parent, and thus probably requires supervision or, at worst, removal of her children from the family.

It may well be that this kind of situation plays into tendencies already inherent in the family to use separation of husband from wife, or parents from children, as a form of survival mechanism in times of stress. Social workers have already recognised that many families have a tendency to deal with crises in this way. In such families[21]

separations have become part of the pattern of life, and are seen as a necessary and desirable way of ensuring a degree of security. The underlying assumption seems to be, 'if we didn't get a break from each other now and then, something really bad would happen which might split us up altogether. At least this way we get a chance to start again later on.' Some families are able to do this quite constructively by the use of kinship networks or close friends, with whom refuge can be taken when the pressure is on. But in other families which do not have such good opportunities for escape from each other, there can come to be an identification of safety and protection from dangerous feelings with various kinds of institutions, access to which is controlled, to some extent at least, by social workers. There are families in which one parent is repeatedly in and out of hospital or prison, or the children are frequently in care, or one by one depart for approved school when they reach the age of fourteen.

These patterns are not necessarily connected with poverty; but the referral of poor people to social services departments for immediate payments may well encourage them to adopt these survival mechanisms. What is therefore at present a characteristic of the transmitted culture of particular families, may come instead to be part of a more generalised culture of poverty.

Another feature of Lewis's characterisation is the tendency to be unable to plan for the future, to seek immediate gratification, to an 'oral' personality structure with weak impulse control. Lewis sees these traits as part of an adaptation to life in which long-term prospects are grim, and therefore the individual seeks compensation in the life of sensations, and a very vivid enjoyment of the present moment.

> Theirs is an expressive style of life. They value acting out more than thinking out, self-expression more than self-constraint, pleasure more than productivity, spending more than saving, personal loyalty more than impersonal justice.[22]

> The low aspiration level helps to reduce frustration, the legitimization of short-range hedonism makes possible spontaneity and enjoyment.[23]

These characteristics tend to be condemned by the authorities who, unlike Lewis, see them as the *cause* rather than the effect of poverty, a sign of the maladjustment which produces material deprivation rather than an adjustment to deprivation. The poor relief authorities therefore devote their principles of assistance to an encouragement of thrift and prudence in the hope of eradicating this kind of fecklessness.

However, like other principles of poor relief, this one is aimed chiefly at impressing those just outside the scope of assistance rather than affecting those receiving it. Rationing principles leave so little margin for thrift and prudence for those actually receiving benefits, that the authorities are forced to make special provisions to deal with needs they themselves create (for example the so-called 'double payments' made in the form of exceptional needs grants for clothing and footwear, which are supposed to be covered by the scale rates). Thus, the very rationing that deters non-claimants and encourages them to plan and provide for adverse circumstances makes it quite impossible for claimants to do so. Low scale rates *have* to be supplemented by discretionary payments from time to time, thus making long-term claimants apply separately for each need as it arises. An adequate income, which would enable those receiving assistance to make realistic provision for long-term needs, is ruled out on the grounds of its effect on the working poor.

In the same way, rationing principles applied to emergency situations reinforce features of the culture of poverty. Changes in the administrative system of supplementary benefits which have already been described have made income from this source less reliable (because of bureaucratic and postal delays), and emergency payments to rectify delays less accessible. The only alternative has been to apply for urgent help from social workers of the local authority. However, these payments have been made in a form which plays straight into the hand-to-mouth culture of the very poor. It seems somewhat harsh to judge the poor for their oral personalities when the largest proportion of 1963 Act payments was made, according to the Manchester research, for *food*; people can hardly be blamed for having oral preoccupations when their needs are determined by the emptiness of their larders. In the same way, the use of payments by voucher and assistance in kind tends not only to be highly stigmatised, but also to have about it the flavour of a day-to-day existence based on making the best of whatever can be scraped together and patched up well enough to get by. Existing from one second-hand bed to the next is hardly a recipe for full participation in a property-owning democracy.

The kind of assistance provided by social services departments according to their very stringent rationing principles put one very much in mind of some of the accounts given in *La Vida* of assistance received from social workers in Puerto Rico. 'I was getting help from the Mothers' Aid and I asked for help also from *El Welfare*. They said they would give me groceries. Every month I got eight packages of rice, two two-pound cans of lard, a big five-pound cheese and three cans of spiced ham.'[24] If anything, *El Welfare* sounds somewhat more generous than its British counterpart, but equally prone to reinforcement of its clients' oral personalities and their tendency to focus on short-term needs.

But if the income maintenance and the personal social services tend to collude with features of the culture of poverty, the aspect of social policy which has been most instrumental in its creation has been in the field of housing. It is bad housing and homelessness which in the past ten years have come to represent the most conspicuous evidence of the inequalities in our society, and the failure of social policies to provide a decent life for a substantial proportion of our citizens. The re-creation of urban squalor that seemed to be disappearing in the wake of the Beveridge revolution is the most important contributory factor in the formation of a new culture of poverty in this country, which is related both to the particular conditions under which our social services are provided, and to the overall position of the poor in our economy. The existence of whole communities living in conditions of overcrowding and decay is enough, taken with these other factors, to ensure that a proportion of the population grow up in a culture of poverty through the misfortune of living in a particular area. The scandals of the early 1960s which surrounded the original revelations by Jeremy Sandford and the Rachman furore have subsided, not because the housing conditions of the poor have improved, but because they now occupy a separate sector of community, a world apart. Those who enjoy better accommodation and a decent standard of living have become first blasé and then insulated from the problem. The slums have come to be the ghettoes of people who are seen to be from a separate, inferior class. Whereas they first aroused pity, increasingly they now provoke indifference or fear.

There is one approach by social scientists to the housing problem (which is to be found in Donnison's book *The Government of Housing*) which suggests that there really is no answer to this 'problem' anyway. He points out that this country compares quite well with others in Europe on various scales, by which quantity and quality of houses might be measured. It is second only to Belgium in rates of dwellings per 1,000 inhabitants and rooms per 1,000 inhabitants. In household equipment, it is third to Switzerland and Germany in rates of houses with piped water, and top of the league table in rates of fixed baths. He also draws attention to the fact that a comprehensive housing policy would have to take account of such complex factors as population growth, immigration, distribution of industrial expansion, changes in life expectation, size of families and so on. Furthermore, all these changes in turn give rise to altered expectations, and he concludes that:[25]

housing targets, programmes and policies are always provisional and always superseded before long. The more determined a nation is to resolve its problems, the faster will be the tempo of social change, and the sooner will new aspirations take the place of the old.

In other words, dissatisfaction with housing standards as they are can be seen as an inevitable feature of a dynamic economic system, and a healthy sign of a fast rate of social change.

If Donnison is right to draw attention to the constant necessity to modify housing targets, it is equally true that those who have made confident predictions about progress in this field (as he did in 1967), are constantly having to eat their words. It would seem that he, like many others before him, had underestimated the compulsion of the market economy to provide accommodation for luxury needs and for commercial purposes before it meets the demand for homes for the poor. Indeed, as far as domestic provision is concerned, the trend towards owner occupation, which in part reflects the larger profits now to be gained from new developments, speculation and land hoarding than from letting houses, can never solve the problem of housing for the worst-off sector. The proportion of owner-occupiers has risen from one-tenth before the First World War to over half today.[26] However, government intervention in the field of owner occupation takes the form of tax relief on mortgage interest, so that those who pay no tax at all get no assistance, whereas the better-off get more relief the higher their mortgage. This means that the only way to remedy the more acute and conspicuous housing problems (of homelessness and the slums), is by increasing the availability and raising the standard of rented accommodation in both the public and the private sectors.

As far as private tenancies are concerned, the attractiveness of owner-occupation for the better-off has had the opposite effects. High demand for old houses as well as new ones has forced prices up steadily, and given landlords strong motives for selling rather than letting. The various Rent Acts since 1957 have reinforced this trend, and the result has been that in general only extremely inferior housing has been either profitable for landlords to let or within the means of the poor. Houses on their last legs have been used for multi-occupation, and the last drops of profit squeezed out of them before they fell down or were demolished. Because of the slow rate of building of new private and council housing (well below the average for Western European countries since the war),[27] shortages have ensured that slum landlords have had no difficulty in finding tenants.

Council tenants were thus a privileged group. Because of the various complicated forms of subsidy attached to this type of housing, they paid a low rent for the standard of home they occupied—even though council rents were on average higher than private rents. Council housing policies tended to favour longer-term residents who were not the poorest or those living in worst conditions, and the system of subsidies was criticised on the grounds that many tenants could afford to pay a higher rent. It was this criticism among others that gave rise to the policies of the recent Government. The Housing Finance Act now requires local authorities to charge a 'fair' (i.e. commercial) rent for their houses. This was offset by a system of rebates (now extended to include private tenants), which subsidised households according to a means test. The intention was, presumably, to force better-off tenants to choose between paying a much higher rent or moving out into owner occupation. However, the timing of the Act was such that it coincided with the release of enormous sums of Building Society money on to the market, when new houses were not being produced at anything like the rate required to soak up these funds. Too much money chasing too few houses sent the prices soaring. As well as accelerating the rise in rents, this has greatly reduced the number of council house tenants who could contemplate owner occupation as an alternative to their present situation. Thus, all that has happened has been that council rents have risen, and a very high proportion of tenants have required subsidisation by way of rebates. These rebates are, of course, a form of poverty trap, which operate like the Family Income Supplement, keeping low-wage earners at the same level within a broad band of actual earnings.

Thus, for the homeless and those living in substandard rented accommodation, the recent Government's measures have provided no encouragement or relief. Instead, what has been happening for some time is that a new tier of provision is being developed to deal with the needs of the poor. For some time in many city areas, housing authorities have used 'short-life' property (scheduled for demolition under road or development schemes) for those families in the most desperate situations. In Birmingham, for instance, this was done in close co-operation with the social services department, as a way of providing for families whose standards were considered to be not yet up to those required of a tenant of a council-built property. While this policy staves off what could otherwise be a flood of homelessness, it is difficult not to see it as a kind of official counterpart to the rack-renting of slum properties by private landlords. Councils are creating a new stratum of substandard provision for poor families, often reinforcing their low morale and their problems of providing their children with a sense of decency and worth, by placing them in shabby, sometimes even vermin-infested dwellings, depressingly situated among rubble and boarded-up buildings. Coloured immigrants are particularly liable to find themselves a target group for this policy. 'The correlation of coloured tenants and sub-standard property is no accident; the authorities admit that they regard this type of housing as being

particularly suitable for immigrants, even if this is genuinely intended only as a temporary arrangement.'[28] The Institute of Race Relations's study in 1967 reached the conclusion that 'what can be
shown is how through the normal machinery of housing allocation the coloured family tends, for a number of reasons, to be
classed as one of second or third-class citizens'.[29] This is increasingly
true of a wider sector of people, who through being forced to live
in areas of deterioration, squalor and overcrowding, are already at
a disadvantage in slum clearance schemes because 'houses in multi-
occupation tend to be deferred in favour of clearing smaller houses
in single family occupation which may, anyway, come nearer to
the narrow physical definition of a "slum" '.[30] Such people are
more likely to be shifted, if at all, 'out of sight to patched-up
housing in an area which will later be condemned and which
offers no better facilities or schools than before'.[31]

However, in most respects, even these families are fortunate
compared with some others. The Institute of Race Relations's investigations showed[32]

> how easy it is for an immigrant family (and many others) to
> slip through the public housing net altogether, even when
> residence in a clearance area might be presumed to qualify
> them for a council tenancy ... the only house-holder almost
> sure of a place is the working-class archetype, the long-stand-
> ing tenant of an unfurnished self-contained house.

The remaining group finds itself in the hands of the local authority
social services departments. The range of provisions available to
these departments reflects the piecemeal assortment of measures
taken to combat the rising tide of homelessness since the early
1960s. Homelessness was not a problem which was very seriously
considered when our social services were set up in the period
immediately after the war. The Part III accommodation provided
by many local authority Welfare Departments consisted mainly of
old workhouse buildings, and little was done to improve or add to
these facilities in the next ten years. Then, during the summer of
1961, came the first signs of a sudden rise in the number of homeless families in London; at that time the increase to 643 families
was considered a crisis, and the rise by November 1962 the figure
of 1,014 families was thought alarming.[33] Yet by 1966 there were
12,400 people in hostels for the homeless in London, and by 1969
18,800.[34] The scandal of revelations like those in *Cathy Come
Home* produced a policy in Welfare Departments of improving
facilities in Part III accommodation and of keeping families together wherever possible. But this improvement was only brought
about as a reaction to the sharp *deterioration* in the housing situation for the poorest group. Most authorities responded to the joint

Ministerial circular of 31 October 1966, which drew attention to the need to improve temporary accommodation, because they were experiencing an increase in the need to receive children into care through shortage of places in temporary accommodation for homeless families. Thus, while the new expenditure on Part III accommodation since that time is certainly a better alternative than the separation of families, and more especially of children from parents, it none the less represents a failure of the notion of preventive 'community care', and a return to a policy of providing institutional care for destitute and homeless families—a policy which appeared to have been abandoned at the time of the break-up of the Poor Law and the closure of the workhouses.

Some idea of the expansion in provision of temporary accommodation can be gained from local authority treasurers' statistics. In 1971-2, all local authorities spent an average of £70.22 per 1,000 population on temporary accommodation, and the average number of persons in such accommodation was 24,832. In London, the boroughs spent £247.71 per 1,000 population on an average of 14,216 people in temporary accommodation.[35] If this is compared with figures for 1959-60 the enormous rise becomes apparent. National figures were £5. 9s. per 1,000 population and a figure of 5,876 people in temporary accommodation on 31 December 1959. In London, there was an average of £2. 2s. per 1,000 population and 2,146 people in temporary accommodation on that night.[36] A county like Devon, which has made no extra provision in terms of new buildings for temporary accommodation since 1948, has estimates in its ten year plan for an expenditure of £74,000 by 1982-3 in the revenue account, and plans for a modern new unit for homeless families; Torbay plans an outlay of £30,000 on capital account, and an increase from revenue from £422 to £8,000 in the next ten years. In 1959-60 Devon (including Torbay) spent seven shillings per 1,000 population on temporary accommodation.[37]

In face of the mounting pressure from homeless families, social services departments adopted other methods of staving off the need to receive children or families into institutions. One such is the payment of bed and breakfast or boarding house charges. Expenditure on this form of emergency provision has risen sharply, and represents yet another form of urgent need payment by the local authorities. Most authorities do this out of funds earmarked for the 1963 Children and Young Persons Act, and here again operate a scheme of dubious statutory validity which frequently infringes their clients' rights to exceptional circumstances payments from social security. Another policy forced on local authorities by the homelessness crisis has been co-operation with squatters; several urban authorities have entered into formal negotiations with squatters' organisations to put squatting on a more-or-less official basis. Those authorities which resisted this policy have sometimes run into trouble with their social workers (as in Southwark), or with squatters themselves (as in Plymouth, where the office was occupied and painted with slogans).

Yet another area of social services departments' intervention in the field of homelessness (which began under the Children's and Welfare Departments), is the provision of rent guarantees to housing departments for council house tenants in arrears of rent. The research done by Heywood and Allen showed that in areas they investigated such schemes were either created or extended under the financial terms of the 1963 Children and Young Persons Act after temporary accommodation came under pressure from 1966 onwards. Some idea of the extent of these provisions can be gained from figures from Devon, where expenditure on rent indemnification and intermediate accommodation (bed and breakfast) are kept separately from other direct financial assistance to families. Here the figures for 1971-2 are, at £4,215, nearly as high as those for direct grants (£4,923), and the estimates in the ten year plan are for an increase by 1982-3 to £11,000 for this form of provision alone.

This patchwork of involvement in the field of homelessness by social services departments represents a response to a mounting crisis since the early 1960s, and has been largely unplanned, un-co-ordinated and piecemeal. Under increasing pressure from housing experts, the Government is now considering transferring all responsibility for homelessness from social services to housing departments, ostensibly in order to try to get the homeless seen as a housing need rather than a social nuisance. However, in the absence of an adequate supply of new council houses, this must surely only mean that a different department will take over the paraphernalia of dealing with the poorest and neediest applicants in some way other than by giving them proper houses. The institutions, the boarding houses and the patch-repair slums will still be standard ways of holding back the flood of urgent applications, and it would seem likely that if housing departments do take on this responsibility, they will employ social workers to do the job of coping with the angry, frustrated and desperate families in need.

The field of housing thus represents yet another area in which mechanisms of poor relief have been transferred from the income maintenance services to the local authorities. On the financial side, rate and rent rebates have proliferated as a vast new form of selective benefits, wider in scope than the centrally administered Family Income Supplement, and with the same poverty-trapping effects. Social services departments' acceptance of responsibility for rent indemnities and urgent needs payments for the homeless in overnight accommodation, have relieved the Supplementary Benefits Commission of what would otherwise have been a tremendous pressure for discretionary payments. Finally, on the institutional side, the increased provision of temporary accommodation for homeless families has recreated, in the local authority setting, the institutional side of the Poor Law. Economic forces which brought about the housing shortage ensured that one of the primary values associated with the development of social work services, the avoidance of institutionalisation, has had to be renounced for a large group of homeless families. Improvements in temporary accommodation and the policy of keeping families together represent only secondary gains for those forced to accept the stigma and loss of autonomy associated with this form of accommodation. Social workers are all too aware of the dangers of transmission from one generation to another of dependence on institutional care. In this instance, the poor are again being put at risk because housing policy has failed to provide homes for them.

The contribution all this makes to the development of a culture of poverty scarcely needs to be emphasised. Areas of slum housing create a common identity among the poor and, as Lewis says 'a sense of territoriality results from the unavailability of low-income housing outside the slum areas'.[38] The struggles for survival, the battles with housing authorities, the traumas of receptions of children into care and of families into temporary accommodation, all build up a pattern of existence which, through its hopelessness and insecurity, require the kind of defensive and defiant methods of self-preservation which are embodied in the culture of poverty. Just as a secure home contributes more to a feeling of belonging to a community than any other factor (an explanation for the high priority given to housing by immigrants),[39] so the lack of adequate long-term accommodation is the major factor in creating a life style in which there is no planning for a future which holds no hope of improvement. Housing policy and the practices of the social services combine to give rise to a hand-to-mouth existence which is a reproduction of the patterns documented by Lewis in his studies of Puerto Rican slums.

In many ways, Lewis's choice of the term 'culture of poverty' is misleading. As he has shown, this culture is not characteristic of *uniformly* poor communities (as in peasant societies), but of *stratified* social structures, in which affluence coexists with a particularly demeaning form of poverty—the poverty of the discarded failures, the maimed, the redundant and those whom the economy needs only for short-term exploitation. This culture is characteristically urban, and reflects the need of advanced productive processes to draw large numbers of unskilled people into cities, to use them as cheap casual labour, and then to discard them, temporarily or permanently, to rot in the slums. The most obvious example in this country was the deliberate attraction of Commonwealth immigrants to do our dirty work during the prosperous Macmillan era. The disruption which such inflows of population cause to traditional community and family patterns, both among the immigrants and the local population, is discounted so long as there are strong economic justifications for it. The recognition of the social problems which are a product of this form of economic growth comes later. Theories like the 'cycle of deprivation' are conjured up to explain the existence of pockets of human misery and squalor.

Lewis's observations on the culture of poverty are borne out by British studies like Kerr's *The People of Ship Street* and Spinley's *The Deprived and the Privileged*. It would seem that the continuities in family patterns observed by social workers as contributing to deprivation are part of a subcultural adaptation to the conditions of life in city slums, overlaid with reactions to the policies of officials of those social services which characteristically are involved with the urban poor. As the consequences of these patterns on family life and the upbringing of children have begun to be recognised, new strategies for intervention in the lives of the slum-dwellers have been sought by the authorities, who have become alarmed at the phenomena they have helped to create. The results of official deprivation both in housing policy and in the income maintenance services, have had to be tackled as part of a growing recognition of a crisis in our cities.

9
'Positive discrimination'

In the past five years, social policy has increasingly focused upon the problems of the city slums and their inhabitants. Part of the diagnosis has been the 'rediscovery of poverty', and the remedies for this have been new selective benefits and the growth of discretionary poor relief functions in the local authority social services. But, as Sir Keith Joseph's theory of the 'cycle of deprivation' indicates, increasingly official concern has concentrated on other phenomena associated with urban squalor, and particularly in the effects of this style of life on young children. Because 'deprivation' has been recognised as going deeper than the financial and material circumstances of families, government intervention has increasingly sought to have a direct influence on the standards of education, health and social adjustment of the poorest inhabitants of the big cities.

Along with the culture of poverty, another theoretical influence which has clearly moulded Sir Keith Joseph's thinking about the 'cycle of deprivation' has been the research findings of the National Children's Bureau. In his speech to the Pre-School Playgroups Association he said,[1]

> there is evidence mounting from the National Child Development Study of a clear sequence of social disability from parent to child. There is a continuing follow up study of nearly all children born in Britain in a single week in 1958, known as the 1958 cohort. I am sure you will have seen only a few weeks ago accounts of a new report on this study entitled *From Birth to Seven*. This shows the many ways and extent to which children in working class families, particularly those with semi-skilled and unskilled fathers, are disadvantaged from birth.

At a policy level, some of Sir Keith Joseph's proposals seem to have been borrowed directly from the National Children's Bureau's publications. For instance, his notion of 'preparation for parenthood', outlined in the original speech, mirrors a paragraph from the section on 'primary prevention' in *Born Illegitimate*: 'all schools should include in their curriculum a course on human relationships and child development, with particular emphasis on what is now known about the importance of the earliest years of life for optimal physical, emotional and intellectual growth'.[2] Similarly, his proposals for research into the cycle are very much on the lines proposed by the Bureau;[3]

> at present our knowledge of child development, family dynamics, the interaction of economic, social and personal factors—indeed most of the major questions regarding normal and deviant behaviour in both children and adults require further study, both theoretical and applied; partly due to lack of knowledge, our methods of detection, assessment and intervention are still crude.... A multi-disciplinary approach must be adopted, with the emphasis shifted to the earliest stages of a child's development; with information and counselling services being readily available; and with preventive planning pushed back very much earlier—for optimal effectiveness to conception or before.

What the Children's Bureau's own researches show is the crucial nature of early influences in determining a child's chances of attaining desirable standards—both educational and social—in later life. For instance, children deprived of normal family life fail to develop the most basic skills. 'Language development among children in care was found to be more seriously affected by deprivation than any other aspects of development and achievement.'[4] Other disadvantages give unequal chances to children in different ways.[5]

> A number of tests and assessments were used to explore and compare the abilities and attainments of the illegitimate, adopted and legitimate groups of children respectively. Consistent and significant differences were found between them on all the aspects which were examined. Time and time again the illegitimate sample were at the bottom of the league table, be it for general knowledge, oral ability, creativity, perceptual development, reading attainment or arithmetical skills.

They have also, as Sir Keith Joseph pointed out, shown that children whose fathers are in manual occupations are already disadvantaged educationally at the age of seven; and that there is 'a marked trend for the incidence of "maladjustment" to increase the lower the social class'.[6]

However, the Bureau does not go on from this to link poverty with emotional deprivation in the way suggested by Sir Keith Joseph's 'cycle of deprivation' theory. In spite of this last finding, they do not endorse the view that emotional deprivation is more prevalent among underprivileged families; 'a home may be rough and ready, or even dirty and disorganised, and yet there can be real affection between parents and children'.[7] They suggest that 'there are stronger grounds for believing that intellectual neglect and deprivation are more common among underprivileged children since their parents are usually ill-educated, if not of limited ability'.[8] However, this does not lead them towards a selective type of provision for the problems they identify. Instead, their proposals for a preventive family advice service are universalistic in approach.[9]

> This needs to be done at the earliest possible time, recognising that early learning is basic and that defective family relationships are not confined to any one strata of society. While poor housing and financial strain contribute to or may cause impaired relationships and intellectual neglect, the converse is not true; the absence of these adverse factors does not ensure adequate intellectual stimulation or harmonious family relationships.

This was written before Seebohm, and suggests the sort of service that local authorities might have provided, had public assistance responsibilities not determined the role of the new social services departments. Kellmer Pringle and her associates seem to imply that a properly established public service to deal with *emotional* deprivation is more likely to be effective than a service which attempts to select 'at risk' groups according to criteria such as low income or social class. The proposal also implies that a service which dealt effectively with emotional and family problems would be making a contribution towards eliminating the kind of disadvantages in education and health (particularly mental health) which poorer people suffer.

However, their revelation of the disadvantages of lower-class children and other special deprived groups seems to provide evidence for those who would recommend the development of special preventive services on the principle of 'positive discrimination'. The Bureau recognises this, and seems to see this principle as unlikely to provide enough to counteract the problems it has revealed. 'The various schemes being tried out in community development projects, educational priority areas, urban aid programmes and family advice services are all a beginning in this direction. But only the merest beginning.'[10] The principle of 'positive discrimination' is neither warmly endorsed nor definitely rejected. This reaction is not surprising. The kind of policies advocated by Kellmer Pringle and her colleagues are based on the notion of attempting to raise standards of parenthood and improve methods of child care at all levels of society and in every kind of community. The National Children's Bureau recommend a range of services available to all mothers aimed at supporting them in their childrearing tasks, and reinforcing their sense of the importance of their parental role.

There is evidence in Sir Keith Joseph's more recent speeches that he is coming to see this as a worthwhile end in itself, but it was certainly not the intention behind the original policies which concentrated resources on the city slums. The purposes which underlay efforts towards 'positive discrimination' (started under the previous Government) were quite clearly connected with alarm at the growing evidence of lawlessness, squalor and a culture of poverty in the deteriorating areas of the large cities. They were very much a political reaction to the threat of an urban crisis similar to those in France and the USA; their introduction was hastily announced in the wake of a political storm over Mr Powell's 'rivers of blood' speech. Thus the adoption of 'positive discrimination' as a basis for official intervention had little to do initially with the researches of the National Children's Bureau, or with the advocacy of this principle by social scientists. They represented a sort of crisis intervention, the form of which was influenced by American practice, rather than a policy which had been developed out of a deep theoretical consideration of the problems. No great effort had been made to think how they could be reconciled with other principles of social policy. Accordingly, it is not surprising to find that these interventions have raised all sorts of problems, and that the principle of positive discrimination has not been built into new developments in the social services outside these particular programmes.

The most distinguished advocate of positive discrimination was Professor Titmuss. While recognising that 'separate discriminatory services for poor people have always tended to be poor quality services',[11] he argued that 'there is no escaping the conclusion that if we are effectively to reach the poor we must differentiate and discriminate'.[12] In *Commitment to Welfare*, he suggested that our social services had reached a point of development where[13]

we face the positive challenge of providing selective, high quality services for poor people over a large and complex range of welfare; of positively discriminating on a territorial group or 'rights' basis in favour of the poor, the handicapped, the deprived, the coloured, the homeless, and the social casualties of our society. Universalism is not, by itself alone, enough. . . . If I am right, I think that Britain is beginning to identify the dimensions of this challenge of positive, selective discrimination—in income maintenance, in education, in housing, in medical care and mental health, in child welfare, and in the tolerant integration of immigrants and citizens from overseas; of preventing especially the second generation from becoming (and seeing themselves as) second-class citizens. We are seeking ways and means, values, methods and techniques, of positive discrimination without the infliction, actual or imagined, of a sense of personal failure and individual fault.... The real challenge resides in the question; what particular infrastructure of universalist services is needed in order to provide a framework of values and opportunity bases within and around which can be developed socially acceptable selective services aiming to discriminate positively, with the minimum risk of stigma, in favour of those whose needs are greatest?

Titmuss places great emphasis on the avoidance of stigma, and argues that this can be achieved so long as the 'residual' model of welfare, as a 'burden', is abandoned. Tests of eligibility, aimed at keeping people out, treating them as applicants or supplicants rather than beneficiaries or consumers, are intended to discriminate by deterrence, and to induce a sense of personal failure. Positive discrimination, by contrast, is intended to provide the *best* services for its recipients, and discrimination thus becomes a process of inclusion rather than exclusion. Within a universalist system of values and a sense of membership of a community, positive discriminatory services can be provided 'as rights of categories of people and for classes of need in terms of priority social areas and other impersonal classifications'.[14]

One of the answers to the problem of stigma suggested at the time of the introduction of first programmes of 'positive discrimination', was that of increased participation by recipients of this kind of selectivity in its provision. In some ways this may simply have been a coincidence, in that the notion of 'participation' was being canvassed as a solution to all sorts of industrial, administrative and social problems in the late 1960s. The Seebohm Report advocated that both consumers and ratepayers should be more actively involved in the work of the local authority social services departments. The revival of community work represented an expression of the recognition of participation as an important element in the successful provision of social services. Abel-Smith recommended, even more broadly, 'consumer sovereignty of a new kind to be exercised within the public services so as to widen the freedom of the individual'.[15]

However, there is some reason to believe that there was another explanation for the connection between the first positive discrimination programmes and the new interest in participation in the social services. The new programmes were clearly influenced by similar government interventions in the USA. The Kennedy and Johnson administrations had used this kind of federal intervention as the characteristic method of their New Frontier and Great Society programmes. The influence of American policies on our own is shown in the choice of terminology : 'urban aid', for instance, was the name given to one of the American schemes. It is therefore instructive to examine the results of American experience with this type of policy, to see the results of their attempts to discriminate in favour of disadvantaged individuals and communities. In doing so, we shall see that the notion of participation was an integral one in these programmes, both for administrative and political reasons, and it therefore seems likely that it was imported along with the notion of positive discrimination as a strategy to tackle the problems of our own under-privileged minorities and deteriorating neighbourhoods.

The first of the American programmes was launched by President Kennedy in 1961, and was concerned with juvenile delinquency; there followed in 1963 the Community Mental Health Centre Act which gave federal support to the provision of community centres. In 1964, 1966 and 1967, the Johnson administration pumped massive government resources into community action, community development and neighbourhood services as the main instruments of anti-poverty programmes. The targets of all these injections of federal funds were the large urban centres of population. Furthermore, although they seemed to be concerned with different aspects of social deviance they in fact shared very similar aims and methods.[16]

One of the Great Society programs presumably was concerned with juvenile delinquency, another with poverty, still others with mental health and blighted neighborhoods—a veritable melange of social maladies and programs to deal with them. But the diversity of labels is deceptive. These programs ostensibly had different functions, to be sure, but they carried them out in remarkably similar ways. Each program singled out the 'inner city' as its main target; each provided a basketful of services; each channeled some portion of its funds more or less directly to new organisations in the 'inner city', circumventing the existing municipal agencies which traditionally controlled services; and, more important, each made the service agencies of local government, whether in health, housing, education or public welfare, the 'mark'—the target of reform.

The reasons for these strategies were mainly political. Piven and Cloward show that they can be traced to an attempt by the two Presidents to consolidate their own support among the urban poor, and especially in the urban black communities.[17]

The language of the new statutes and policies referred to the 'inner city', or to 'slums', or to the 'urban core'. But these terms were only euphemisms for the ghetto, for it was the ghetto neighborhoods that these programs were chiefly designed to reach—and by tactics reminiscent of the traditional political machine.... A neighborhood leadership was cultivated called 'community workers' ... to receive program patronage. The neighborhood leadership, in turn, became the vehicle for involving large numbers of people in the new programs, for spreading the federal spoils. It made little difference whether the funds were appropriated under delinquency-prevention, mental-health, anti-poverty, or model-city legislation: in the streets of the ghettoes, many aspects of these programs looked very much alike.

There is thus one obvious difference between the American and British versions of 'positive discrimination', for there has been no attempt by British administrations to create a direct relationship between the national government and the urban poor. Neither the Labour nor the Conservative party had any great hopes of the poor as potentially important supporters, and thus neither Government had the same direct political impetus towards such policies that existed under a Democratic Presidency in the USA. However, both had much to fear from urban disorder and consequent Powellite backlash. In addition, what they did share with their American counterparts was a dilemma about the extent to which they should involve existing local government institutions in their new programmes. In the USA, these were initially quite explicitly bypassed. 'From the beginning of the Great Society programs, city government was defined as a major impediment by many federal officials, an obstacle to be hurdled or circumvented if federal funds were to reach blacks.'[18] Although this was far from popular, particularly in traditional Democratic strongholds, 'the risk of antagonising local political figures had to be run, for if the funds were simply given to local white ethnic political leaders, there was little reason to think that the black poor would benefit'.[19] While it is unlikely that any British commentator would put the case against local authorities quite so strongly, a number of studies have shown how their processes tend to favour better established groups of long-term residents as against various kinds of newer immigrants (for instance in housing policies).[20] Similarly, Davies's researches in the field of education revealed that:[21]

> total expenditure per primary school pupil is uncorrelated with low social class, while total expenditure per secondary school pupil is negatively correlated with it. In expenditure on secondary education, at any rate, what we have at the moment is negative not positive discrimination.

The very notion of central government intervention through positive discrimination programmes implies a failure by local authorities to produce a pattern of services which meets the needs of the most needy members of their communities.

Thus, if British governments have been more willing to involve local authorities in their attempts to introduce positive discrimin- ation, and to work through them, they have not been without their critics for doing so. Holman suggested that local authorities were unlikely to tolerate the sort of conflicts which are inevitably created by attempts to engage the poor in more active participation in obtaining their social rights.[22] Others have drawn attention to the ways in which they have traditionally operated according to highly stigmatising principles, and have developed their own methods of rationing the poorest sector. Reddin calculated a total of some 1,500 different means tests administered by local authorities as a way of making selective benefits less eligible.[23] Others still have shown how unwilling local authorities are to take heed of the views of those who actually consume their services. 'It may well be that one of the reasons for the low esteem in which local government is held is derived from its reluctance to recognise the growth of consumer consciousness.'[24]

Because the American programmes chose to bypass local govern- ment institutions, the conflicts they engendered were overtly political ones. A detailed analysis of the histories of some of the programmes at local level is given in R. M. Kramer's book *Partici- pation of the Poor*. He shows the fear and resentment felt by elected representatives and better-off constituents about the active involvement of racial minority group leaders in the work of the programmes. For instance, in San Francisco, the Mayor initially tried to control the Economic Opportunity Council, but found him- self challenged by a coalition of civil rights workers and community groups. 'From the beginning a prevailing pattern of rancorous con- flict was established, which remained the dominant mode of confronting most program and administrative issues.'[25] Speeches by the Mayor referred to 'power play and politics' by his opponents, and when they finally gained control of the Economic Opportunity Council, he announced 'I have a very definite feeling that this program is headed in a direction we don't want ... it has the potential for setting up a great political organisation. Not mine. Because I have had nothing to say about it.'[26]

Similarly, in the Santa Clara County Economic Opportunity Com- mission, the increased involvement of Mexican Americans in the programme did not go unchallenged.[27]

Part of the price for some of this social action was continuing criticism from various conservative elements in the com- munity. Charges of a 'left-wing revolution' within the E.O.C. were made by a Congressman who asked for a federal investigation of possible subversive elements in the E.O.C. A three-part newspaper series appeared, in which the 'radical' backgrounds and connections of various area board members were delineated.

Thus, in general,[28]

if local white politicians were agitated at the outset because a great deal of patronage escaped their control, they became hysterical when the federal government permitted, and often encouraged, its new apparatus of local agencies to put pressure on municipal services themselves—pressure to get more for blacks.

The issues came to be about the distribution of resources and of political power.

The conflicts which positive discrimination programmes engendered between the poorest groups and those who had traditionally enjoyed the privileges associated with a slightly more eligible status are thus characteristic of the American history of this type of government intervention. Because of the less overtly political nature of British programmes, and because of the relative absence of racial overtones, we are unlikely to encounter the same direct confrontations over the issues involved here. However, fundamentally, the difficulty inherent in any such policy is exactly the same, wherever and however it is carried out. It is essentially a problem of how a group which has traditionally been treated as the least deserving, which has previously been allocated the fewest resources, whose every characteristic has formerly been taken to be synonymous with degradation and inferiority, can suddenly be given priority and, through a process of getting more than its 'fair' share, be brought up to the standards of the rest. This is more than simply a technical problem of social administration; it is a problem that is part of the whole balancing act of social policy which has been discussed in this book. If the income maintenance services and the personal social services are being used to maintain differential status according to deservingness, how can positive discrimination programmes be carried out without upsetting this delicate operation? If the poor and dependent have traditionally been seen as poor and dependent because of their inferiority, and the less poor and independent encouraged to define their slightly more eligible status in terms of their virtue, how can rewarding the inferior at the expense of the virtuous be justified?

This is a problem which has been recognised by writers about social policy. Pinker, for instance, acknowledges that 'positive discrimination programmes are likely to invoke intense hostility from the public'.[29] He also suggests that social scientists have a role to play in helping the government deal with this hostility.[30]

There are already signs of a greater willingness on the part of government to make a more systematic use of social research in order to define and cover categories of greatest need. There are, for example, the research projects of the Department of Health and Social Security, which will investigate the special problems of fatherless families and the chronic sick, as well as the more general social factors that influence the quality of family life. In education, there are the area-based research projects set up after the manner recommended by Plowden.... Any policy based on positive discrimination principles is totally dependent on adequate research if its aims are to be recognised as being reasonable and just.

Thus, the links between the Government's positive discrimination programmes and the kind of research done by the National Children's Bureau become clearer. Sir Keith Joseph makes a great deal of use of research findings in his theory of the 'cycle of deprivation', and indeed argues as if the theory itself springs directly from research. The object is to present a thoroughly *social* (as opposed to political) justification for the kinds of programmes set up by the Department and the Department of Education and Science. This explains the emphasis in Sir Keith Joseph's speeches on *social deviance*—'the problem families, the vagrants, the alcoholics, the drug addicts, the disturbed, the delinquent and the criminal'— rather than simply on emotional or material deprivation. Whereas the National Children's Bureau emphasises deprivation and its consequences in terms of attainment, Sir Keith Joseph mentions their findings and then links poverty with maladjustment, thus justifying positive discrimination by appealing to the dangerous social consequences of allowing slum areas to become breeding grounds of disorder and vice. It is a very subtle shift of emphasis that reveals the motivation behind his policies. For Conservatives at least, positive discrimination can really only be justified by reference to the negative consequences of allowing a culture of poverty to flourish unchecked by government intervention. Apparent links between research and new programmes serve all sorts of useful functions. They justify government intervention to its supporters, to local authorities and, above all, to those who do not benefit from them and might thus be hostile to them. It is much easier to get non-beneficiaries to accept programmes that claim to be dealing with the poor for their deviance and moral inferiority than it is to obtain their acquiescence in providing them with special advantages. However, while this kind of justification is politically helpful and ideologically useful in reconciling positive discrimination with principles like less eligibility, it makes nonsense of the original aims of these programmes. How, for instance, can the notion of giving resources to an area to check its high rate of juvenile delinquency be reconciled with aims such as Plowden's of making 'schools in the most deprived areas as good as the best in the country'?[31] Those who endorse positive discrimination programmes on the grounds that they will reduce social deviance in slum areas, are unlikely to be willing to carry them through to this kind of conclusion.

Very much the same rationale was used to explain the American programmes where 'there was every reason to expect a backlash from urban white voters', and there, as well, academic and professional jargon served to appease these interests.[32]

> One tactic was the emphasis on 'community development'. This concept was reassuring to whites; they understood it to mean that the assault would be on the 'pathology of the ghetto', not on white stakes in neighborhoods, schools, jobs or public services. . . . Juvenile delinquency, family deterioration, poor work habits, and welfare dependency among the black poor were, after all, precisely what many whites thought the 'urban crisis' was all about. By promising to solve these problems, and to do so through black 'self-help' projects within the confines of the ghettoes themselves, the programs not only conciliated blacks but appealed to whites as well, thus easing the way for federal intervention in the face of growing political divisiveness in the cities. There were other reasons why the political interests at stake were not widely recognised, at least in the beginning. One was the large role played by various professionals, especially social workers and social scientists, who provided the rationales for the Great Society. Each measure was presented at the outset as a politically neutral 'scientific cure' for a disturbing social malady. Each concrete program that evolved was couched in the murky, esoteric terminology customarily used by professionals, a terminology that obscures the class and racial interests at stake. . . . Finally, the professionals and social scientists lent an aura of scientific authority to what might otherwise have been perceived as political rhetoric. By thus obscuring the fact that the federal government was about to give something to the blacks, opposition by white groups was deflected.

Piven and Cloward make it clear that this was only a short-term expedient; in the longer run, as we have seen, conflict was not avoided, and in so far as the programmes gave the black poor anything tangible, conflict was inevitable. In the same way, in this country, while the use of explanations in terms of social deviance serves as a temporary measure for reducing hostility, the government eventually has to choose between programmes which really do raise standards for the poor (and thus incur the hostility of other groups), or programmes which are intended only to provide social control in potentially disruptive neighbourhoods (which could not really be described as positive discrimination).

Another clear dilemma for the recent Government was the question of participation by the poor in any programmes. The decision to involve local authorities more directly than in the USA has already meant that less emphasis has been put on participation here than there. However, the features of the culture of poverty already discussed in the last chapter must tend to reduce the effectiveness of interventions that are based on conventional local government institutions. The poor are already heavily involved with local authority social services departments because of their responsibilities for public assistance and homelessness, and for these reasons are already as distrustful of them as of the income maintenance services. In many ways, their attitudes to the 'Welfare' are akin to the American black poor's perceptions of their public welfare agency or the Puerto Rican's of El Welfare. With such an approach, they are likely to take what they can get in the way of direct assistance or material aid, but unlikely to be won over by any attempt to present the local authority as serving their interests. Similarly, in education, negative attitudes stemming from a culture of fatalism will tend to undermine any attempt to improve standards which proceeds simply from putting more resources into existing methods and institutions. In so far as the Government is aware of this it is forced instead to recommend the adoption of new methods which try to enlist a more active involvement of the poor in their attempts to improve the standards of their lives. This requires a new approach by social workers and teachers, who have to be trained to see themselves taking a role of being among and with the poor, helping them to discover strengths within themselves rather than grabbing at the resources offered them in an alienated fashion. The new breed of community workers, youth leaders and teachers are thus encouraged to adopt a more idealistic view of the potential of the poor; instead of seeing themselves as appointed to control or stamp out the negative elements in the culture of poverty, they are more likely to identify with the poor, and appreciate the survival value and positive contribution of their way of life. Hence those who see themselves as allies to the poor people amongst whom they work are, by the same processes through which they make positive discrimination programmes more effective, also potential agents for conflict. If they do achieve identification with their neighbourhood or minority group, they are likely to perceive the attitudes of the rest of the community, the majority, as selfish, depriving or repressive. While social scientists' research reduces conflict by emphasising social pathology among the poor, community work tends to increase conflict because those professionals actually involved in it see their role, in engaging the participation of the poor, as stimulating their involvement in fighting for a better deal for themselves from the rest of society.

This kind of difficulty has already been encountered in this country. Local authorities have been encouraged to give community workers and unattached youth workers considerably more independence and scope than they allowed to social workers within their conventional settings—particularly in government-sponsored schemes. This has given community workers a special kind of envied professional status, and their ethos has undoubtedly been influential, and spilled over into conventional social work. For example, an article in *Case Con* about 'Victimisation in the Hackney Seebohm factory' focuses on the disciplinary action taken against a senior social worker whose approach favoured community work.[33]

> David F... was a threat to the Hackney Social Services hierarchy and his victimisation was an attack on all social workers who seek new ways of working and control over their work situation.... As a radical social worker, he was responding sensitively and 'responsibly' to the Seebohm Report demand for social workers to be more effective by accepting 'greater responsibility', developing and initiating 'more varied work', to promote 'community involvement' and to actively encourage people to 'self help'. He and his team were working along these lines. They had a coffee corner in their office for clients; clients were encouraged into their office; they worked with local community groups like the Claimants' Union; and David had been critical of his department and on one occasion he went against departmental policy by placing a homeless family in a hotel.

Elsewhere, too, concern has been expressed about the influence of '"change agents" outside the existing power structure', and the need to incorporate them before they become models of 'a new kind of animal'.[34] All this is reminiscent of the USA's experience, where[35]

> the federal programs channeled funds directly to groups forming in the ghettoes, and they in turn often used these monies to harass city agencies ... community people, social workers, and lawyers were stationed in ghetto storefronts, from which they badgered housing agencies to inspect slum buildings or pried loose payments from welfare departments. Later, the new agencies began to organise the poor to picket public welfare departments or boycott school systems. Local officials

were flabbergasted; one level of government and political party was financing the harassment of another level.

The strategy of positive discrimination is, therefore, beset with difficulties, especially for a Conservative regime. It represents an attempt to offset the effects of its measures which reinforce the harmful features of the culture of poverty. It uses research in the field of emotional and educational deprivation to justify intervention into fields of social pathology which are in part the creation of its own policies for income maintenance. It identifies forms of social deviance with areas of material, environmental and cultural deprivation, and proposes special measures to intervene in their processes of self-perpetuation. In doing so, it lays itself open to the charge of inconsistency, because the rest of its social policy is dedicated to preserving distinctions between the treatment of different sectors according to criteria of deservingness. Furthermore, even if it succeeds in defusing these conflicts by skilful use of technical and professional justifications at the planning stage, it eventually encounters direct opposition from those who do not benefit if schemes produce tangible results, or conflict with the professional workers it employs to implement the schemes if they do not.

Apart from these practical difficulties, there remains a question of principle about whether programmes for positive discrimination can ever achieve their aim (at least the aim avowed in conferences of academics and Ministry officials), of bringing the standards of services in the poorest neighbourhoods up to the *best* standards elsewhere. Even supposing that the recent Government was not committed to policies in income maintenance and local authority social services which were totally opposed to this aim, it is very doubtful whether these programmes could ever succeed. Services in poor areas do not exist in isolation; they form part of a complex pattern which is determined by many other criteria besides the amount of local or central government funds at their disposal. Above all, they take their place in a competitive economy, in which the standard of social services, like other services, is determined to a large measure by the economic forces of the market. The laws of economics are at least as important a factor in the analysis of what it is possible to achieve from positive discrimination as the principles of social administration.

Pinker acknowledges that one major contribution to the recognition of a need for positive discrimination has been 'the monopolization of the best social services by middle-class citizens practising positive discrimination on their own behalf'.[36] The most obvious fields in which this applies are education and health. It can readily be shown that private education and private health are parasitic upon the public sectors of these services, and draw off the best resources from them without making an economic contribution to their cost. The public schools not only enjoy state support, but also use teachers who have been trained at the State's expense without paying for them—and make no apologies for attracting the best teachers away from state schools. Private medicine uses hospital buildings and equipment, as well as trained staff, which it could not possibly afford to provide for itself, and for which it does not pay an economic price. But even more importantly, the economic forces which determine standards in these fields have much to do with the commercial market, and little to do with the educational and medical needs of individuals. Davies's finding about the relationship between social class and expenditure per pupil in education within the state system is not the result of coincidence. Because industry and commerce place more value on highly trained personnel than they do on unskilled labour, there will never be a shortage of resources for higher education. The cultural attainments of the poor have little relevance for the efficiency of companies; education, like the other social services, ultimately serves production, and the low productivity of the poor means that they cannot justify the kind of expenditure which is lavished on the better-off.

Thus Plowden's aim of providing 'schools in the most deprived areas as good as the best in the country', would have to be achieved against the whole tide of economic forces. It could be done, but it would mean a redistribution of educational resources away from those whose privileges are considered to be a measure of their value to society, and on to those who have traditionally been re-garded as a burden, and who are unlikely to repay expenditure on them by making the kind of 'positive contribution' to the com-munity which is normally measured in terms of the productive process. This explains why the very high standards reached by a few isolated schools in deprived areas are usually the result of injections of funds and personnel by projects financed out of private trusts, which see artistic, cultural or educational excellence as ends in themselves. This has not been the rationale of the State's provision for education, which is quite specifically geared to training people for their roles in an industrial society, through 'a subtle indoctrination in a scientific ideology that ignores or plays down any conception of human beings as persons'.[37]

Similarly, Aneurin Bevan's intention (expressed in presenting the National Health Bill) to 'universalise the best' in health provisions can be seen as largely having failed in face of economic forces which distribute resources according to criteria other than medical need. Before the National Health Service was established, inequali-ties existed not only between private medicine and the rudimentary public services, but also between regions, between teaching and general hospitals, between hospitals treating acute conditions and those treating long-term illnesses, and between physical and mental health.[38] While there has been more equalisation between these needs in this country than in others, differentials established under a 'free market' system have persisted in slightly modified forms.[39] These work against the poor, for they suffer disproportionately from some very common long-term conditions (like rheumatic heart disease, bronchitis and other respiratory complaints),[40] and from other conditions such as spinal injury, whose treatment has not advanced as rapidly as that for more acute illnesses. Thus, it is not surprising to find that while the working class uses the National Health Service most,[41] the better-off tend to get better-quality service.[42]

The fact is that the Health Service has become the market for an enormous industry which is a very important factor in determining its pattern. The explosion of the drugs market (which resulted in almost a doubling in the national drug bill between 1949 and 1956),[43] accounts for only a part of this commercial empire. The role of doctor has, with more and more sophisticated aids and equipment, come to be increasingly one of a technician, so that 'the medical profession has to a great extent lost control'.[44] This includes the practice of firms of keeping doctors up-to-date with latest scientific developments in their advertising literature.[45]

That commerce should attempt to take over the task of academic instruction, using its immense resources in the palatable presentation of scientific facts, is a matter of deep significance. For if doctors are, in fact, reduced to receiving instructions from trade, what becomes of their claim to be considered a learned profession?

Even more significantly, the pattern of distribution of medical resources comes to be determined by the possibility of developing sophisticated techniques of treatment, requiring profit-creating investment in expensive equipment. Thus, some acute illnesses which require advanced technology in their treatment (as heart and kidney transplants do), get enormous resources, while diseases with much higher incidences in the population receive low priority.

Thus in health, as in education, positive discrimination in favour of the poor would require an enormous effort of redistribution of resources to overcome the effects of market forces. This was never the intention of the small-scale government interventions represented by the programmes of positive discrimination so far initiated. They were, as we shall see in the next chapter, *ad hoc* responses to the problems of the slums, and particularly to the threat of a breakdown in law and order.

10
Law and order

> In effect, Beveridge's five giants, Want, Ignorance, Disease, Idleness and Squalor, are still undefeated, not least because in combination they tend to nullify the effect of services offered separately for different conditions.... To remedy this situation in a total way will require a massive transfer of resources. To fail to do so may be to create future conflicts as racial riots have reminded the USA.[1]

This kind of warning was given to the Government in a series of official reports between 1965 and 1969—the Milner Holland Report, the Plowden Report and the Seebohm Report for example—and in recommendations from other bodies, such as the National Committee for Commonwealth Immigrants. Thus the use of expenditure on social services in selected areas came to be seen as a potential instrument of social policy, designed to forestall the danger of a breakdown of law and order, especially in those areas with high concentrations of coloured immigrants.

This is clearly seen in the timing of the 'Urban Programme' announced by Mr Wilson in 1968. It was on 20 April of that year that Mr Enoch Powell made his notorious 'rivers of blood' speech in which he referred specifically to the 'tragic and intractable phenomenon which we watch with horror on the other side of the Atlantic'. It was the lawlessness and the riots in the American cities which he took as the model for his prophecies of violence and bloodshed in this country. It was this speech, linking immigration, urban unrest, poverty and civil disorder with the resentment of the British-born poor over housing shortages, unemployment and the decay of city slums that galvanised the Government into action. The sight of dockers and other trade unionists marching through the streets in support of Mr Powell was enough to bring about the announcement of a transfer of resources to the 'special problem areas'.

On 4 May, Mr Wilson told a Labour rally at Birmingham. 'I am not prepared to stand aside and see this country engulfed in the racial conflict which calculating orators or ignorant prejudice can create.' He announced a 'new urban spending programme to include areas containing a high proportion of immigrants'. He said that there were fifty-seven local authority areas where the immigration problem was substantial. After drawing attention to the increase in expenditure by those local authorities during the previous five years, he said,[2]

'We are ready to embark on a new urban programme over and above the massive increase in expenditure since 1963-64 to which I have referred.' Mr. Wilson said many big towns faced tremendous problems in education, housing, health and welfare, even where there was virtually no immigrant problem. He added that 'expenditure must be on the basis of need, and the immigration problem is only one factor....' He warned, however, that 'every penny spent would have to be met by corresponding economies somewhere else.'

Thus, what was instigated as a result of Mr Powell's threats of a breakdown of law and order, and of open racial conflict, was not a massive transfer of resources, but a minor injection of funds. What was initiated was not a new principle for the organisation of the social services, but a new urgency in tackling problems, provoked by the political repercussions of Mr Powell's speech. In this chapter, I wish to examine the implications of using this kind of selective measure as an attempt to deal with conflict situations and with the problems posed by mounting crime rates and the threat of disorder.

If the immediate spur to the urban programme was political, the longer-term pressure for this policy came from increasing evidence of 'social disorganisation' among the urban poor; this was reflected in criminal statistics long before the racial problem flared up. In their different ways, both the programmes of 'positive discrimination' and the new selective benefits on the income maintenance side were attempts by successive governments to apply first-aid to the running sores of slums and squalor, and both were linked with a deep-rooted fear of the poor, and a recognition of the connections between poverty and crime and disorder. Criminal statistics are one sphere in which research in the social sciences would largely support Sir Keith Joseph's theory of the 'cycle of deprivation', in that deteriorating, overcrowded and squalid neighbourhoods do tend to have high rates of juvenile delinquency and crime, and it is among the poor that inter-generational continuities of criminal behaviour are characteristic. It is generally agreed that if the poor have a social problem other than their poverty, it is their tendency to break the law.

However, it would be difficult to get such a consensus about the causal connection between poverty and crime, or the significance of lawlessness among the poor. The 'cycle of deprivation' approach would emphasise the personal attributes of the poor, their psychological characteristics, their low educational attainment and individual achievement. But some sociologists have drawn attention to the fact that the culture of poor neighbourhoods condones many forms of juvenile delinquency and adult behaviour that the law defines as crime. Still others go further to suggest that the norms of such groups represent a rejection of the values of larger society (or at least the approved means of achieving desirable ends), and thus constitute a rival subcultural definition of permissible behaviour.

There is therefore room for considerable disagreement about the scope and functions of the culture of poverty in relation to law and order. The 'cycle of deprivation' school would tend to see the poor as generally aimless, chaotic and self-destructive in their disruptive and disorderly behaviour. The others would stress the supportive functions of a subculture which tolerates lawbreaking as a means of survival or the attainment of limited material success. Some would even suggest that this culture is potentially a force for social change, in that it challenges existing values and priorities, and represents a rallying point for the poor in their struggles to further their interests. Shared hostility to the forces of law and order is thus seen as capable of providing solidarity or even political significance in any movement by the poor to achieve their own ends. The rejection of the larger society's standards in questions about ownership and property rights in this way becomes a potential revolutionary focus. Even within the tradition of official thinking about poverty which is represented by the 'cycle of deprivation' theory, there is a good deal of uneasiness about possible connections between movements of the poor and the total breakdown of law and order. While they refuse to see political significance in the plight of those suffering poverty, they none the less fear militant combinations of poor people who might be tempted to use illegal means of asserting their claims to better treatment from the authorities.

Thus, the poor are officially perceived as potentially lawless and, worse still, as constituting a risk of mass action of a rebellious nature. The relationship between acts of individual deviance and collective disorder is unclear, but the authorities would much rather deal with the former than the latter. Accordingly, principles of poor relief have always taken account of the potential threat to law and order posed by the poor, and have made provision as far as possible for individualising claimants, and encouraging them to see themselves in terms of their own particular needs for relief, rather than to identify with a group or class of others in a similar situation. The authorities prefer the risk of a claimant's violent reaction to stringent tests of his eligibility for relief to the dangers of combinations of claimants which would be increased if such tests were relaxed. The cubicles in supplementary benefits offices both symbolise and physically accomplish the individualisation of claimants of public assistance.

Occasionally, however, circumstances have made this process difficult to accomplish. In the 1920s and 30s for instance, mass unemployment was perceived by the unemployed as a common problem shared by those who suffered it, and movements of unemployed workers flourished and had political significance. The National Unemployed Workers' Movement's oath contained the vow 'to never cease from active strife against this system until capitalism is abolished and our country and all its resources truly belong to the people'.[3] The NUWM organised six massive 'Hunger Marches' between 1922 and 1936, in which contingents of the unemployed from various parts of the country converged on London for a rally and demonstration. Their protest was both against unemployment and against low rates of assistance, 'work or full maintenance at trade union rates' being their recurrent demand.[4]

In a recent article about the marches, Maureen Turnbull concludes that:[5]

> the militancy of the unemployed was a constant source of apprehension to every government in the twenties and thirties, [and that] what emerges from the state papers is that the marchers presented an enormous administrative headache and that every effort was made by officials of both central and local government to thwart them.

In spite of the lawful and orderly nature of all the demonstrations, the Government made every possible attempt to prevent them, initially by use of the mechanisms of poor relief. When the marchers found ways around the regulations which were used against them and their families, the police were involved, arrests were made, and prosecutions took place under a statute of Edward III. In an atmosphere of great alarm about the march of 1932, a Cabinet committee was set up to look at ways of applying stricter sanctions against the marchers. A Bill declaring marches to be illegal was drawn up, and eventually several leaders were imprisoned. The Government's attempts to counteract the NUWM's campaign was a concerted effort of intrigue involving police spies and informers, the press and the Prime Minister. 'The fact then that the marches took place and reached their destination is in itself no inconsiderable achievement.'[6]

Along with the attempt to individualise claimants, the authorities have dealt with militancy among the poor by treating it as they do abuse of the system of relief. They have always had powers, since the days of the Poor Law, to deal with idlers, vagrants and troublemakers either by their own punitive controls, or by invoking the criminal laws against vagrancy and fraud. Those who press their claims with undue firmness, or who claim too often for too many needs, are thus under threat of investigation or prosecution for alleged fraudulence; or, if they make their presence felt at the office, they may be arrested for causing a breach of the peace. The same methods inhibit vigorous representation by members of claimants' organisations, as the experiences of the Claimants' Unions described in chapter 5 indicate. Claimants' Union literature has stressed the dependence of social security officials on the police to back up their controls and rationing procedures. They also recognise the intentions behind the appointments system, aimed at keeping waiting rooms empty and reducing the feeling among claimants of belonging to a like-interest group. 'Putting out propaganda and organising mass-action is thus going to be made difficult, if not impossible. Divisions and isolation amongst claimants may become worse.'[7]

Although the activities of Claimants' Unions are disorderly and militant, their tactics in social security offices could hardly be said to be a threat to the whole fabric of society. Yet the Unions have pronounced themselves to be intent on a total overthrow of the system of poor relief, and, by implication, of the rest of the establishment. Stronger evidence of the revolutionary intentions of the Unions was contained in the revelation at the 'Angry Brigade' trial that several of the Stoke Newington Eight were or had been members of Claimants' Unions. Even so, it could be argued that political activists like these were members of many organisations, and their views and activities do not necessarily reflect those of the majority of union members, let alone the majority of claimants. The attitude of the authorities towards the ideological commitment of some articulate Claimants' Union members is ambivalent. On the one hand, official pronouncements suggest that militancy, like straightforward abuse, is confined to a tiny minority. On the other hand, the authorities behave towards militants, as towards those suspected of abuse, as if they constitute a great moral danger to the rest. It is as if they suspect that militancy, like abuse, could if unchecked spread like wildfire. While their statements suggest that the majority of claimants would be the last people to adopt a militant ideology or practise abuse, their actions suggest that there is an imminent danger of their doing both.

The same ambivalence which is characteristic of the officials who have to deal with the practicalities of poor relief is found in the works of theoretical writers about revolution. Marx himself dismissed the poorest class as unreliable, because conditions of poverty 'prepare it far more for the part of a bribed tool of reactionary intrigue'.[8] However, this conclusion, based on study and detailed examination of evidence, was paradoxical, since Marx believed that revolution could only come through the 'increasing misery' of the whole working class. If the misery of the poorest made them unsatisfactory material for revolution, it is difficult to see how a presumably similar form of misery would have a different effect on the rest, unless Marx took the view that what he described as 'the social scum, that passively rotting mass thrown off by the lowest layers of old society'[9] were reduced to that state by a form of natural selection which cast the most inferior in the lowest position.

During the century since Marx's exposition of his theory, the 'increasing misery' he predicted has been felt more by the traditional poor whom he condemned, and the peasants of the underdeveloped countries whom he dismissed, than by the proletariat of industrialised countries in whom he put his faith. Accordingly, revolutionary theory has been revised to take account of the apparent 'embourgeoisement' of affluent workers, and the poor have been given a much more important role. 'It is within this mass of humanity, this people of the shanty towns, at the core of the lumpen proletariat, that the rebellion will find its urban spearhead', was Fanon's conclusion from his experiences of the Algerian War of Independence.[10] Marcuse, too, stresses the role of 'the substratum of outcasts and outsiders, the exploited and the persecuted of other races and other colours'[11] who are more likely to recognise the essential falsity of the alienated enjoyment of material wellbeing which is characteristic of a 'repressed society'.

It is difficult to square these theoretical perspectives with the empirical studies made of the political reactions of people living in poverty. Lewis is quite categorical that:[12]

> my own studies of the urban poor in the slums of San Juan do not support the generalisations of Fanon. I have found very little revolutionary spirit or racial ideology among low-income Puerto Ricans. On the contrary, most of the families I studied were quite conservative politically and about half of them were in favour of the Republican Statehood Party.

However, Lewis notes in Cuba 'the Castro regime—unlike Marx and Engels—did not write off the so-called lumpen proletariat ... but rather saw its revolutionary potential and tried to utilise it'.[13] He felt that the evidence of a culture of poverty in Cuba had diminished with the revolution.

It is probably more accurate to describe the characteristic political attitude of the poor as indifference rather than conservatism. Studies have repeatedly shown that the poor vote less than any other class;[14] and the poorer they are in relation to the rich, the less they vote—in the USA for instance, only 49 per cent of those eligible voted in the Presidential election of 1920, and only about 60 per cent in more recent national elections.[15] If they do take part in politics, the reactions of the poor are unpredictable. Unlike other groups, they cannot be relied upon to vote according to their economic interests, because no political party in the kind of democratic system that has evolved in Western societies represents their interests. The exceptions to this rule are those countries like France and Italy, which have large Communist parties, which tend consistently to attract the votes of the urban poor.[16] Elsewhere, the poor tend only to participate in politics in times of crisis, and then unpredictably. They tend to identify with extreme programmes from left or right, and to support those who promise quick solutions to the economic conditions of which they are victims. The poor are also said to favour authoritarian methods of solving problems (hence their support for Communist parties) and to be more willing to condone the use of violence and intimidation to achieve political ends.[17]

The poor in democratic countries are thus apolitical because they see no good reasons for participating in the complexities of the political game. They favour simple and if necessary violent solutions, and they recognise that only drastic measures are likely to effect any changes in their situation. Attempts to 'politicise' the poor under normal conditions fail because there is never anything sufficiently dramatic to be achieved by a participation in politics. In crises they may suddenly throw their weight behind a group which promises them some immediate direct action in the matters which concern them most.

It is this unpredictability of the poor, who can under normal circumstances be discounted as a political force, that in part explains the jumpiness of the authorities in relation to them, and the concern about their threat to law and order. It also links the phenomenon of crime with that of political activism among the poor. At first sight the two appear totally unrelated, because crime seems to represent an individualistic solution to problems of poverty, and a form of acquisitive materialistic status-seeking behaviour which is the very antithesis of collectivist political action. However, where whole communities condone criminal behaviour, the borderline between a multiplicity of individual deviant acts and a wholesale mass uprising, rioting and looting, is a fairly narrow one. As far as the poor are concerned, it is not their political organisation that is feared, but their chaotic, unpredictable disorganisation and its violent expression, often in the form of a group or crowd attack on some particular target. This may not necessarily take an overtly political form, but any collective action by the poor is potentially of political significance because of their position in society, and their awareness of how little they have to lose. The example which springs to mind from literature is in Dickens's *Tale of Two Cities*, in which the first pre-revolutionary mob action stems from a child being run over by a nobleman's carriage. I once heard a white middle-class South African telling a very similar story of being attacked by a crowd after running over a child in an African township.

A high crime rate, and particularly a rise in the rate of violent crimes such as has occurred in this country in recent years, is thus a phenomenon to cause governments some concern, as much from the point of view of political stability as for the other obvious reasons. Even though crimes may take a bizarre and gruesome form, lack apparent motivation, or be committed by poor people against each other, the tendency for social controls to break down, particularly in areas in which there is a culture of poverty, poses some kind of threat to the authorities. It is impossible to predict when those who have previously shown no common cause may suddenly join together and attack the outsiders. A clear example of such a process can be seen from the very rapid 'politicisation' of prisoners in America and in this country during brief campaigns in recent years. Prisoners share all the conservative and individualistic tendencies of non-institutionalised criminals, and have added to these the divisive influence of prison discipline. Contrary to popular opinion, they rarely feel solidarity with each other, and under normal circumstances prison officers are able to maintain control by using them against each other—the extreme case being the use of 'inmate guards', who in some American states carry guns, and in one actually murdered large numbers of their fellow prisoners. However, during the wave of gaol riots in America, black prisoners adopted the militant ideology of the black political activists; the martyrdom of George Jackson in one such disturbance and the violence and bloodshed in many others made prison discipline suddenly a major problem for the authorities. On a much smaller scale, and in a much smaller way, the influence of PROP, a 'trade-union'-like movement for prisoners, which organised the series of protests and sit-ins in British prisons during the summer of 1972, was totally unpredictable from earlier prison disturbances, which have tended to be confined to élitist groups like top-security prisoners in special wings. The lack of precedents and warning of these disturbances made them all the more difficult for the authorities to handle.

The overall relationship of poor relief to crime rates is not a subject much discussed by social investigators. The exception to this general rule was the Poor Law Report of 1834. It was one of Chadwick's strongest points that the system of allowances had led to an increase in crime. He emphasised in his Report that those parishes which had abolished allowances had experienced a drop in the crime rate.[18]

Whatever impels any class into courses of sustained industry must necessarily diminish crime; and we find that one characteristic of the dispauperised parishes is the comparative absence of crime. In Bingham, before the change of system took place, scarcely a night passed without mischief; and during the two years preceding 1818, seven men of the parish were transported for felonies; now there is scarcely any disorder in the place. In Uley and Southwick parishes crime has similarly ceased.

What is significant about this interest in the relationship between crime and poor relief in 1834 is that it followed on a very dangerous breakdown in law and order in the southern counties in 1830. The Labourers' Revolt, which took the form of an uprising in several counties with the burning of machinery and (in Hampshire), of two workhouses, came as a severe shock to the Government, which had successfully suppressed all overt expression of rebellion for the previous ten years. It did not escape the Government's notice that the rebellion occurred precisely in those counties where the Speenhamland system was most widely operated, and accordingly, the appointment of the Royal Commission to enquire into the operation of the Poor Law had the issue of law and order very much in mind. It was only the threat of revolution itself that caused the authorities to consider the possible connection between methods of poor relief and the level of criminal activity. The same processes of reduction that had led them to explain crime in terms of individuals' moral weaknesses forced them to explain rebellion in terms of crime. The phenomenon of a mass uprising, unlike that of a host of separate criminal acts, demanded a theory which accounted for the demoralisation of a whole *class*, rather than individual members of it. Chadwick's theory supplied that need.

In modern times, social scientists, administrators and politicians have been too preoccupied with more technical details of public assistance to give serious consideration to the issue of its effect on crime rates or respect for the law. The intricacies of balancing poor relief provisions with wage levels, and of devising the right mixture of stigma and deterrence have precluded attention to this very broad and complex issue. Pinker acknowledges 'the failure of social scientists in our own time to predict either the American race-relations crisis or the French disturbances'. In the wake of the American crisis, several writers went so far as to blame social scientists for it. For instance, Moynihan points to 'those liberal, policy oriented intellectuals who gathered in Washington, and in a significant sense came to power, in the early 1960s',[19] as responsible for getting programmes adopted which encouraged black militancy, harassed the welfare system, and gave rise to a breakdown of law and order. It was this type of accusation that prompted Piven and Cloward to undertake their analysis of the relationships between poor relief, political decisions and public disorder, as a result of which they suggested that the increase in welfare payments was 'a response to civil disorder caused by rapid economic change'.[20] They go on to develop a general theory that such disorder tends to provoke central government to intervene and override local authorities' provisions.[21]

> Political incumbents try to use the power and resources of government to intervene in the institutional arrangements that breed dissension or to develop public programs intended to recapture the allegiance of disaffected blocs.... It is this objective—the political 'reintegration' of disaffected groups—that impels electoral leaders to expand relief programs at times of political crisis engendered by economic distress.

In other words, they reject Moynihan's thesis that disorder was caused by the relief explosion, and suggest instead that the relief explosion was the result of 'a distinctively managerial kind of politics'. The Great Society programmes which brought about the expansion of welfare rolls were motivated by a rise in civil disorder, but they did not cause it.

However, their own analysis also shows that the programmes themselves did cause conflict, and certainly contributed to disorder. While it is true that the expansion in poor relief started in the early 1960s, and accelerated in 1964 (i.e. before the Great Society programmes started to take effect), the really violent disturbances of the 'long hot summers' (1966 to 1969) took place in the immediate wake of these programmes. They make it clear that the policy of 'maximum feasibility participation' by the poor led to an increase in black militancy to the point that[22]

> even some agencies funded with quite pedestrian designs, such as day-care centers or family-planning services, found themselves forced to adopt aggressive postures and undertake agitational activity in order to maintain their credibility in the face of challenges by the militants whose stature rose as the ghetto masses became more volatile.

Militancy became closely connected with a strategy of welfare rights agitation, and welfare rights workers were often ideologically committed to wider aims in terms of social change and black power. The officially sponsored programmes which provided premises and staff for organisations which made it their business to harass local welfare agencies were thus an essential part of the movement towards organised militancy which burst into violent action in disturbances like the Watts riots and the Chicago protests.

Piven and Cloward's book was written in anticipation of an imminent restrictive 'reform' of the poor relief system in America following the election of the Nixon administration. They expected this as the logical next step in a cycle of expansion and contraction of welfare payments which their studies had identified in the previous fifty years of American history, and thus their book tended to play down the part of the Great Society programmes in provoking disorder. Instead, they suggested that the explosion in public assistance that it brought about was

> the *true relief reform*, that it should be defended and expanded.[23]

> From our perspective a relief explosion is a reform just because a large number of unemployed or underemployed people obtain aid, for many of them would otherwise be forced to subsist without either jobs or income.[24]

Their suspicion of Nixon's proposed measures to tighten up the provision of poor relief and to enforce low-wage work, thus led them to underestimate the connection between the expansion of public assistance and the breakdown of law and order. What they, in fact, describe is a classic example of the process first identified by de Tocqueville in *L'Ancien Régime et la revolution*. An underprivileged group, trapped in a subservient position, first attracts attention by disorderly or rebellious behaviour; it wins some concessions from those in power, which in turn raises its expectations; fresh concessions increase expectations, and a belief that the government is too weak to withstand pressure; but the government has no intention of going all the way with the new militants; it tries to clamp down on the pressure for reform that it has generated; the result is conflict, violence and, ultimately, open revolt. Expectations cannot suddenly be damped down, and the government cannot explain that it never intended to grant the subservient group higher status or increased power to control its destinies.

This process in relation to poor relief can be observed in situations other than the one in the USA. Although Piven and Cloward see the period between the end of the Napoleonic Wars and 1834 as a gradual contraction of allowances, neither contemporary commentators nor the Poor Law statistics support their view. It seems that Chadwick was right to conclude that the high crime rate and rural disorders were associated with increased dependence on poor relief, and that attempts to bring about reductions in expenditure on assistance met with mass resistance, both before and after 1834. The expectation of allowances, combined with the dependant status of rural paupers, had made them a volatile and potentially revolutionary class. Middle-class radicals exploited the threat of this violence to win electoral reform concessions in 1832, and places in the Whig governments which followed them, but it was the rural paupers whose violent revolt triggered off the political crisis.

It may well be that both the combination of welfare dependence and violent political disturbance, and the importance of resentment of public expenditure on the poor in causing backlash, have been underestimated in other contemporary analyses of quasi-revolutionary situations. Northern Ireland is a case in point. It is a well known fact that a disproportionate share of welfare expenditure in Northern Ireland goes on Catholics; in fact, some people have suggested that Ulster Catholics are failing to follow their true interests by espousing Republicanism, for union with the South would involve the loss of social security benefits and other subsidies on a massive scale. This typically English misunderstanding of an Irish political situation assumes that dependence on poor relief gives rise to submissiveness and a willingness to accept second-class status. Englishmen who tend to ascribe irresponsibility to Ulster Catholics as part of a racial character trait should consider the contrast between them and their now staid and stolid co-religionists in Eire. The comparison shows clearly the difference made by full citizenship and a share of political power; participation in the processes of self-government has apparently given the vast majority of Southern Catholics, many of whom are poorer than their Ulster counterparts, a sense of obligation towards the law of their land which Northern Ireland Catholics do not feel. It is not poverty but dependence and inferior status that gives rise to political extremism. While Ulster Protestants were willing to subscribe their portion towards the cost of keeping Catholics on public assistance so long as they remained subservient, their resentment of the welfare budget flared as soon as Catholics became disorderly and made political demands. Their backlash, like that of American whites, was very much related to hostility to 'concessions to violence' in the form of public expenditure on Catholics. A final similarity between the American and Irish uprisings lies in the fact that both began with small, liberal, middle-class civil rights movements, which focused on welfare rights, and emphasised stigma and the second-class treatment of those preponderantly receiving welfare benefits.

The tendency amongst English people to see Northern Ireland as a foreign country (like Aden or Cyprus) and our unfortunate soldiers as caught up in an incomprehensible local feud, obscures the fact that the situations in Belfast and Londonderry are as much the product of British economic and social policies as of Irish history and religious bigotry. The social services of Northern Ireland which gave rise to the original civil rights protests (particularly over housing), are organised on the same basis as those of England. Religious discrimination merely adds a dimension to the partiality and class distinctions which are equally characteristic of our own systems of allocating resources. It could well be argued that Northern Ireland represents a kind of barometer of British social unrest, and that change in our political climate can be measured by events in that turbulent province. This theme was brilliantly illustrated in George Dangerfield's book *The Strange Death of Liberal England*, in which he showed how the apparently calm and unruffled surface of pre-1914 society was about to be shattered by a series of violent political eruptions, so that 'only our submersion in a general European catastrophe averted a crisis of our national fortunes'.[25] The constitutional struggles over Lloyd George's budgets, the suffragette movement and the threat of a General Strike were part of an atmosphere of violent political conflict which found expression in the Mutiny at the Curragh and the arming of a Protestant volunteer force in Ulster. There was a plot involving the Ministry of Defence, some Army chiefs and a section of the Tory Party which was prepared for a unilateral declaration of independence in Northern Ireland, and could have led to a civil war. In the same way today, Irish bombs exploding in our streets, our undergrounds and our public offices trigger off a reaction in our own political life which reflects the violent undercurrents in British society. When Mr Heath talks about 'a small group of desperate men' his words have the hollow Canute-like sound of a man attempting to deny the groundswell of disorder and turbulence both in Ulster's cities and our own.

What all these examples suggest is that an expansion of poor relief *provided on a selective basis for an identified group or class* leads to an *increased* danger of a breakdown in law and order, or ultimately a politically unstable situation. Many factors contribute to this effect. Above all, the processes of selection by which benefits are rationed tend to increase the self-identification of the group that benefits, and to increase the hostility to that group of those that do not benefit. The same processes also tend to reinforce the culture of poverty, to increase contempt for the authorities and disregard of the law. The selected target group which is seen as in need of special welfare provision because it is unable to get resources that others enjoy through participation in the normal political and productive processes becomes more aware of itself and of its position in the larger society through being the object of such expanded provision. It recognises that more generous subsidies and allowances are only given because other civil rights are denied; that these increases in benefits do not make it more equal but more dependent. In Chadwick's phrase, it becomes 'demoralised'; in more contemporary language, it becomes volatile, unstable, a potential force for political unrest and sudden unpredictable violence.

It might be argued that there is no danger of such things happening in this country because the group which receives the increases in benefits is not identifiable, as in the USA and Northern Ireland, by race or religion. However, there are strong reasons to believe that claimants of social security here are coming to see themselves increasingly as a group with common interests; the Claimants' Unions are only part of the evidence for this. Furthermore, non-claimants are more and more able to identify this group, both by their areas of residence and their dependence on benefits. The widening net of selective allowances provided by local and central government pulls the group together and separates it from those who do not qualify; the two are becoming different social classes, with different interests and different rights. The politics of selectivity feed into the already-present danger of conflict between militants on both sides.

Neither politicians nor social scientists are willing to recognise the trend in this direction. It is too much in the interests of both to deal with poverty as a social problem, to increase social security and other selective provisions rather than to attempt, by economic measures, to reintegrate the poor into the mainstream of productive and political life. For instance, during the negotiations over Phase three of the Pay Pause, Mr Heath stated that he would prefer to deal with the problem of low-paid workers by increasing Family Income Supplement coverage rather than raising the level of permitted wage rises at the lower end of the scale. It may be significant that the only Member of Parliament to comment critically on the broader implications of the introduction of the Family Income Supplement was Mr Enoch Powell.[26] In the long run, those who assert their resentment of the beneficiaries of this scheme may well be his supporters.

It was Mr Powell's outburst that first provoked the use of 'positive discrimination' as a measure of selectivity in the provision of benefits to try to ward off the threat of civil disorder. At present, the very limited use of this principle avoids the exacerbation of conflicts by the processes described in this chapter, but in the longer run this form of discrimination is likely only to deepen the divisions which it is intended to heal.

11
Conclusion

I have based this book upon a consideration of the developments in the social services which have concentrated resources on a selected group alleged to be in greatest need. The starting point was Sir Keith Joseph's theory of the 'cycle of deprivation', because this theory encapsulates a number of myths that are very prevalent in both the academic and the political spheres of social policy at the present time. One of these myths is that it is possible to provide, on a selective basis, the best services for the poorest members of the community. Another is that the poorest group is the one which is most in need of every kind of social service. A third is that more generous provision of social services to areas with high concentrations of poor families can reduce tensions and conflicts between rival groups.

In some ways, it is surprising that a Secretary of State for Health and Social Security has put forward such a theoretical formulation of the basis of the Government's social policies. Perhaps he was confident of an academic consensus in favour of an allocation of resources in the directions he felt to be indicated by the notion of the 'cycle'. In the hope of stimulating further inquiries into the phenomena he had identified, his department summoned a distinguished gathering of social scientists together in April 1973 to hear a paper prepared by an inter-disciplinary group of eminent specialists on 'Approaches to research on transmitted deprivation'.[1] Their paper in large measure reflects the thinking of its patron. After distinguishing between 'personal characteristics or qualities which we will call "attributes", and inadequacies in the physical or social environment as they impinge on an individual which we will call "burdens"'[2] it goes on to list homelessness as a burden, but poverty as an attribute. The full list of attributes for research investigation into their 'inter-generational continuities' is 'economic status, occupational skill, job stability/instability, education skills, emotional or behavioural attributes, and defects in interpersonal relationships.'[3] Thus the group's approach is already heavily weighted towards a selective concentration on 'bad factors' which, though financial or material in effect, are seen as belonging in the individual. By contrast, bad housing and homelessness are the only burdens (factors in the social environment that are not to be investigated) which the group mentions.

The promise of research funds appears to have affected the group's memory, for in their haste to number the many phenomena which require further investigation, they seem to have ignored a hundred years of previous sociological research on both sides of the Atlantic. For instance, in a section on 'multiplicity of attributes', they pronounce that 'knowledge is needed on the extent to which different attributes occur together, and the extent to which disabilities are multiple rather than single'.[4] With presumably unconscious irony they add[5]

> in addition to the attributes listed there are several others which need to be taken into account in the research, although the mechanism of their inter-generational transmission is not in question. The two very different attributes of this kind which most warrant attention are, on the one hand, colour of skin and, on the other physical impairment. Skin colour is known to be transmitted genetically and it is unlikely that there is any *necessary* connection between skin colour and social disability. Nevertheless, skin colour may be a powerful indicator of certain kinds of social disadvantage. The research would need to determine why this is so and by what mechanisms skin colour is associated with disadvantage.

One wonders how many millions of pounds of research funds it will take to reveal that the reason why certain skin colours are associated with disadvantage is the frequency with which their occurrence is correlated with other attributes, such as low economic status, a lack of occupational skill, poor educational attainment and high job instability.

The paper received a critical reception from the conference, and Sir Keith Joseph's subsequent speeches suggest that he may have modified his own presentation of his theory in line with some of these criticisms. His speech to the National Association for Maternal and Child Welfare in June 1973 makes much fewer claims about connections between poverty, deprivation and maladjustment. Indeed, poverty is only referred to in one short section. He acknowledges that the problems of devising ways of supporting parents 'may not be altogether simple'.[6] He also admits that[7]

> attempts at intervention to offset early disadvantage by, for example, what is referred to as 'positive discrimination' have been disappointing in their results. But we are beginning to see that the interventions we have so far attempted have been inadequate in scale, in term, in method, in understanding of what we are about.

Thus, although Sir Keith Joseph recognises the difficulties inherent in his policies, there is no indication of a fundamental change in them.

Furthermore, although there have been numerous detailed criticisms of both his theory and his policies, there is unlikely to be a concerted challenge to them from academic circles. The lure of financial support for social investigations is not the only cause of the convergence between political, administrative and academic views of the phenomena of poverty and deprivation. The notion that there are conflicting *principles* of social administration is becoming increasingly unfashionable. Pinker argues that in social policy 'the academic debate is more imbued with ideological imperatives than its parliamentary counterpart'[8] but that 'if a discipline is to play any effective part in the short-term amelioration of social problems, its practitioners must be prepared to compromise on issues of principle'.[9] He suggests that a tendency towards ideological excesses in academic circles is curbed through the democratic process and 'the "rules of the game" that govern the practice of civilised discourse'.[10] Furthermore, the practicalities of social administration exert a similar influence, because 'relatively frequent contact with the realities and complexities of human need quickly sobers the enthusiasm of ideologists and utopians'.[11] Pinker goes on to conclude that conflicts between social and economic policy have been exaggerated by protagonists at both ends of the academic and political spectrum, and suggests that it may be that[12]

> there is no intrinsic conflict between social and economic policy.... In relation to the wider social system, welfare systems contribute in very real terms to the maintenance of stability and consensus.... Social services are one of the more civilised ways in which societies maintain themselves and survive. Social services receive and reallocate resources in order to ameliorate social conflict and strengthen the bonds of social solidarity.

Similarly, Donnison's view is that

> there can be no generally and permanently valid principles of social policy and no book of rules for the social administration.[13]

> The social services are a continually developing response to continually changing needs and problems.... The evolution of these services is not an impersonal or automatic response to external pressures of supply and demand; neither is it simply dictated by legislation; it is largely brought about by the people who work in the services.[14]

This kind of view is derived from a fairly narrow consideration of the development of the British social services since the war, and reflects a kind of myopia which seems equally to afflict theorists, politicians and practitioners who take a specialist interest in the evolution of detailed administrative procedures. The functionalist model of the social services assumes that they serve the same ends, whatever the principles of the government in power, whatever the nature of the State they serve. If regimes are to be judged for their 'civilised ways of maintaining themselves' according to the quantity they spend on social services, then the Republic of South Africa, with the highest *per capita* expenditure on its African population's welfare in the continent, comes out of this measurement very well. The fact that many of its citizens have to be forcibly moved onto their new housing estates is not reflected in the statistics. Our own longer-term history shows that it is quite possible to devote large sums of money to 'social welfare' provisions which promote the economic objectives of particular powerful factions. The system of out-relief in the Speenhamland era was as carefully geared to the productive requirements of the landowners who ruled England at the time of the Napoleonic Wars as were the principles of 1834 to the interests of the new industrial entrepreneurs. It was not economy alone that dictated that widows and orphans should be kept in conditions of 'less eligibility' in the workhouse until the breakup of the Poor Law. Institutionalisation was often an expensive as well as an effective way of stigmatising those who could not support themselves. The particular methods employed to implement the principles of social policy always have been those which best suited the interests of the most powerful political group.

Our own new pattern of services is not, as Pinker and Donnison suggest, simply the result of the great diversification and complexity of conflicting interests in an advanced technological society that only a democratic compromise can reflect. It follows very closely the development of social services in that more advanced economy, the USA. The need to deal selectively with the poor as a separate group by means of 'positive discrimination' is not, as they would have us believe, the result of research discoveries of 'the persistence of gross inequalities', but a political response to a social and economic crisis. The crisis represented by the urban poor was of an increasingly disaffected, lawless group, economically redundant or functioning only with low earning power as cheap casual labour; a disorderly, squalid reproach to the system which produced it. It is easy enough to recognise the two nations in American society—the affluent white middle class and the prosperous workers on the one hand, the black and immigrant inhabitants of the ghettoes on the other. Equally, we can see the splits in their social services. Social insurance gives adequate protection against misfortune and old age to the better-off; public welfare gives highly stigmatised assistance to the poor. In the personal services, the middle class monopolises specialist skills, while the poor make do with 'casework' from untrained social workers acting as poor relief officers, and social control by the law enforcement agencies and the psychiatric services. These inequalities in standards and institutional divisions are being recreated in our own welfare state, in response to changes in our social structure as we move in the direction of becoming a society more like the USA.

The fact is that capitalist economies developed their own distinctive kind of social services long before they were influenced by either social scientists or an electorate. From the first beginnings of the break-up of the feudal system, poor relief was used as a way of dealing with the consequences in social disruption of changes in the system of production. It was used as a way of intervening in the lives of the poor to enforce the work ethic, to encourage families to take responsibility for each other, and to keep law and order. Capitalism needed poor relief to regulate the rootless class it created. Left to its own devices therefore, capitalism is in no danger of producing no social services at all—it will simply produce them according to these particular principles. It will produce more of such services the more disruption it causes, so the size of services is no guide to their benevolence. The point about this particular form of economic organisation is not the quantity of social services it engenders, but their particular quality. Even at the height of the era of *laissez-faire*, the Poor Law was being adapted, not disbanded. Thus if democracy and the social sciences do not challenge these *principles* of poor relief, they cannot be said to be having any influence on the shape of the social services at all.

Of course, there have always been other kinds of social services for groups other than the poor. In the nineteenth century, these were developed quite separately by the middle and working classes; the middle class through the churches, the banks, the law firms, the insurance companies and the public schools; the working class through the chapels, the Friendly Societies, the building societies and the trade unions. Government social policy in the twentieth century has often been in terms of strengthening these provisions—for instance, by making grants to public schools, or allowing tax relief on insurance premiums and mortgage interest repayments, or, as in 1911, nationalising the financing of the Friendly Societies. However, a more important question about government policy is the extent to which it attempts to extend the *best* of such provisions to include a wider, or if possible, a total coverage of the population. At the opposite end of the scale, governments may be judged by the percentage of the population who are forced to rely on various forms of public assistance provided according to the old principles of means test, less eligibility and work enforcement.

There have been times in our history when the combined influence of social scientists and the electorate challenged the government's policy of applying Poor Law principles to a broad section of the worst-off members of our society. On a small scale, one such time was the period between 1905 and 1914, which was marked by the Royal Commission on the Poor Laws and the Liberal schemes for sickness and unemployment insurance. Another such time was during the Labour Government of 1945 to 1951. It was characteristic of both periods that what was challenged, criticised and ultimately changed, was not merely the application of Poor Law principles to the business of providing *relief*, but also their influence on the *personal* social services that the authorities were supposed to be offering. Conversely, during times when principles of poor relief are extending their dominion over a wider sector of the population, there is a tendency for them to invade the public provisions for personal social services as well as the income maintenance services, as they are invading the local authority social services departments at present.

We have seen how the plight of children in the care of Public Assistance Committees inspired the creation of the new social work departments in 1948. It was something of a moral crusade to set children free from the shackles of the workhouse and less eligibility, and the new services could grasp a clear principle in their work. The provision of the best possible life for deprived children was a noble aim, and within the administrative structure created at the time, a fairly realistic one. Also the identification of a single object for compassion, and one worthy of compassion, enabled the best principles of casework to be called for in the service of children. However, while the exclusion of parents probably simplified the focus of the new departments' work, and the narrow functions assisted the development of an efficient administrative structure, in the long run it was clearly wrong and against the interests of children to deny the importance of family and preventive work. Unfortunately, the attempt to widen provision to include these aspects coincided with a decline in the initial idealism of the services, a loss of the original crusading zeal, and a subtle shift of responsibility for poor relief away from the central government department. Thus, the development of a family casework service, which would have been the logical evolution from the Children's Departments, has been bedevilled by professional confusion, loss of confidence and the building up of administrative structures and practices adapted to the public assistance side of the local authorities' new duties.

The principle's of casework can, as the work of the best Children's Departments showed, represent an effective challenge to the principle of poor relief. Compassionate identification with those suffering from basic deprivations can lead to a personalised and humanised provision of services which is very different in kind from the spirit of public assistance provisions. Although the personal social services always carry stigma, the best services do so more by virtue of the dread attached to such misfortunes as bereavement and mental illness than because of the way they treat those who receive them. There is no reason why a family casework agency should not represent the same principles in its dealings with its clients as the best Children's Departments did, provided it was given an equally clear mandate to work with them as *persons*, human beings in various kinds of adversity, not cases to be assessed on their financial eligibility for bureaucratically defined benefits or, worse still, their deservingness of any assistance at all.

The attempt to provide a Family Service, as Seebohm departments were originally intended to be, is complicated by the difficulty of focusing social work on the family rather than the individual in need of help. To set up an agency committed to the support of the institution of the family would require a very special kind of skill, not so much in organising its structure, as in defining its aims and providing reinforcement of its norms and values. Perhaps only the Family Service Units in this country (as they were in the 1950s) represent a model of a social work agency committed to the preservation of families in emotional and material distress, and in tune with the strong bonds of feeling between even the most disrupted and disruptive parents and their apparently neglected and rejected children. It is a response to the felt attachment within the family group that is required of any social work provision which is going to strengthen parents in their task of bringing up children in an atmosphere of conflict or despair. While poor parents may be specially prone to such feelings, and poverty may add a dimension to their distress, the imposition on the social worker of *statutory responsibility for the relief of poverty* virtually destroys any possibility of the commitment to the emotional task of helping parents live with the agonising pulls and pressures of family life. This task requires a kind of single-minded dedication, based ultimately on an act of faith in the value of parents to children and children to parents; it is a special kind of faith which was precisely what Relieving Officers and National Assistance Board men lacked. The new generation of social workers is inclined to scoff at the tender-hearted and soft-headed dedication of the earlier generation which was raised on Bowlby and the Robertson films; but it is very doubtful whether without this kind of dedication social work has anything to offer parents experiencing real conflict about their parental roles. Here it may be that social work has something to learn from the National Association for the Welfare of Children in Hospital, a middle-class mothers' organisation which, by committing itself wholeheartedly to Bowlby's principles, has successfully made considerable inroads into the cycle of deprivation which occurred when young children were separated from their parents on admission to hospital. By securing the admission of mothers with their children, and longer visiting hours, they have reduced not only distress but probably longer-term emotional damage among the under-fives; but this would not have been done without the dedication which came from those who had experienced the traumas of separation. Essentially the family is a network of feelings, and it is only by recognising the prime importance of helping parents and children to deal with their emotional attachments to each other, that social work will begin to make its interventions in the emotional 'cycle of deprivation' count.

Not everything that has happened since the local authority services were combined has been bad. Some useful experience of work with families under the new generic approach has been gained in many areas; in others, new initiatives in community work have yielded some encouraging results. Family and community work are both important new developments (or rather, revivals) in social work, which would achieve an exciting new pattern of public provisions if the local authority services were free to develop them; but this will never be done until a clear distinction is made between such truly personal social services, and public assistance provision for emergency and exceptional need.

Whatever form of income maintenance system is adopted, there will need to be some form of service to make payments to meet extreme forms of financial emergency, on at least a short-term basis. I have argued that such a service will always tend to be provided according to Poor Law principles, and that therefore the aims of a true Welfare State should be to keep this service as small and residual as possible. This was Beveridge's aim. It should also be as local and community based as is feasible and this, too, was the original conception of the National Assistance Board; as Aneurin Bevan said, 'Where the individual is immediately concerned, where warmth and humanity of administration is the primary consideration, there the authority which is responsible should be as near the recipient as possible.'[15]

There could be a case, therefore, for basing this service on the local authorities. Indeed, the development of the social services departments, and their increasing resemblance to the old Public Assistance Committees, suggests that the best plan might be to use their field work services for precisely this purpose. However, if this were done, public provision for personal services, staffed by professional social workers, and for residential services, would have to be moved to a quite separate local authority department. It is the mixture of public assistance and social work that is so fatal to the social worker's professional task, and to the interests of their clients in need of either kind of service.

A personal social service department which had no connection with poor relief would not be in danger of selecting its clients according to their need for financial assistance. It could then concentrate on human deprivation, on the emotional traumas of childhood and the conflicts of family life in all strata of society, without having to consider the Poor Law principles of less eligibility, means test and work enforcement. If physical, educational and emotional disabilities are transmitted from one generation to the next as Sir Keith Joseph suggests, it could work with families to break such patterns without the burden of responsibility for their financial and material well-being. At present, local authority social workers are often doing little more than hand out emergency payments to get families from one crisis to the next, and in that process reinforcing the culture of poverty, and acting out a cycle of official deprivation of the poor. The connections between poverty and the cycle of deprivation are thus mainly contained in the present administrative structures of our social services. If public assistance and the personal services were separated, the two problems would be seen to be largely distinct from each other.

However, such a separation could only be achieved by means of a revolutionary change in our income maintenance services. I have argued that the reason why the supplementary benefits system requires underpinning in the form of emergency and exceptional needs payments from local authority departments is the shifting emphasis in the functions of social security. Since the failure of the principle of National Insurance to provide universal subsistence-level maintenance led to the abandonment of universality and the notion of flat-rate benefits in the contributory sector, supplementary benefits have increasingly taken over the role of being the fundamental social security provision for a very broad sector of the population. This has meant that the residual concept of National Assistance has had to be abandoned, and Poor Law principles have been modified to suit the wider role given to the Supplementary Benefits Commission. Above all, flexibility and responsiveness to immediate need have been sacrificed in an attempt to reduce stigma and make the administration of benefits more impersonal. Supplementary benefits thus represent an uneasy compromise between notions of old-fashioned public assistance and more recent provisions of benefits as of right. They satisfy neither criteria, with the result that while the 'deserving' grumble about means test and stigma, the 'undeserving' have had to be passed over for emergency assistance to the local authorities.

Superimposed upon these changes has been the much more basic crisis heralded by the 'rediscovery of poverty'. The post-war era of prosperity had the side-effect of producing a new class of urban poor, the flotsam and jetsam of economic change, drawn into the cities and then left struggling for survival in the sordid and insecure world of the slums. The recent Government has tried to deal with this problem according to Poor Law principles; it has introduced new benefits and allowances for the 'working poor' aimed at keeping those who are subsidised in a slightly less eligible situation than those who are not. But, as the experience of the Speenhamland system showed, this method is particularly efficacious in producing a demoralised 'culture of poverty', and the pauperised attitudes which follow from this 'second class' status can be seen to lead to high crime rates and an increase in civil disorder. The price which in the long run has to be paid for employing this method to deal with the social problems generated by increased affluence is a 'law and order' crisis, similar to that in the USA, and the possibility of organised conflict between the pauper class and those who resent its dependence and demoralisation.

The question of discovering new principles for the provision of income maintenance therefore goes much deeper than the kind of technicalities which preoccupy government publications and Child Poverty Action Group pamphlets. It is not simply a matter of finding new ways of giving more money to those who have a low income. It is a question of what sort of society we wish to live in. In the USA, deep divisions between rich and poor have led to a situation in which many better-off people in the cities carry guns; few feel safe to venture into the ghettoes; most are unprepared to risk a walk in the public parks. A higher standard of living is enjoyed at the expense of an astronomical rate of crime, especially crimes of violence, armed police, massive security provisions and an atmosphere of paranoid anxiety. While racial and religious differences always exacerbate distinctions between paupers and independent citizens, any country which divides itself on these lines is virtually ensuring for itself an atmosphere similar to the one in the USA, as our own experience at the start of the nineteenth century proved.

To avoid this kind of situation in this country, better-off people would be required to sacrifice some of their high standard of living; economic growth would have to cease to be our overriding priority; and above all, the work ethic, already badly eaten away at the edges, would have to be abandoned as a basic value underlying income maintenance. The insurance principle has been shown to be an inadequate way of providing for interruptions of earnings; now interruptions of earnings have come to be only one of a number of situations giving rise to the need for income maintenance. What has to be faced squarely sooner or later is that the economic motivation which must henceforth underlie income maintenance provision is that of providing people with enough to maintain an adequate level of consumption. Instead of trying to devise methods of forcing people to work, social security should seek to give people an adequate, decent standard of life. The other side of the coin from this is that if our economy has advanced to a point that a proportion of the population are doing work that is of such low value (compared with the productivity of machines) that they cannot command a wage sufficient for subsistence, then the notion that people *should* subsist on wages must be scrapped. If work at the bottom end of the pay scale is to be so degraded, so menial, so spasmodic and so badly paid, we should certainly not expect human beings to assess their status, their worth and their family's welfare according to its measure. If we have no intention of bringing low wages up to a level that will drastically reduce differentials between rich and poor, between status-giving and debasing employments, then we must be prepared to supply an income to people, as of right, which is nothing to do with their willingness to work.

Proposals for a guaranteed income as of right, irrespective of work, usually provoke strong objections from those who believe that the poor only work because they are forced to do so by economic necessity. It is interesting that such objectors usually define their own work motivations in other terms—satisfaction, fulfilment, self-realisation, achievement or sheer gain. Like all the other principles which underlie poor relief, the enforcement of work rests on the notion that the poor do not share the same human feelings that move the rest of the population to behave decently. It is not considered likely that the middle classes would suddenly abandon their wives or fail to maintain their children unless they were forced to take responsibility for them; yet the means test is designed precisely to *compel* the poor to do what the rest of society is assumed to do by choice. The tax system is not organised in such a way as to assume that each taxpayer is a potential fraud whose declarations must be checked in every detail, yet the social security system is designed precisely on the basis that abuse can only be prevented by assuming that no claimant is eligible until he *proves* his eligibility. Abuse and fraud are thus taken to be the norms among the poor; honesty and frankness among the better-off. It is a mark of the double standards by which our social services are administered, that only those services which deal selectively with the poor assume that coercion alone will produce the behaviour which most decent citizens would, of their own accord, consider desirable.

As far as work is concerned, it is likely that, if a guaranteed adequate income as of right was provided, few if any people would be prepared to do some of the filthy and degrading low-paid jobs that still exist—a situation which threatened in the 1950s, and led to the encouragement of mass immigration from the Commonwealth. This would mean that, as in some other advanced countries which do not have a menial pauper class, our industries and public services would have to find some other way (mechanical perhaps) of doing their dirty work. A guaranteed income might well also mean a larger proportion of people unwilling to work at all; but even this is questionable. The present system, which makes the payment of most benefits conditional on doing *no* work, or only a very limited amount, means that people have to choose between trying to support themselves completely out of earnings, or being entirely idle. If the guaranteed income was not affected by any work done, everyone who was at all fit would have an incentive to do *some* work. Those who were so old, sick or disabled as to be completely unfit could, perhaps, be given increments to their guaranteed income to compensate for their inability to supplement it from work. The whole system would thus assume that people *want* to work, and encourage them to do so, unlike the present one, which assumes that the poor and dependent do not want to work and, while they are in receipt of benefits, ensures by every method (including spying and prosecutions) that they do not.

Although a guaranteed income would not necessarily cause great disincentives to work at the lower end of the pay scale, it would probably involve considerable ones at the upper, because it would need massive increases in taxation to finance it. It would necessarily involve a transfer of income from the rich to the poor. It would mean a fundamental alteration in our national priorities, a sacrifice of economic growth as the primary objective of all political and economic life, and the deliberate cultivation of a different kind of society in which traditional relationships between groups and classes were basically altered. However, only such major changes can avert the difficulties and dangers inherent in a divided society such as present social policy is producing.

The recent Government took a step which looks as if it is in the direction of a kind of guaranteed income in its proposals for the introduction of tax credits.[16] The Green Paper declares the aims of the scheme as being 'to improve the system of income support for poor people',[17] to reduce the element of means testing in the social services by superseding Family Income Supplement in the case of those in the scheme and by relieving 'hundreds of thousands of pensioners from the need to draw supplementary benefit';[18] and 'to extend the benefit of tax allowances to people who have insufficient income to pay tax'.[19] However, the method of financing any additional cost of the scheme is not discussed in any detail, the paper dismissing it as an issue by saying that 'with the growth of national income, more resources will become available'.[20] The implication would appear to be that the Government wished to carry out the scheme without increasing taxation to finance it. As critics of the Green Paper have pointed out, the 'illustrative levels of credit' used in the paper are relatively meaningless because, while they assume that incomes will rise considerably, they make no allowances for other changes, for example, rises in prices or in the level of other benefits, in the period between now and the introduction of the scheme.

Accordingly, it is difficult to assess the scheme in very precise terms, but certain features of it stand out clearly. Even under the illustrative figures only some 800,000 pensioners out of 2·2 million dependent on supplementary benefit would be taken off supplementary benefit.[21] If a 'revenue neutral' basis is adopted (i.e. if we assume that the scheme is financed without the rate of existing taxation being raised, or at no net cost in extra taxation, an assumption which makes more sense than those implicit in the illustrative examples), then 'the reduction would be considerably smaller, leaving some 1¾ million pensioners dependent on means testing'.[22] 'For the large numbers who would still have to have their pensions supplemented, there would be no net benefit from the tax-credit scheme.'[23]

Thus as far as pensioners (who form the majority of those claiming supplementary benefit) are concerned, the effect would be to take out of that system a group which is not the poorest or the neediest. It is a group which has the greatest resentment of the means-test procedures of supplementary benefit, the most 'deserving' of the elderly poor, the group which has, in the main, only come to be included in the supplementary benefits system since the creation of the Ministry of Social Security in 1965. Furthermore, the pensioners who benefit most from the proposals according to the Green Paper are those 'who at present neither pay tax nor are eligible for supplementary benefit'.[24] However, Barbara Castle calculated that 'the gain to this group would be seriously reduced by the fact that they would become liable to tax on all their other income' so that 'as a result, even with the illustrative levels of credit, single pensioners with some other income can actually be worse off under the scheme'.[25] Whatever the eventual outcome, the Government's intention was clearly to prevent this group joining the ever growing numbers dependent on supplementary benefits, since the latter system had proved unacceptable to the enormous bulk of 'deserving' old people who had come to be eligible for it.

For the sick and the unemployed, the scheme involves the taxation of National Insurance Benefits, giving rise to tax credits, but the loss through taxation, although it allows a slight advantage under the illustrative examples, 'reduces the net benefit quite considerably and with a revenue-neutral scheme some families with children would become substantially worse off'.[26] Also, the long-term unemployed who had run out of National Insurance Benefit would be excluded from the scheme, and still have to depend on supplementary benefit.

As far as families with the breadwinner in work are concerned, the Green Paper's proposals have already been modified in line with criticisms made to the Select Committee. Tax credits have been dropped in favour of a child credit, payable as a cash benefit to the mother. However, the effects of child credits in relieving poverty and eliminating Family Income Supplement would depend on the level of credits and the way they are financed. According to evidence given to the Select Committee about the effects of a 'revenue neutral' scheme 'on this basis, families now claiming F.I.S. could actually be worse off than they are now'.[27] As the proposed scheme is at present organised, it would not be possible to eliminate Family Income Supplement without distributing enormous sums to people in the other ranges of income. It 'would involve providing £425 million to those with incomes over £2,000 a year in order to eliminate one means-tested benefit costing £7 million per year'.[28] In general terms, the proposed scheme has little effect in relieving poverty, as even according to the illustrative figures, of the total £1,300 million which the scheme would cost, 'only £150 million would go to households with incomes of £1,000 a year or less ... compared with £745 million going to those with annual incomes over £1,600'.[29] Furthermore, the scheme specifically excludes self-employed persons who, according to the Child Poverty Action Group, have four times as high a rate of poverty as other employed persons[30] and families with an income of less than £8 per week, which will affect many unsupported mothers.

Finally, the scheme would do nothing to affect the local authority means-tested benefits which are rapidly replacing Family Income Supplement as the major form of poverty trap in the income maintenance system. According to Holman, 'it is estimated that some 2¾ million council and up to 700,000 private tenants will be due for rent rebates and allowances'.[31] These benefits have an even lower take-up rate than the 52 per cent estimate for Family Income Supplement. 'From the available evidence, it appears that little more than half actually claim their rate rebates while the Birmingham scheme for rent rebates for private tenants had a take-up rate of only five per cent.'[32] If the Government were really determined to eliminate means-tested benefits and selective allowances, these and the free school meals and milk schemes would surely be targets as much as Family Income Supplement. In fact, it would seem instead that means-tested benefits will come to be concentrated in the local authorities, while a tax credit system will take over only a small proportion of those formerly dealt with by supplementary benefits.

It will be interesting to see what effects the removal of the most 'deserving' of the poor from the supplementary benefits scheme will have on the work of the Supplementary Benefits Commission. It might be considered that this would enable it to return to the residual role occupied by National Assistance, to use its discretionary powers more generously, to deal more sensitively with those in greatest need, and to be more responsive to emergency and exceptional situations. However, it is not clear whether the Green Paper's reference to a saving of 10-15,000 civil servants[33] includes a running down of the staff of the Supplementary Benefits Commission, and, if so, whether this would mean a further move in the direction of centralisation and a reduction in the services for urgent and exceptional need. If so, the way could be open for the wholesale transfer of provisions under Section 7 and Section 13 of the Ministry of Social Security Act to local authority social services departments. The needs of the 'undeserving' and especially of poor parents with young children, would thus be concentrated in the hands of social workers.

The tendency towards giving local authorities the whole obligation for this kind of provision has been played down by writers on social administration. For instance, Holman states 'the expenditure under these Sections (of the Children and Young Persons 1963 Act and Social Work Scotland Act) is not large, is not continuous and is not intended to replace income due from the Supplementary Benefits Commission'.[34] He substantiates this point by referring to figures from the Scottish Education Department for the year 1968-9, which was the one immediately after the introduction of the new Act there. In fact, as I showed in chapter 6, an examination of recent expenditure by local authorities under these sections shows that it is rapidly overhauling the Supplementary Benefits Commission's very modest provisions for exceptional needs, which form only 0.7 per cent of total expenditure on supplementary benefits. While there is no question of local authorities taking over the payment of scale rates, it is quite conceivable that they might take on the whole task of providing for urgent and exceptional needs, since they already do a large part of it.

The proposals for a tax credit scheme therefore have important implications for the future of both the income maintenance and the personal social services; but they do not represent a step towards a true guaranteed income. Instead, they are simply adaptations, taking account of unsatisfactory features of the present social security system, such as the inclusion of enormous numbers of 'deserving' old people in a means-tested scheme, and the low take-up rate of Family Income Supplement. They do not represent a new principle, but a modification of the old principles to take account of changes in the economic situation. The long-established principles of poor relief will, at the most ambitious estimates, still apply to some four million recipients of supplementary benefits. The government's own calculation is that 10 per cent of the population will be excluded from the tax credit scheme altogether. Of those included, many hundreds of thousands will still be forced to undergo various forms of local authority means tests.

Thus none of the fundamental problems raised in this book about income maintenance and deprivation will be solved by this measure. These problems must persist and give rise to the kinds of conflicts described so long as the old principles of poor relief continue to underlie our social policies. Only an increasingly ruthless application of these principles can sustain the system of income maintenance as it now exists, for economic changes and the social disruption that has followed them have given rise to irreconcilable contradictions in the productive system and allocation of our national resources. In the enforcement of the work ethic, of family responsibility and of law and order, punitive measures will have to be employed to counteract the disincentives of low pay, the dislocations of the culture of poverty, and the disorder of city slums and the culture of crime. Increasingly institutions, such as those currently employed to deal with homelessness, will have to replace the notion of 'community care' as a way of enforcing the norms required by social policy.

The alternative of a guaranteed income would, while breaking the work-income connection, set poor families free to pursue other priorities than merely struggling for survival. It is assumed that leisure and culture are beneficial and ennobling for the better-off; is there any reason to suppose that freedom from the compulsion to work long hours merely to survive will demoralise the poor? Most of the evidence suggests that 'a psychology of scarcity produces anxiety, envy, egotism (to be seen most drastically in peasant cultures all over the world). A psychology of abundance produces initiative, faith in life, solidarity.'[35] The fundamental change in society's attitudes which would be necessitated before a guaranteed income could be provided for all, would be likely to affect priorities in production as well as methods. Instead of taking part in the wage slavery which at present turns out luxuries for the rich, and the futility of production for waste, people would have the chance of engaging in work which was directed towards social needs. Instead of useless gimmicks, we might for the first time find ourselves possessing an adequate supply of hospitals, schools and houses.

Sir Keith Joseph's concern for deprived children, and his avowed intention of providing support for their parents, are belied by the ways in which the recent Government's policies have affected the development of the social services. As long as Poor Law principles hold sway, those who require help from the social services will suffer the brutalities which are an integral part of the treatment provided according to those principles. Family life as it is known to those who are well enough off to appreciate the sweeter and gentler aspects of human existence has always been, and always will be, systematically denied to recipients of poor relief by the overseer, the workhouse master, the sex snooper and the social security bully boy. The social services will never truly contribute towards the appreciation of those values associated with the lives of our more fortunate and contented family groups until the principles of the Poor Law are abandoned for ever.

Notes

1 The cycle of official deprivation

1 Sir Keith Joseph, Speech to Pre-School Playgroups Association, 29.6.72, p.4.
2 Ibid., pp.4-5.
3 Ibid., p.10.
4 Ibid.
5 Ibid., p.7.
6 Ibid., p.6.
7 For example, see R. E. Park and E. W. Burgess, *The City*, University of Chicago Press, 1925.
8 P. Sainsbury, *Suicide in London*, Chapman & Hall, 1955.
9 T. Morris, *The Criminal Area*, Routledge & Kegan Paul, 1957.
10 R. K. Merton, *Social Theory & Social Structure*, Free Press, 1957, p.146.
11 A. B. Hollingshead and F. C. Redlich, *Social Class & Mental Stress*, John Wiley, 1955.
12 J. K. Myers and L. L. Bean, *A Decade Later: A Follow-Up Study of Social Class and Mental Illness*, John Wiley, 1968.
13 W. McCord and J. McCord, *Origins of Alcoholism*, Tavistock, 1960.
14 E. M. Schur, *Narcotic Addiction in Great Britain and America*, Tavistock, 1963.
15 M. Davies, *Probationers in Their Social Environment*, A Home Office Research Unit Report, HMSO, 1969, p.118.
16 Ibid., p.34.
17 W. Jordan, 'Intolerable behaviour in a Cathedral city' (unpublished).
18 M. B. Clinard, *The Sociology of Deviant Behaviour*, Holt, Rinehart & Winston, 1964.
19 W. J. Goode, *Women in Divorce*, Free Press, 1956.
20 J. P. Gibbs, *Suicide*, Harper & Row, 1968.
21 Joseph, op. cit., p.8.
22 Sir Keith Joseph, 'The next ten years', *New Society*, 5.10.72.
23 Joseph, Speech to Pre-School Playgroups Association, p.5.
24 Jean Packman, *Child Care: Needs and Numbers*, Allen & Unwin, 1969.
25 Ibid., p.170.
26 Ibid.
27 Ibid.
28 Ibid., p.171.
29 Ibid.
30 Janet Mattinson, *Marriage and Mental Handicap*, Duckworth, 1970, p.113.
31 D. P. Moynihan, *The Negro Family: The Case for National Action*, Department of Labour (Office of Policy Planning and Research), 1965, p.14.
32 I. Lurie, *An Economic Evaluation of Aid to Families with Dependent Children*, Brookings Institution, 1968.
33 Joseph, 'The next ten years'.
34 M. Brill, 'The local authority

social worker', in K. Jones (ed.) *Yearbook of Social Policy; 1971*, Routledge & Kegan Paul, 1972, pp.93-4.

35 R. Pinker, *Social Theory and Social Policy*, Heinemann, 1971, p.97.

36 Ibid., p.107.

37 Ibid., p.108.

38 Packman, op. cit., p.228.

39 Jean Packman, 'Incidence of "need"', in J. Stroud (ed.), *Services for Children and their Families; Aspects of Child Care for Social Workers*, Pergamon, 1973, pp.73-4.

40 Joseph, Speech to Pre-School Playgroups Association, p.10.

2 Official theories of deprivation

1 Quoted in R. Pinker, *Social Theory and Social Policy*, Heinemann, 1971, p.26.

2 Herbert Spencer, *The Man Versus the State* (ed. D. MacRae), Penguin, 1970, p.107.

3 Poor Law Act, 1598, Section 7.

4 Poor Law Act, 1930, Section 41.

5 Poor Law Act, 1598, Section 7.

6 Ibid.

7 Ibid., Preamble.

8 F. F. Piven and R. A. Cloward, *Regulating the Poor*, Tavistock, 1972, p.3.

9 Quoted in M. Bruce, *The Coming of the Welfare State*, Batsford, 1961, p.42.

10 Piven and Cloward, op. cit., p.27.

11 Report of the Royal Commission on the Poor Laws, 1834.

12 Ibid., p.227.

13 Conclusions to Edwin Chadwick's report in *The Extracts*, 1833, p.338.

14 Report of the Royal Commission on the Poor Laws, 1834, p.240.

15 Sir Keith Joseph, Speech to Pre-School Playgroups Association, 29.6.72, p.12.

16 Report of the Royal Commission on the Poor Laws, 1834, p.261.

17 Ibid., p.241.

18 Ibid., p.227.

19 Report on the Sanitary Conditions of the Labouring Population, 1842.

20 Select Committee on the Administration of Relief of the Poor (1864), Parliamentary Papers, 1864/8, pp.189-93.

21 Beatrice Webb, *My Apprenticeship*, Longmans, 1926 (1950 ed.), pp.172-3.

22 Ibid., p.172.

23 Herbert Spencer, *The Study of Sociology* (ed. S. Andreski), Macmillan, 1969, p.340.

24 Charity Organisation Society, Second Annual Report, 1870, p.5.

25 Charity Organisation Society, Fifth Annual Report, 1875, pp.5-6.

26 Charity Organisation Society, Twenty-first Annual Report, 1889, p.2.

27 Charity Organisation Society, Second Annual Report, 1870, pp.5-6.

28 Ibid.

29 Charity Organisation Society, Third Annual Report, 1871.

30 Charity Organisation Society, from Hammersmith Committee Report, 1873; quoted in C. L. Mowat, *The Charity Organisation Society*, Methuen, 1961, p.36.

31 Charity Organisation Society, Islington Committee, Twelfth

Annual Report, 1882-3, p.16.

32 J. W. Bready, *Doctor Barnardo*, Allen & Unwin, 1930, ch.XII.

33 Beatrice Webb, *Our Partnership*, Longmans, 1948, p.317.

34 Ibid., p.369.

35 Ibid., p.386.

36 T. Jones, *Lloyd George*, Oxford University Press, 1951, p.34.

37 Quoted in Sir H. Bunbury and R. Titmuss, *Lloyd George's Ambulance Wagon*, Methuen, 1957, p.24.

38 Webb, *Our Partnership*, p.369.

39 Bruce, op cit., pp.223-4.

40 'Social Insurance' Part 1, Cmd 6550, 1944, p.6.

41 Ibid.

42 Beveridge Report, *Social Insurance and Allied Services*, Cmd 6404, 1942, p.120.

43 One such history is at present being written by Jean Packman, Senior Lecturer in Social Work, Exeter University.

44 Poor Law Act, 1930, Section 15 (i) (6).

45 Children's Act, 1948, Section 12.

3   The triumph of the Poor Law

1 Mr James Griffiths, Second Reading of National Insurance Bill, House of Commons, 6.2.46.

2 V. N. George, *Social Security; Beveridge and After*, Routledge & Kegan Paul, 1968, p.23.

3 Beveridge Report, *Social Insurance and Allied Services*, Cmd 6404, 1942, p.121.

4 Lord Beveridge, 'Social security under review', *The Times*, 9.11.53.

5 George, op. cit., p.33.

6 Mr Norman McKenzie at the Labour Party Conference, *The Times*, 2.11.57.

7 George, op. cit., p.36.

8 M. Pilch and V. Wood, *Pension Schemes*, Hutchinson, 1960, p.143.

9 George, op. cit., p.38.

10 Ibid., p.52.

11 HMSO, *Provisions for Old Age*, Cmd 538, 1958, p.7.

12 F. Lafitte, 'The future of social security', *Social and Economic Administration*, vol. 1, no. 1, 1967.

13 Beveridge Report, p.108.

14 Mr Aneurin Bevan at the Labour Party Conference 1955, *The Times*, 14.10.55.

15 'The future of pensions', *The Times*, 2.3.55.

16 George, op. cit., p.224.

17 A. B. Atkinson, *Poverty in Great Britain and the Reform of Social Security*, Cambridge University Press, 1969.

18 *Poverty and the Labour Government*, Poverty Pamphlet no. 3, Child Poverty Action Group, 1970.

19 Report of the Royal Commission on the Poor Laws, 1934, pp.227-8.

20 *Poverty and the Labour Government*, p.7.

21 Ibid., p.10.

22 National Assistance Board Annual Report, 1956, pp.39-43.

23 Frank Field and Margaret Grieve, *Abuse and the Abused*, Poverty Pamphlet no. 10, Child Poverty Action Group, 1972, p.6.

24 Mr David Ennals in *Poverty and the Labour Government*, p.30.

25 Supplementary Benefits Commission, *The Administration of the Wage Stop*, HMSO, 1967, para.45.

26 Ruth Lister, *The Administration of the Wage Stop*, Child Poverty Action Group, 1972.

27 Department of Health and Social Security, Press Release, 17.12.69. Quoted in Field and Grieve, op. cit., p.4.

28 Ibid., p.12.

29 Ibid.

30 Supplementary Benefits Commission, *Exceptional Needs Payments*, HMSO, 1973, p.15.

31 Field and Grieve, op. cit., p.1.

32 Andrew Sinfield and Fred Twine, 'The working poor', *Poverty*, no. 12/13, 1969.

33 P. Townsend and B. Abel-Smith, *The Poor and the Poorest*, Bell, 1965, p.46.

34 *Poverty and the Labour Government*, p.11.

35 C. V. Brown and D. A. Dawson, *Personal Taxation Incentives and Tax Reforms*, PEP, 1969.

36 *Poverty and the Labour Government*, p.12.

37 Ibid., p.17.

4 Wages and the work ethic

1 Interview with Sir Keith Joseph, 'The family way', *Guardian*, 4.6.73.

2 S. E. Finer, *The Life and Times of Sir Edwin Chadwick*, Methuen, 1952, p.45.

3 Report of the Royal Commission on the Poor Law, 1834, p.54.

4 *Employment and Productivity Gazette*, May 1969, p.411, and *Ministry of Labour Gazette*, June 1961, p.247. Quoted in *Poverty and the Labour Government*, Poverty Pamphlet no. 3, Child Poverty Action Group, 1970, p.9.

5 A. R. Thatcher, 'The distribution of earnings of employees in Great Britain', *Journal of the Royal Statistical Society*, 1968, series A, vol. 131, part 2. Quoted in A. Sinfield and F. Twine, 'The working poor', *Poverty*, no. 12/13, 1969.

6 G. Routh, *Occupation and Pay in Great Britain: 1906-60*, Cambridge University Press, 1965, p.152.

7 F. F. Piven and R. A. Cloward, *Regulating the Poor*, Tavistock, 1972, pp.32 and 196.

8 R. Blackburn, 'The unequal society' in R. Blackburn and A. Cockburn (eds), *The Incompatibles: Trade Union Militancy and the Consensus*, Penguin, 1967, p.25.

9 E. H. Phelps-Brown and E. P. Hart, 'The share of wages in the national income', *Economic Journal*, vol. LXII, 1952. Quoted in R. Blackburn, 'The unequal society', in Blackburn and Cockburn, op. cit., p.25.

10 Piven and Cloward, op. cit., p.216.

11 Ibid., p.186.

12 K. Marx, *Gundrisse der Kritik der Politishen Ökonomie*. Quoted in M. Nicholaus, 'The unknown Marx', *New Left Review*, no. 48, March-April 1968.

13 G. Calvert and C. Neiman, *A Disrupted History*, Random House, 1971, p.96.

14 Marx, op. cit.

15 Piven and Cloward, op. cit., p.177.

16 Ibid., p.147.

17 Frank Field and Margaret Grieve, *Abuse and the Abused*, Poverty Pamphlet no. 10, Child Poverty Action Group, 1972, p.16.

18 Supplementary Benefits Commission, *The Administration of the Wage Stop*, HMSO, 1967, para. 45.

19 'The secret machinery of the poverty code', *Sunday Times*, 8.8.71.

20 Ruth Lister, *The Administration of the Wage Stop*, Poverty Pamphlet no. 11, Child Poverty Action Group, 1972, p.6.

21 Piven and Cloward, op. cit., p.175.

22 J. Hughes, 'Low pay. The case for a national minimum wage?' in D. Bull (ed.), *Family Poverty*, Duckworth, 1971, p.96.

23 V. N. George, *Social Security: Beveridge and After*, Rout-

ledge & Kegan Paul, 1968, p.20.

24 S. Yudkin and A. Holme, *Working Mothers and their Children*, Joseph, 1963, pp.44, 45, 168.

25 Sinfield and Twine, op. cit., p.4.

26 Piven and Cloward, op. cit., pp.171-2.

27 Yudkin and Holme, op. cit., p.170.

28 Ibid., p.171.

29 See for instance S. R. Parker, 'Work and non work in three occupations', *Sociological Review*, vol. 13.

30 For a fuller discussion of the situation see Bill Jordan, *Paupers*, Routledge & Kegan Paul, 1973.

5 Rationing, conflict and the Claimants' Unions

1 A. Sinfield and F. Twine, 'The working poor', *Poverty*, no. 12/13, 1969, p.7.

2 R. Pinker, *Social Theory and Social Policy*, Heinemann, 1971, p.114.

3 *Claimants' Union Guidebook*, National Federation of Claimants' Unions, 1972, p.22.

4 National Federation of Claimants' Unions Journal, no. 3, Summer 1972, p.8.

5 G.A.I. Campaign, *Ideas & Proposals resulting from the Whitsun Conference on the Campaign for a Guaranteed Adequate Income*, NFCU, 1972, pp.1-2.

6 Newssheet of a London Claimants' Union, April 1972.

7 Newssheet of a London Claimants' Union, April 1972.

8 Newssheet of a Lincolnshire Claimants' Union, 1971.

9 People's News Service, 14.7.73, p.3.

10 *Guardian*, 14.8.72.

11 *Exceptional Needs Payments*, Supplementary Benefits Administration Papers no. 4, HMSO, 1973, p.12.

12 Ibid., p.10.

13 Ibid., p.11.

14 Ibid., p.7.

15 Ibid., p.17.

16 Ibid., p.3.

17 Tyneside Claimants' Union Bulletin, December 1972.

18 O. Stevenson, *Claimant or Client?*, Allen & Unwin, 1973, p.26.

19 Ibid., pp.25-6.

20 Ibid., p.26.

21 Ibid.

22 Ibid., pp.28-9.

23 For a discussion of tax credits see chapter 11.

6 The making of a public welfare agency

1 N. Middleton, *When Family Failed*, Gollancz, 1970, pp.266-7.

2 Ibid., p.194.

3 Ibid., p.68.

4 Ibid., p.305.

5 Ibid., p.309.

6 D. M. Deed, 'Family case-work' in C. Morris (ed.), *Social Casework in Great Britain*, Faber & Faber, 1950 (1961 edition), p.64.

7 Report of the Committee on the Care of Children (Curtis Report), HMSO, 1946.

8 K. Woodruffe, *From Charity to Social Work*, Routledge & Kegan Paul, 1962.

9 Report of the Working Party on Social Workers in the Local Authority Health and Welfare Services, HMSO, 1959, p.241.

10 Middleton, op. cit., p.267.

11 B. P. Davies, 'Welfare departments and territorial justice', *Social & Economic Administration*, vol. 3, no. 4, Oct. 1969.

12 Report of the Working Party on Social Workers in the Local Authority Health & Welfare Services, HMSO, 1959, p.241.

13 U. M. Cormack and K. Mc-Dougall, 'Case-work in social service', in Morris, op. cit., p.31.

14 Clare Britton, 'Child care', in Morris, op. cit., p.172.

15 Children Act, 1948, Section 12.

16 Report of the Committee on the Care of Children (Curtis Report), para. 441.

17 Britton, op. cit., p.168.

18 Cormack and McDougall, op. cit., pp.23-4.

19 Ibid., p.31.

20 Ibid., p.34.

21 Middleton, op. cit., pp.308-9.

22 Cormack and McDougall, op. cit., p.33.

23 B. Wootton, *Social Science and Social Pathology*, Allen & Unwin, 1959, p.296.

24 J. Streather, 'Welfare rights and the social worker', *Social Work Today*, vol. 3, no. 15, 1972.

25 Cormack and McDougall, op. cit., p.33.

26 Ibid., p.34.

27 O. Stevenson, *Claimant or Client?*, Allen & Unwin, 1973, pp. 58-9.

28 Cormack and McDougall, op. cit., p.34.

29 E. Younghusband, 'Conclusion', in Morris, op. cit., p.202.

30 *Summaries of Local Authorities' Returns of Children in Care*, Home Office, 1967-70; and *Children in Care of Local Authorities at 31st March 1972*, DHSS Statistics & Research Division, Dec. 1972.

31 J. S. Heywood and B. K. Allen, *Financial Aid in Social Work*, Manchester University Press, 1971.

32 S. Watson, 'The Children's Departments and the 1963 Act' in J. Stroud (ed.), *Services for Children and Their Families*, Pergamon, 1973, pp.51-2.

33 Heywood and Allen, op. cit., p.77.

34 Letter to the Editor, *Social Work Today*, vol. 4, no. 1, 5.4.73.

35 Stevenson, op. cit., p.52.

36 Supplementary Benefits Commission, *Exceptional Needs Payments*, Supplementary Benefits Administration Papers, HMSO, 1973, no. 4, p.19.

37 Ibid., p.11.

38 Stevenson, op. cit., p.208.

39 Report of the Committee on Local Authority & Allied Personal Social Services (Seebohm Report), para. 274.

40 R. M. Titmuss in Standing Conference of Organisations of Social Workers, Discussion Paper no. 1 (1966); also, *Commitment to Welfare*, Allen & Unwin, 1968, pp.88-9.

41 Stevenson, op. cit., p.52.

42 R. W. L. Wilding, 'Telephones', *Social Work Service*, 1973, no. 1, March.

43 Alan Keith-Lucas, *Some Casework Concepts for the Public Welfare Worker*, University of North Carolina Press, 1957.

44 Alan Keith-Lucas, *Decisions about People in Need*, University of North Carolina Press, 1957, p.244.

45 Wilson, 'Public welfare and the new frontier', *Social Services Review*, Sept. 1962.

46 F. F. Piven and R. A. Cloward, *Regulating the Poor*, Tavistock, 1972, p.177.

47 Keith-Lucas, *Some Casework Concepts for the Public Welfare Worker*, p.6.

48 Ibid., pp.6-7.

49 Keith-Lucas, *Decisions about People in Need*, p.248.

50 Heywood and Allen, op. cit., p.71.

7 'Front line troops in the war against poverty'

1 Report of the Committee on Local Authority and Allied Personal Social Services, Cmnd 3703, 1968, paras 474 and 492.

2 Sir Keith Joseph, 'The next ten years', *New Society*, 5.10.72.

3 R. Pinker, *Social Theory and Social Policy*, Heinemann, 1971, p.151.

4 That is the period between April and October 1970.

5 J. Connor, 'Casework: The antidote to Bolshevism?', *Case Con*, no. 10, Jan. 1973, pp.13-14.

6 C. Cannan, 'The ideology of casework and professionalism', *Case Con*, no. 3, 1972, p.5.

7 Ibid., p.4.

8 Ibid.

9 B. J. Heraud, *Sociology and Social Work*, Pergamon, 1970, p.193.

10 Ibid., p.196.

11 Cannan, op. cit., pp.3, 5.

12 J. Handler, 'The coercive Children's Officer', *New Society*, 3.10.68.

13 P. Halmos, *The Faith of the Counsellors*, Constable, 1965, p.74.

14 P. Halmos, *The Personal Service Society*, Constable, 1970, p.38.

15 Ibid., pp.57-60.

16 Halmos, *The Faith of the Counsellors*, p.47.

17 G. Hamilton, 'Helping people —the growth of a profession', in *Social Work as Human Relations*, 1949, p.14.

18 A. Walker, 'Child guidance at the crossroads', *British Journal of Psychiatric Social Work*, 1970, vol. X, no. 3.

19 Report of the Committee on Children in Care (Curtis Report), HMSO, 1946, para. 445.

20 A. Etzioni, *A Comparative Analysis of Complex Organisations*, Free Press, 1961.

21 A. Etzioni, *Modern Organisations*, Prentice Hall, 1964.

22 A. Etzioni, *The Semi-Professions*, Free Press, 1969.

23 Claudine Spencer, 'Seebohm: problems and policies', *Social & Economic Administration*, vol. 4, no. 3, July 1970.

24 Ibid., p.176.

25 Ibid., p.178.

26 Ibid.

27 Claudine Spencer, 'Seebohm: problems and policies', *Social & Economic Administration*, vol. 4, no. 4, Oct. 1970, p.306.

28 Claudine Spencer, 'Seebohm: problems and policies', *Social & Economic Administration*, vol. 4, no. 3, July 1970, p.179.

29 Letter to the Editor, *Social Work Today*, vol. 4, no. 2, 19.5.73, p.63.

30 National Federation of Claimants' Unions' Handbook, 1971.

31 Jean Packman, *Child Care: Needs and Numbers*, Allen & Unwin, 1969, p.51.

32 Ibid., p.31.

8 The social services and the culture of poverty

1 Sir Keith Joseph, 'The family way', interview with John Cunningham, *Guardian*, 4.6.73.

2 See chapter 1.

3 Jean Packman, *Child Care: Needs and Numbers*, Allen & Unwin, 1969.

4 Ibid., p.229.

5 Oscar Lewis, *La Vida*, Panther, 1968, p.48.

6 Ibid., pp.48-9.

7 Ibid., p.50.

8 Ibid., p.51.

9 Ibid., p.54.

10 Ibid.

11 Ibid., p.57.

12 Ibid., pp.49-50.

13 Ibid., p.58.

14 Ibid., p.53.

15 N. Middleton, *When Family Failed*, Gollancz, 1970, p.304.

16 Frank Field and Margaret Grieve, *Abuse and the Abused*, Poverty Pamphlet no. 10, Child Poverty Action Group, 1971, p.16.

17 *Cohabitation*, HMSO, 1971.

18 O. Stevenson, *Claimant or Client?*, Allen & Unwin, 1973, p.144.

19 'Paper tiger', *Tyneside Claimants' Union Bulletin*, Jan. 1973.

20 Stevenson, op. cit., p.130.

21 W. Jordan, *The Social Worker in Family Situations*, Routledge & Kegan Paul, 1972, p.66.

22 Oscar Lewis, op. cit., p.29.

23 Ibid., p.58.

24 Ibid., p.82.

25 D. V. Donnison, *The Government of Housing*, Penguin, 1967, p.19.

26 S. Alderson, *Housing*, Penguin, 1962, p.82.

27 Donnison, op. cit., ch. 2.

28 E. Burney, *Housing on Trial*, Institute of Race Relations, Oxford University Press, 1967, p.65.

29 Ibid.

30 Ibid., pp.63-4.

31 E. J. B. Rose, foreword to ibid., p.vi.

32 Ibid., p.65.

33 D. Barton, *A Hope for Housing?*, Mayflower Books, 1963, p.62.

34 Des Wilson, *I Know it was the Place's Fault*, Oliphants, 1970, p.10.

35 Institute of Municipal Treasurers and Accountants,

Local Health and Social Services Statistics, 1971-2.

36 Institute of Municipal Treasurers and Accountants, Welfare Services Statistics,

1959-60.

37 Ibid.

38 Lewis, op. cit., p.53.

39 Burney, op. cit., p.32.

9 'Positive discrimination'

1 Sir Keith Joseph, Speech to Pre-School Playgroups Association, 29.6.72, p.7.

2 E. Crellin, M. L. Kellmer Pringle and P. West, Born Illegitimate, National Foundation for Educational Research, 1971, p.114.

3 Ibid., pp.123-4.

4 M. L. Kellmer Pringle, Deprivation and Education, Longmans, 1965, p.293.

5 Crellin, Kellmer Pringle and West, op. cit., p.104.

6 Ibid., p.90.

7 Kellmer Pringle, op. cit., p.273.

8 Ibid.

9 Ibid., p.286.

10 Crellin, Kellmer Pringle and West, op. cit., p.117.

11 R. M. Titmuss, Commitment to Welfare, Allen & Unwin, 1968, p.134.

12 Ibid., p.159.

13 Ibid., pp.134-5.

14 Ibid., p.135.

15 B. Abel-Smith, Freedom in the Welfare State, Fabian Tract no. 353, p.16.

16 F. F. Piven and R. A. Cloward, Regulating the Poor, Tavistock, 1972, p.260.

17 Ibid., pp.260-1.

18 Ibid., p.262.

19 Ibid., pp.262-3.

20 For example see E. Burney, Housing on Trial, Institute of Race Relations, Oxford University Press, 1967.

21 B. Davies, Social Needs and Researches in Local Services, Joseph, 1968, p.59.

22 D. Holman, 'The wrong poverty programme?', New Society, March 1969.

23 M. Reddin, 'Local authority means-tested services' in P. Townsend et al., Social Services for All?, Fabian Tract no. 383, Part one, p.49.

24 L. J. Sharpe, Research in Local Government, Greater London Research Papers, no. 10, London School of Economics, 1965, p.11.

25 R. M. Kramer, Participation of the Poor: Comparative Community Case Studies in the War on Poverty, Prentice Hall, 1969, p.66.

26 Ibid., p.60.

27 Ibid., p.103.

28 Piven and Cloward, op. cit., p.263.

29 R. Pinker, Social Theory and Social Policy, Heinemann, 1971, p.197.

30 Ibid., pp.176-7.

31 Central Advisory Council for Education, Children and their Primary Schools, HMSO, 1967, vol. 1, para. 174 (1), p.66.

32 Piven and Cloward, op. cit., pp.276-8.

33 J. Connor, 'Victimisation in Hackney Seebohm factory', Case Con, no. 7, April 1972, p.11.

34 Evidence of Professor Donnison to the Study Group on Training for Community Work, Community Work and Social Change. A Report on Training, Calouste Gulbenkian

Foundation, Longmans, 1968, p.27.

35 Piven and Cloward, op. cit., p.266.

36 Pinker, op. cit., p.188.

37 Morris in J. D. Sutherland, *Towards Community Mental Health*.

38 R. Klein, 'An anatomy of the N.H.S.', *New Society*, 28.6.73, pp.740-1.

39 Ibid., p.741.

40 Ibid., p.740.

41 M. Rein, 'Social class and the health service', *New Society*, 20.11.69.

42 A. Howlett and J. Ashley, 'Selective care', *New Society*, 2.11.72.

43 Titmuss, op. cit., p.218.

44 F. Roberts, *The Cost of Health*, 1952, p.80.

45 Ibid.

10 *Law and order*

1 A. Forder (ed.), *Penelope Hall's Social Services of England and Wales*, Routledge & Kegan Paul, 1969 edition, p.300.

2 *The Times*, 6.5.68.

3 M. Turnbull, 'The "hunger marches" of the 1920s and 30s', *Journal of Social Policy*, vol. 2, part 2, April 1973, p.132.

4 Ibid., p.131.

5 Ibid., p.142.

6 Ibid.

7 'Paper tiger', *Tyneside Claimants' Union Bulletin*, Jan. 1973.

8 K. Marx and F. Engels, *Manifesto of the Communist Party*, Foreign Languages Publishing House, 1959, p.59.

9 Ibid.

10 F. Fanon, *The Wretched of the Earth*, Grove Press, 1965, p.103.

11 H. Marcuse, *One-Dimensional Man*, Beacon Press, 1966, p.256.

12 Oscar Lewis, *La Vida*, Panther, 1968, p.56.

13 Ibid., p.55.

14 For example, see E. Banfield, *The Moral Basis of a Backward Society*, Free Press

1958; and G. Knupfer, 'Portrait of the underdog', *Public Opinion Quarterly*, 11, 1947.

15 S. M. Lipset, *Political Man*, Heinemann, 1960, p.181.

16 H. Cantril, *The Politics of Despair*, Basic Books, 1958, pp.3-10.

17 Lipset, op. cit., p.97 and ch. iv *passim*.

18 Report of the Royal Commission on the Poor Laws, 1834, pp.240-1.

19 D. P. Moynihan, *Maximum Feasibility Misunderstanding: Community Action in the War on Poverty*, Free Press, 1969.

20 F. F. Piven and R. A. Cloward, *Regulating the Poor*, Tavistock, 1972, p.196.

21 Ibid., p.41.

22 Ibid., p.273.

23 Ibid., p.348.

24 Ibid., p.342.

25 George Dangerfield, *The Strange Death of Liberal England*, preface by Paul Johnson, MacGibbon & Kee, 1966, p.10.

26 *The Times*, 11.11.70.

11 Conclusion

1 SSRC/DHSS Day Conference on Transmitted Deprivation. 16.4.73.
2 Joint SSRC/DHSS Working Party, *Approaches to Transmitted Deprivation*, 1973, p.2.
3 Ibid., pp.8-9.
4 Ibid., p.10.
5 Ibid., pp.9-10.
6 Sir Keith Joseph, Speech to National Association for Maternal and Child Welfare, 27.6.73, p.12.
7 Ibid., p.14.
8 R. Pinker, *Social Theory and Social Policy*, Heinemann, 1971, p.97.
9 Ibid., p.106.
10 Ibid., p.134.
11 Ibid., p.108.
12 Ibid., p.102.
13 D. V. Donnison *et al.*, *Social Policy and Administration*, Allen & Unwin, 1965, p.29.
14 Ibid., pp.27-9.
15 Aneurin Bevan, quoted in M. Bruce, *The Coming of the Welfare State*, Batsford, 1961, p.290.
16 Government Green Paper on proposals for a tax-credit system, Cmnd 5116, 1972.
17 Ibid., p.2.
18 Ibid., p.28.
19 Ibid.
20 Ibid., para. 118.
21 Select Committee on tax credit. Report and Proceedings of the Committee (Mrs Castle's Draft Report), HMSO, 1973, p.80.
22 Ibid., p.80.
23 Ibid.
24 Green Paper on proposals for a tax-credit system, Cmnd 5116, para. 107.
25 Select Committee on tax credit, Report and Proceedings of the Committee, p.81.
26 Ibid., p.81.
27 Ibid.
28 Ibid., p.84.
29 Ibid., p.79.
30 Child Poverty Action Group, Evidence to the Select Committee, Section III, 'The excluded groups', p.10.
31 R. Holman, 'Poverty, welfare, rights and social work', *Social Work Today*, vol. 4, no. 12, 6.9.73, p.359.
32 Ibid.
33 Green Paper on proposals for a tax-credit system, Cmnd 5116, para. 47.
34 Holman, op. cit., p.358.
35 E. Fromm in R. Theobald, *The Guaranteed Income*, Doubleday.